5 12/14

4 4/16

Helen M. Plum Memorial Library
Lombard, Illinois
www.helenplum.org
A daily fine will be charged for
overdue materials.

AUG   2013

UNDERCOVER COP

UNDERCOVER COP

How I Brought
Down the Real-
Life Sopranos

MIKE RUSSELL
with Patrick W. Picciarelli

THOMAS DUNNE BOOKS
St. Martin's Press
New York

THOMAS DUNNE BOOKS.
An imprint of St. Martin's Press.

UNDERCOVER COP. Copyright © 2013 by Mike Russell with Patrick W. Picciarelli. All rights reserved. Printed in the United States of America. For information, address St. Martin's Press, 175 Fifth Avenue, New York, N.Y. 10010.

www.thomasdunnebooks.com
www.stmartins.com

Design by Kathryn Parise

LIBRARY OF CONGRESS CATALOGING-IN-PUBLICATION DATA

Russell, Michael, 1950–
    Undercover cop : how I brought down the real-life Sopranos / Michael Russell with Patrick W. Picciarelli.
        Pages cm
    Includes bibliographical references and index.
    ISBN 978-1-250-00587-8 (hardcover)
    ISBN 978-1-250-02111-3 (e-book)
    1. Russell, Michael, 1950–   2. Police—United States—Biography.
3. Undercover operations—New Jersey.   4. Mafia—New Jersey—
Case studies.   I. Picciarelli, Patrick.   II. Title.
    HV7911.R86A3 2013
    364.106′609749—dc23

                                                    2013009367

St. Martin's Press books may be purchased for educational, business, or promotional use. For information on bulk purchases, please contact Macmillan Corporate and Premium Sales Department at 1-800-221-7945 extension 5442 or write specialmarkets@macmillan .com.

First Edition: August 2013

10   9   8   7   6   5   4   3   2   1

Dedicated to the many victims of these wiseguys and
in memory of Big Jim Sweeney,
who passed away on July 25, 2011.

For Detective Robert D. Martin, PAPD 1947–2012.
The world is a diminished place without you.
Rest well, my friend.

Contents

 1. Fitting In   1
 2. No Hard Feelings   13
 3. Mikey Ga-Ga: Back in the Life   23
 4. Balancing Act   34
 5. Striking Oil   52
 6. We're Talking Real Money Here   73
 7. Gathering Dirt   92
 8. Here's Looking at You, Mikey   110
 9. On the Wire   132
10. One Man's Garbage . . .   151
11. Fed Up   178
12. Back with a Vengeance   196
13. Gangsters "R" Us   216
14. Getting Bombed   242
15. No Second Takes   257

CONTENTS

16. Takedown   280

Epilogue   293
Appendix: Cage Crew   305
Acknowledgments   309

UNDERCOVER COP

1

Fitting In

March 1982

I was in King's Court, a mob hangout on the west side of Newark, New Jersey, with two wiseguys. We were doing what wiseguys do: talking about pussy and money, not necessarily in that order.

The club was in a commercial area, which for Newark at that time meant more vacant storefronts than viable businesses. The Court was what passed for a health club back then: four racquetball courts and a weight room the size of a closet. The main attraction was the disco, a club within a club, located in the center of that mecca to healthy living. Play a few games of racquetball to get the cardio up and the hamstrings loose, then repair to the bar to drink yourself silly, dabble in some coke, maybe get laid.

It was the eighties; disco was still in bloom, but waning, slowly being replaced by hip-hop and rap. In this primarily Italian and Irish neighborhood, disco wasn't going down without a fight.

That night the disco was packed with a diversity of types. Mobsters mixed with college students, off-duty firefighters and cops, with a smattering of junkies and underage girls looking to trade some free tight snatch for drugs. There was no shortage of takers. The racquetball courts were deserted.

Despite the variety of the clientele and the size of the crowd, peace was usually maintained in the disco. The owners, made guys from the Lucchese crime family, saw to it, as did the small army of bouncers who were as big as Buicks. The Lucchese family ran this section of Newark and had a mostly peaceful yet contentious relationship with the Gambino and Genovese families, who whacked up the rest of the city.

Anthony Acceturo was the capo who ran the Lucchese crew. Acceturo—or Tumac as he was known on the street—was a heroin addict and all-around scumbag. Born and raised in Newark, his claim to fame was killing some black bookmakers back in the sixties to make his bones with the Luccheses.

Like-minded groups gathered at the bar and in corners, shrouded by smoke and trying to maintain private conversations under the din of blasting music. As an homage to the old days, the joint also boasted a live singer a few days a week who focused on the old standards, giving people with taste a respite from the noise. The current Sinatra wannabe was Frank Vincent, who had a pretty good voice and would later go on to appear in the HBO series *The Sopranos* and numerous other TV shows and movies, always typecast as a gangster. He's best known for telling Joe Pesci to get his "fucking shine box" in the movie *GoodFellas,* and exiting the scene via bullets, stab wounds, and numerous kicks to the head.

Tonight, those patrons who weren't sweating on the dance floor to the rhythmic beat of Gloria Gaynor made frequent trips to the bathrooms to partake in as much cocaine as they could shovel up their noses. Coke isn't a mellow drug, it causes users to seek action. The resurgence of coke in the eighties fueled the success of clubs everywhere. These were the days before random drug tests, and it was in the best interest of partygoers to keep the peace and blow their brains out with impunity. This included cops, bad guys, doctors, lawyers, politicians, and everyone else. It was party time.

An eclectic crowd if there ever was one.

With me were Joey Ricardi and Rory DeLuca, two Lucchese associates, young guys looking to get made and maybe someday get rich as bosses of their own crews. Or maybe wind up in the trunk of a Cadillac in the long-term-parking lot at Newark Airport, whichever came first.

My name's Mike Russell and I was a New Jersey state trooper working undercover, playing the role of an up-and-coming mobster looking to work with a crew and make a ton of money. My cover was that I was once a cop but was fired for being excessively violent and had been accused of criminality by my cop bosses, charges that had never been substantiated. I had been given the nickname Mikey Ga-Ga by my new best friends in the Court, a street name that truly meant nothing. A drunken capo had coined it one night and it stuck.

I was thirty-two years old, from the Newark area, had spent my life on the street, and had the well-deserved reputation of being a tough guy. The local Mafia contingent believed my bullshit story, but it was still taking a while for me to work my way into the confidence of Acceturo. I had plenty of time. Cops are nothing if not patient. While patience might be a virtue, trying to work your way into a Mafia family made it a necessity.

It can sometimes take many months or even years to convince normally suspicious gangsters that you are one of them. My object was to build a good criminal case, one that would stick in court and send the bad guys to jail for a long time. To what extent my supervisors would have me go to get convictions would soon become evident, but for now I was simply biding my time by tending bar, managing the health-club portion of the Court, and talking up a good background for myself.

It was a typically brisk winter evening, cold and dank. I'm convinced God gave Newark what seemed like a permanent overcast to fit in with the palpable feeling of despair and defeat that hung in that economic DMZ. The race riots after the Bobby Kennedy and Martin Luther King assassinations of the 1960s had permanently labeled Newark as a slum that needed to either be bombed off the map or rehabilitated with massive amounts of federal funds, depending on your political point of view.

We occupied a table in the back near the office, surveying the throng of guys bellying up to the bar or to the butts of the women they were trying to score.

"Lotta off-duty cops," Joey observed.

"Yeah," Rory agreed.

Joey Ricardi was in his twenties, like Rory, and dressed like a typical mob associate: tight jeans, black silk shirt, black leather jacket, and slicked-back hair, what I referred to as a ninety-mile-an-hour hairstyle. He was dark and couldn't be mistaken for anything but Italian. Rory DeLuca looked like Joey, except for the black silk shirt. His was red. Both had enduring sneers and were adorned with enough gold chains to anchor a battleship. If and when they got inducted into the Brotherhood as made guys, the thug look would get replaced with $2,000 suits. They'd still look like hoodlums, only better dressed.

I looked as if I was trying to fit in, dressing the dress and walking the walk, but while these guys were dark and swarthy, I was more Newark-noir, fair skinned and brooding.

These guys could spot an off-duty cop with a paper bag over his head. I knew what was coming next: We were going to boost cars for guns. This was the practice of looking for the cars that belonged to the off-duty cops, who would invariably stash their pieces in their rides before entering the club. Nothing turned off a nubile, young thing like grabbing a guy around the waist and coming up with a fistful of iron.

With almost a hundred cars parked in the vicinity, how could we pick out a cop's car? For me it was easy: I *was* a cop. For Joey and Rory it was a matter of survival; if they couldn't spot a cop at fifty yards, they were destined to be handcuffed by a lot of them.

It didn't take a clairvoyant; most cops parked as close to their destinations as possible, traffic laws be damned. Their cars could be identified to other cops by placing a police-union card on the dashboard. Subtle. This was the eighties, before the term *politically correct* was hammered into the American lexicon. Cops could park by fire hydrants, in crosswalks, on sidewalks, in driveways. If there were a way to pull their cars into someone's living room, they'd do it.

So, with little difficulty, we went hunting for cops' private cars. The object was to smash and grab: break a window, rifle the car as quickly as possible for a gun or other valuables, and move on to the next vehicle. Brain surgery it wasn't.

I didn't want to be the window breaker, seeing as how I was the law. I had planned on being the lookout, but that was soon to change. Undercovers were not supposed to break the law. At least that's what the book said. The street dictated a different set of rules. To seem real and, better yet, not get made as a cop, I occasionally committed the random felony. Tonight would be one of those times.

I scored almost immediately. In the club's parking lot I spotted a brand-new, shiny, black Mercedes-Benz with the doors unlocked and a leather briefcase in the backseat. While the vehicle certainly didn't belong to a cop, it was easy pickings.

Joey and Rory were otherwise occupied, peering into the windows of cars adorned with PBA stickers. I decided to give them a heads-up.

"Hey," I called out. "Got an open car here. Briefcase in it."

Joey's head bobbed up. "No gun?"

I shrugged. "Doubt it. Looks like it belongs to a citizen."

"Fuck it then," Joey said, and went back to the hunt.

Rory had wandered down the street and didn't notice the exchange.

I removed the briefcase, glanced quickly inside, and saw a wad of cash and a lot of paper. I walked to my own car and tossed the briefcase in the trunk, a decision I made on the spur of the moment. The briefcase, the expensive car, that it was left unlocked, spelled M-O-B. Wiseguys didn't lock their cars when parked in friendly territory, figuring no one would have the balls to take off a car obviously belonging to a connected guy. A show of bravado, if you will. *I'm a wiseguy, fuck with my car at your own peril.* Or maybe the Benz belonged to Joe Citizen and he was too drunk to remember to lock it. My cop instinct, however, told me it was the former.

Joey and Rory didn't score any guns, but came up with some loose change, a flashlight, a bottle of Scotch, a box of condoms, and a banana. They stole everything but the fruit. Big-time gangsters.

We wound up back in the club, where we spent the rest of the night getting drunk. Tough work, being an undercover. Rory brought up the briefcase, and I told him it only contained paper so I'd put it back in the car. He accepted that and promptly forgot about it. Joey was too drunk to give a damn.

I got home late, briefcase in hand. My wife and kids were asleep, so I quietly emptied the contents of the case onto the kitchen table. The briefcase contained $2,000 in cash and a bonanza of mob pay-off records that listed political bribes paid to individuals to approve a chain of fast-food restaurants on the Garden State Parkway, plus money-laundering records from the proceeds of gambling and narcotics ventures by the Lucchese crime family. I'd hit the proverbial mother lode. The cash and records belonged to James Castagna, one of the Lucchese bosses and the family's money manager.

After gathering up the records and the cash, I drove to the Bloomfield State Police Barracks, where I made copies of the records, called my trooper handler, and told him of the existence of the records and money. I could have copied the records at a local police precinct, but this was the eighties and police corruption in the Newark area was rampant. I didn't want to have some cop who was on the take report my presence to Tumac even before I got home and into my jammies.

The next day I got a phone call from Michael Taccetta, a soldier in Tumac's crew. He was also Tumac's cousin, a fat-slob bookmaker who without the family connection wouldn't have been intellectually qualified to polish bowling balls.

"Yo, Mikey," Taccetta said, "ya got that briefcase you boosted last night?"

I'd told Joey and Rory I'd put the briefcase back in the Benz, but wiseguys lied to each other all the time. Wiseguys understood that lying was justified if there was money to be made, and since I was supposed to be a wiseguy, larcenous intent was justified. But now was the time to come clean.

"Yeah, I got it," I said.

"Well, it belongs to Jimmy C. He needs the fuckin' thing back."

I had to ask myself what a real low-life mobster would do in a position like this. The mob is all about making money, not loyalty, tradition, respect, or anything else you might see in the *Godfather* movies. It's all about being an "earner." The more money you generated and the greedier you were, the more respect you got.

"He can have it back," I said, "for five grand."

A few seconds of dead air ensued, which seemed more like an hour.

"You gotta be fuckin' with me, right, Mikey?" Taccetta said.

"I ain't fuckin' with you. You want the case, it's gonna cost you five large." I knew this was a risky move, but one that made me seem real. To turn over the case, no questions asked, would be unnatural for a wiseguy. There would at least be some negotiations, even if the case wound up being returned for nothing for a favor owed at a later date. If I couldn't negotiate the $5,000 and returned the case gratis, I might be viewed as a stand-up guy. Either way, it was the right thing to do.

"Okay, ya prick," Taccetta said, "I'll call ya back." I detected a tone of respect in his voice.

A week passed and no one got back to me regarding the briefcase. I didn't know what to make of it. While I continued to show up at the Court, no one mentioned the briefcase or its contents and I didn't bring it up. Perhaps I'd passed a test by being hard-nosed and seemingly unafraid. I knew the Luccheses didn't give a damn about the two grand, and their paperwork was undoubtedly duplicated somewhere. They would have no fear of an associate's turning it over to the cops unless it could be used as a bargaining chip in an arrest situation. Since I wasn't collared and was staying below the cops' radar, they probably didn't care about the paper. Besides, the payoff information was written in code, or what passed for code among the wiseguys. Realistically, Stevie Wonder could decipher it in minutes. Superspies these guys were not, but they thought they had invented an undecipherable code that would make James Bond proud.

So, with no trepidation, I agreed to help Rory and Joey, along with another associate, Bobby Alvegi, break into a safe in a warehouse on South Orange Avenue in Newark.

"Safe belongs to a coke dealer," Bobby said. "Supposed to be packed with coke and cash. We'll whack it up. You in?"

I'd told the crew I was a good safecracker, and now I had to prove it. I knew most people who owned safes utilized the practice known as day locking. This was done by advancing the first few numbers on the combination dial to within one number of opening. This method saved time when the guy who owned the safe wanted to get into it; all he had to do was go to the last number and the safe would open. Since most safe combinations consisted of four numbers, beginning with a right turn, I knew the last turn had to be to the left. All I had to do was move the combination dial one click at a time and try the handle after every move. Eventually I'd get to the right number and the safe would open.

Of course the Three Stooges didn't know day locking from Doris Day, and I'd have them looking out for cops or heavily armed drug dealers while I seemingly worked my Jimmy Valentine magic.

"Yeah," I said, "why the fuck not?"

"We'll pick you up in twenty minutes."

I called my handler in the State Police and cleared the caper with him. Break into a safe? No problem. Commit a felony? No problem. Just another brick in the shithouse that would eventually nail the crew on a variety of charges.

The trio of knuckleheads was on time. Rory was driving a beat-up Dodge, probably stolen, with Joey in the front seat. Bobby Alvegi was in the back with me.

Conversation, if you could call it that, centered on the job.

"Piece a cake," Joey said.

"Yeah, cake," Rory said.

Alvegi grunted.

Good thing I didn't have time to wire myself for sound. It would've been a waste of good audiotape.

The ride to the warehouse, which was in a commercial area of mostly deserted buildings and storefronts, took twenty minutes. The building we were going to burglarize looked like any of the others in the area, bleak and in need of maintenance. The stand-alone, two-story brick structure was unadorned by signs or other identifying markings. Two narrow alleyways bordered the building and separated it from two other buildings that looked just like it.

Rory circled the block twice to make certain no potential witnesses were lurking about. Aside from a quartet of junkies standing on a nearby corner waiting for their delivery of dope, we had free rein. We could have parked the Dodge on their feet and would have gone unnoticed, an addict's attention span being that of a gnat.

We parked down the street and walked silently toward the building. Bobby was carrying a duffle bag loaded with power tools, crowbars, and a police-radio scanner.

When we got near the target, Joey said, "We take the alley on the right. There's a door near the end. You guys go down first, I'll be behind you."

Sounded like a plan. We strolled down the alley single file with me in the lead.

The alley was strewn with debris. I was dodging broken glass and a Dumpster when I felt a sharp pain in the side of my face.

Rory DeLuca had sucker punched me. I spun around from the force of the blow, disoriented and in pain. Instinctually I raised my hands to defend myself, but by this time Joey had maneuvered behind me and Bobby was circling me like a lion stalking an antelope.

I knew instantly that I was about to get a payback for not turning over the briefcase. The burglary job was a con just to get me alone. I'd been set up for a hit.

Rory was coming directly at me, screaming obscenities. I consider myself a pretty tough guy, in good shape and able to take a punch. I felt myself recovering from the strike to the head, but not feeling confident that I'd get out of the alley alive.

My peripheral vision picked up Joey with a dark object in his hand. A brick? A sap?

It was a gun.

Before I could react, I felt a dull thud in the back of my head. I'd been shot square in my skull, the force of the bullet ramming my face against the wall of the warehouse. Everything started to go black. I knew I was going to die. The curses began to fade, as if I were hearing them from a great distance. My life didn't flash before my eyes; I had no time to think of my wife and kids. All I thought about was dying. After twelve years doing police work, I was going to die helpless in a filthy alley, alone.

My last conscious thought was one of frustration: Why hadn't I seen this coming?

Then the world went black and I drifted to the ground.

2

No Hard Feelings

For a brief instant I had no idea where I was, didn't remember what had happened to me; not dissimilar from the feeling of waking up in a strange woman's bed after a night of blackout-inducing boozing.

It came back in a rush: the ambush, the beating, the shot to the back of my head.

Was I dead? My eyes were shut and I was afraid to open them, thinking I might be greeted by a guy in a cheap tuxedo with a red face and horns.

I was lying facedown in the alley, arms twisted under my torso. I had a hell of a headache. As I was building up the courage to open my eyes and try to move, I felt a hand in my pants pocket. Turning slightly and squinting through a swollen eye, I saw a wino, crackhead, junkie—pick one—who had my wallet in one hand while he searched my pants for more booty. To add to what was probably the worst day of my life, I was suffering the indignity of being mugged. But to look on the positive side, I was now sure I was alive.

I rolled over onto my back and grabbed the thief by the arm. He was of indeterminate age, somewhere between thirty and death, with teeth that looked as if they belonged to an eighty-year-old chain-smoker. He had probably figured me for dead, what with a bullet hole in the back of my head, and when I latched onto him, he let out a screech and tore out of the alley, leaving a vapor trail, but not before dropping my wallet.

I leaned back against a brick wall and took stock. My finger found the hole in my head, center mass, equidistant between my ears. Joey, the rat bastard, was a regular Angelo Oakley.

There wasn't much blood. My face was swollen and I felt as if I were in a jar of mayonnaise. My movements seemed to be in slow motion.

The end of the alley appeared to be miles away, like looking through the wrong end of binoculars. I knew I couldn't just sit there and wait for help—I could die waiting—and I didn't think the junkie who'd tried to rob me was on the phone with 911 reporting an injured person. If his heart survived the initial shock of a dead guy's coming back to life, he was probably still running and nearing the Holland Tunnel by now.

Ever so slowly I stood up, using the wall as support. I was unsteady on my feet, but propelled myself toward the mouth of the alley and lurched in the direction of the street. Surely a car would come by shortly and I'd get the driver to take me to a hospital.

It seemed like an hour before I reached the street. No pedestrians were in sight. I staggered to the driver's side of a parked car and waited. Within seconds a radio car from the Newark PD turned the corner and cruised slowly in my direction. Who says there's never a cop around when you need one?

I stepped into the middle of the road and made a feeble attempt at waving the cops down. The radio car pulled up alongside me, the cop in the passenger seat rolling down his window.

"Help you, sir?" He was a young guy, maybe midtwenties. Busted up as I was, I was surprised he was treating me like a tourist wanting directions.

I leaned against the radio car for support. "On the job," I muttered, using the phrase that universally identifies a brother in blue. "I've been shot."

The cop stared at me for a brief moment, then said something to his partner. He reached over his seat and popped the back door.

"Get in." He joined me in the back while his partner, an older guy, flipped on the lights and siren and took off amid screeching tires and a cloud of burning rubber.

My head lolled against the backseat, mouth open. I felt I was losing consciousness and was trying desperately to stay awake, thinking if I blacked out, I'd die.

The young cop was peppering me with questions. "You got ID? Where are you hit? What the fuck happened?"

I managed to squeak out, "Undercover," and let the rest of the questions go.

I vaguely recall being hoisted out of the radio car and being placed on a gurney; after that I lost the battle to stay awake and slid into darkness.

*   *   *

The wound turned out not to be that bad, mainly because my hard head had slowed down the relatively ineffective .32-caliber bullet that had entered it. Note to would-be hit men: if you're going to whack someone, use a round that can kill. A .45 bullet would have exploded my head like a pumpkin dropped from a six-story building; all the .32 did was enter my skull, bounce off bone, and exit an inch above the entrance wound. I received twenty-eight stitches and a three-day stay in the College of Medicine and Dentistry Hospital.

It's a big deal when a police officer gets shot. The press plays it up, railing against the proliferation of guns on the street, the mayor and police commissioner drop by the hospital for a photo op, Al Sharpton calls for the wounded cop's indictment. The usual.

In my case it was different. While I was a police officer, no one knew it, other than my family and my handlers in the State Police. My shooting went unreported and was ignored by the press. In the eighties it was news in Newark when a day passed and someone *wasn't* shot. Some guy staggering out of an alley with a bullet hole in his head was as newsworthy as the proverbial cat in a tree.

I supposed I was better off remaining off the media's radar, but I knew my undercover days were over. Police organizations are livid when one of their own gets hurt, and I expected a full-blown investigation and many arrests. Needless to say, I'd be exposed as an undercover operator and my spying days would be over. At least that was what happened to every other UC that was wounded in the line of duty. I would find out that my case was going to set a precedent.

My first visitor was my wife, Angela. She was twenty-nine years old, with coal-black, shoulder-length hair. To say our marriage was contentious was like saying Hitler had a mild disagreement with the Jews. Angela came from a traditional Italian family, meaning the order of business was to graduate high school, get married, have a bunch of kids, and live a contented life with a husband who valued family, home, and stability.

For Angela it was three out of four. The part about a husband who valued family, home, and was stable eluded her. My fault entirely. While I was busy being Indiana Jones, she was raising our three daughters, being a great mother, and trying to be a good wife to a guy who'd rather lock up bad guys than go to a neighbor's party and discuss the complexities of killing crabgrass.

I'm bored easily and craved action; Angela cherished family and friends. Radical thinking on her part, I thought, but this was one of the reasons we were inching toward divorce. It was a glacial movement toward the Big D; we wouldn't sever our relationship until 1999, twenty-seven years after we married. Our love had morphed into more of a disgruntled respect, and we coexisted for the sake of our daughters.

I kept Angela in the dark. She had no idea I was working undercover, and my being shot was explained to her, by Sergeant Nick Orilio, commanding officer of the Organized Crime Unit, as an "accident." She knew better than to press Nick, who, like most cops, didn't share information with civilians unless ordered to do so at gunpoint.

So Angela stood next to my bed with a look that combined disdain, pity, and concern.

"You okay?" she said, hugging me ever so briefly.

I shrugged. "Never felt better." I smiled.

"There was a priest here, you know. Wanted to give you last rites, but your sergeant threw him out."

That hit home. Was I that close to death? Then I realized that priests like to feel useful and assumed a guy who'd been shot in the head was a good candidate to get last rites and any other sacrament that could grease his way into heaven.

"Are the girls okay?" I asked.

Angela pulled up a chair. "I told them you fell. They don't have to know the truth, and it wasn't in the paper. What happened, Mike?"

I respected Angela and knew I could trust her, but she wasn't one of us, trained in the ways of keeping one's mouth shut and not making any slipups that could cause . . . well, a bullet to the head. She had a few cousins that were made guys in the mob, and a slip of the tongue could have dire consequences.

But I didn't want to lie to her. "It's best you don't know. Point is, I'm gonna be okay." A fountain of information it wasn't, but it was the best I could do.

Her lips compressed to a smooth line, eyebrows arched, shoulders stiffening. I knew the signs; she was pissed. The next twenty minutes were an argument that had begun about five years before. The bottom line was, I could make nice because I was sure my undercover days were over. Angela left thinking I'd done a complete reversal and would spend more time with her and the girls doing what families did together, whatever that was. Little did she know that my acquiescence to normalcy had come about because of my circumstances; I was about to become useless as an undercover cop. I saw my future in uniform patrolling the streets and locking up as many people as I could to transition to the rank of detective.

That notion soon changed with my next visitors.

The aforementioned Sergeant Nick Orilio came in accompanied

by James (Big Jim) Sweeney, a detective sergeant with the State Police. Nick actually had tears in his eyes, but that didn't surprise me. He was a big teddy bear of a man, concerned about his troops and a genuinely nice guy. Sweeney was tougher, more pragmatic, and one of the sharpest cops I ever knew.

As I was telling Nick I was okay and to stop blubbering, I noticed Sweeney was bursting at the seams to say something. After the well wishes and being assured the New Jersey State Police valued my contribution to the undercover investigation, Sweeney hit me with the bombshell.

"Mike, we're considering not going after the guys who did this to you."

I was sure the bullet had affected my hearing. "Huh?"

Sweeney repeated his statement, followed by an explanation. "You're okay, Mike, very lucky. If we lock up the crew, the operation is blown. If you go back to King's Court, settle your differences about the briefcase and the money, you should get a pass."

"Should? What happens if they don't let bygones be bygones? Next time they'll come after me with a friggin' rocket launcher."

Nick chimed in, shaking his head. "It won't happen. Yours was a minor infraction. They tried to take you out, and didn't. They'll let it go. This isn't a scene out of a movie, Mike. Shit goes wrong, they walk away, unless you want to make something of it. You be cool, they'll be cool."

I thought about this. Nick was right, I'd have the perfect cover. If I was anything other than what I pretended to be, I'd either flip and go to the cops or come after the guys who ambushed me. To not do anything would prove I was a stand-up guy.

"You know," I said, "you may have something there."

* * *

I was given five weeks to recuperate.

I lived with my family in a row-house apartment over a store in Newark. The building had two separate residences; we had the top floor and my sister and her family lived on the first floor. We'd been there twelve years and were comfortable in the mostly Italian neighborhood, where crime was minimal and families looked after each other.

I heard nothing from the crew that had tried to take me out, and Angela was pleased that I was keeping my word and not leaping back into police work. I'd hit her with the bad news about going undercover later rather than sooner, but she had to be told eventually. A bullet to the head was mild compared to what I'd put up with from my wife when I began trying to work my way back into the Lucchese crime family.

Initially I thought there were no residual effects from the wound. Other than a headache and a bunch of stitches, I felt like my old self inside of a week. Not until two weeks after my arrival home did I realize I had a problem.

Angela was a great cook, not a great stretch for a woman raised in a traditional Italian family. Every time I thought about how unhappy I was playing the conventional husband role, Angela would whip some lasagna on me and my depression would dissipate. The woman knew her way around a kitchen.

So it was with great confusion that when I forked a mountain of lasagna into my mouth, I realized I couldn't taste it. Could this be possible? It tasted like nothing: no savory sauce, no melted cheese, no succulent sausages. I panicked. I'm a basic guy, I love food, sex, sports, and the occasional cocktail. While I couldn't get laid five times a day, I could certainly eat as often as I desired. Was one of the great pleasures of life gone?

I lunged for the refrigerator.

I bit into an apple, gulped milk, folded a piece of bologna and jammed it into my mouth. Nothing. I might as well have been eating wallpaper.

"Angela!" I yelled.

She came running, arms laden with freshly laundered clothes. When she saw the expression on my face, she looked concerned.

"What?" she asked, eyes wide.

"I've got no taste," I said, unsure of what to do next.

"*You've* got no taste? *I've* got no taste; I married you."

I stared at her blankly, a slightly eaten apple in my hand.

When she saw I wasn't joking, she said, "What happened?"

I explained the revelation, unsure as to how long I'd been without the ability to taste anything. The longer I thought about it, the more I realized I couldn't smell anything either. The bullet had rendered it impossible for me to taste or smell, which would plague me for the rest of my life.

I'd never realized how much I took the simple pleasures of tasting and smelling for granted; I guess everyone does. Acclimation to the problem came with some difficulty, but what choice did I have? The anticipation of getting back to work was a distraction, and after a while I eased myself back into police work.

I told my wife I would be working at an inside job, regular business hours, and would be home at a reasonable time, Newark traffic permitting. In reality I was planning a strategy to confront my attackers and get back into the game.

3

Mikey Ga-Ga:
Back in the Life

While my wife had to pinch herself every day to see if she was dreaming—I'd been home for five weeks recuperating from my gunshot wound and emulating Ward Cleaver as if I were his clone—I was kicking myself in the ass out of frustration, but inflicting less pain than I was suffering being the perfect husband and father.

Angela was loving having me home and devoting quality time to her and the girls, while I hated most of it. Don't get me wrong, I cherished my family, but my excitement gene was craving action, and if I made one more trip to the local Dairy Queen, I was going to shoot *myself* in the head. So I was greatly elated when my state trooper bosses finally permitted me to go back to work.

I'd healed well. I saw the two holes in my head as more of a trophy of battle than a symbol of a life nearly lost. My senses of taste and smell were still gone, but I was slowly adjusting to the depriva-tion. I was using recall to remember how food *used* to taste. I dis-covered a heightened appreciation for texture. Food tasted good because it was supposed to. How could a veal-and-pepper hero have no taste or aroma? My brain willed my dormant taste buds and olfactory senses to enjoy it anyway. After a while, unless I specifi-cally thought about it, I completely forgot about having lost two of the most basic pleasures of man's existence. It's like living next to railroad tracks: At first the train noise annoys the hell out of you and will surely drive you crazy, but after a while you tune it out. Things could've been worse: I might have been shot in the genitals. I guess you could call me a glass-half-full kind of person.

Sergeant Nick Orilio had come up with an operational cover for me. I was to be the owner of a small oil-delivery business and try to work my way into the good graces of the Gambino or Genovese crime families. No way was I going to go back with the Lucchese crew, and according to Nick's reasoning, even though the other crime families might have heard about my near assassination, they should let me become an associate because I was a stand-up guy for not ratting anyone out. Of course I had to be a good earner, because while omertà, the vow of silence, was a commendable attribute, the ability to make money was the most valued skill in organized crime.

I was warned by Sergeant Nick that he had heard a rumor that a crooked Newark police lieutenant named Eddie Dwyer had found out about my undercover status and ratted me out to the Lucchese crew, and that my getting shot in the head was a planned execution based on Dwyer's information, and not on the theft of the briefcase as previously thought. Dwyer was a known corrupt cop, but he'd never been caught at it, mainly because at the time the Newark Police Department was a cesspool of dirty cops. He just blended in. My gut told me that the rumor was just that, a rumor. I doubted Dwyer knew who I was, but I needed to know for sure before I put myself in harm's way again. (Dwyer eventually branched out into holding up banks while he was still on the job. He was easily recognized during one stickup and wound up getting three years in prison.)

I was given an oil truck from a guy someone knew in the truck-leasing business and a pat on the back and sent on my way. My "oil business" had zero employees, no office, and no phone-directory listing. Occasionally, I would have to switch trucks because the one I was driving either broke down or the guy who owned the legit business needed it. No two trucks looked alike, and it appeared I was an oil magnate with a fleet of vehicles. I was flying by the seat of my pants. I even paid for business cards out of my own pocket. I called the business Premium Oil.

I told Angela none of this, making up some bullshit story about going back into uniform and working day tours and four-to-twelve shifts. Just as long as I left the house and returned after my eight-hour "shift," she didn't care what I was doing as long as I came home in one piece and did what passed for normal police work. I figured she might eventually find out about my undercover status, but in typical male fashion I never thought that day would come.

My first order of business was to confront my attackers, or at least the boss who'd ordered me hit. I felt I had to do this to maintain my reputation as a tough, stand-up guy, and to confirm that the Eddie Dwyer story was bullshit. Sergeant Nick was dead set against it, but it was my ass and I felt the success of the new operation depended on it. If I was made as a cop, I'd know it immediately, and I'd get the hell out of Dodge.

So, with great apprehension, I entered a diner that I knew was frequented by Mike Perna, the capo who more than likely okayed my demise. If it wasn't him, it was someone in the same crew of equal rank. Talk to Perna, talk to them all. I chose Perna because he was tough and well respected. If I stood up to him, the word would get out.

Perna was sitting in a booth near the rear of the diner. He was with another guy—probably a bodyguard—whom I didn't know. He was big enough to look as if he were sprayed with PAM and squeezed into the booth.

Maybe a dozen other patrons were enjoying their meals. All of them stopped eating when I walked in, some with forks almost in their mouths. Dead silence ensued.

Perna said something to the muscle with him, who turned around and dipped a hand under his coat. I made sure they saw my hands as I approached the booth.

Contrary to popular belief, most mobsters aren't the smooth, dapper guys the movies and television make them out to be. Your average wiseguy is poorly educated, couldn't string two cohesive sentences together, and is fat and crude. Perna was a captain, and as a captain he was expected to be an example to his soldiers by fitting the mold of a media Mafia don: well dressed, well-spoken, in good shape, and educated.

When I reached the table, Perna smiled and said, "Learn your lesson, Mikey?"

I knew just by the greeting that he had no idea I was a cop. If he had made me, either from Dwyer or another source, I'd have seen it in his eyes. I stared at him long enough to show I wasn't afraid of him or his beefed-up goon.

"Life's one big lesson, Mr. Perna; I learn something new every day."

After a few seconds of dead air he said, "What's past is past. Stay out of trouble." He went back to his lunch. I was dismissed. Better yet, I was alive. And they never got their goddamn briefcase back either.

I familiarized myself with driving oil trucks, huge tankers that were always empty and easier to maneuver. For the first few days I tooled around northern Newark, home to the Genovese and Gambino crime families. I'd stop by their hangouts, which were invariably bars or restaurants, have one or two beers, maybe grab a sandwich, and get seen without being heard.

I learned from experience that getting close to the wiseguys required that you be subtle. A pushy, mouthy guy is either labeled a cop or a bad security risk. Ingratiating myself would take time, and the way to start was by becoming a recognizable face. I hoped the rest would come in time.

Inevitably people talked to me. Small talk is common among drinkers, and I was determined to fit in by not asking any questions. I'd rap about everything from politics to women to sports. Mikey Ga-Ga was nothing if not the social butterfly. Problem was, time was passing, and I was getting nowhere fast. The wiseguys kept to themselves and acted as if they didn't know I existed.

While barhopping I picked up a lucrative sideline: removing furnaces from buildings. While this was dirty labor, I knew it was the last thing a cop would do. Most undercovers would accept the danger inherent to their work, but get dirty? Never. I was more concerned about showering before I went home so Angela wouldn't get suspicious.

I was soon making pretty good money and ran into an ethical dilemma. What do I do with the extra cash, which was significant. I ran this conundrum past Jim Sweeney, who, I thought, would bounce it off some mysterious trooper ethics board. Instead he said, "Fuck it. Keep the money, you're earning it." He didn't have to tell me twice. Between my trooper salary, my furnace-removal fees, and the occasional oil delivery, I was doing pretty well financially. But my newfound wealth wasn't bringing me any closer to infiltrating the mob.

Another day, another tour of the wiseguy joints. It was like being on autopilot. I'd hit the same places, say hello to the same people, order a sandwich and a beer, and move on to the next establishment. Not only wasn't I accomplishing anything, but I was putting on some weight. My wife recognized this and was wary.

"You got the gourmet-restaurant beat?" she asked, eyeing my extra poundage.

The closest thing to a decent restaurant where Angela thought I was working was a Chinese place where I wouldn't eat if you held a gun to my head—again.

"Crime fighting builds up a hell of an appetite," I said.

She gave me a sideways look. "Uh-huh."

So there I was, once again making my rounds in the oil truck, when I stopped the rig at the intersection of Bloomfield and Roseville Avenues. This was a commercial area littered with mom-and-pop restaurants, factories, warehouses, and other small businesses.

I looked across the street and saw what looked like a businessman: a white guy about forty-five years old, meticulously dressed, leaving a diner and walking toward a late-model black BMW 745. This was an expensive car, the top-of-the-line Bimmer, and it caught my eye. Plus a white guy in this neighborhood stuck out like a black guy at a Ku Klux Klan meeting.

Right behind this businessman type were two black guys, late twenties, maybe early thirties. They were walking too close to him to be out for a stroll, so I decided to pull the rig over and watch them.

Sure enough, the black guys pounced on the white guy and began to pummel him; your classic blitz-type street mugging: overpower the victim with lightning speed, inflict as much damage as you can in a limited time, rifle his pockets, and get the hell away. This type of street crime is over in less than thirty seconds. Normally a good tactic, but I was on them in less than ten seconds.

I'd been a fighter all my life, both in the street and in the ring, having trained in heavyweight champion Anthony (Two-Ton Tony) Galento's gym in Newark. Because my street skills were survival-oriented, I loved a good fight when the odds were against me. Two against one was good odds as far as I was concerned, particularly against street mutts who probably didn't know the first thing about fighting proficiency.

These were pretty big guys, but in less than a minute both were unconscious. No fancy footwork or kung fu moves, just a few body jabs followed by two roundhouse punches for the coups de grâces. The victim was still getting his footing by the time everything was over.

"You okay?" I asked. He looked familiar but I couldn't place him. The guy gave me a once-over. "Yeah, I'm fine. You?"

"No problem here." I glanced over my shoulder at the two prostrate figures. "I'll go call the cops." I turned to go into the diner from which the victim had emerged.

He grabbed me by the arm. "No cops." A few cars had slowed down to check out the two unconscious muggers. "Come with me back inside Joe's."

We went into Joe's Diner, a spotless, small, four-booth eatery. The place looked as if it had been there since the 1930s: Formica counter, chrome-and-red-leather stools, old-fashioned sugar jars, black-and-white-tile floor. A big, shiny brass espresso machine was perched on the counter against a wall. The thing must have cost at least five grand and definitely looked out of place. An old lady was behind the counter, and I heard rattling pots in the kitchen. No patrons, no waiters.

The old lady said in a heavy Italian accent, "Everything okay, Mr. Gerardo?"

"Yeah, yeah, I'm okay, thanks to this guy." A nod to me. "Couple of black guys tried to mug me. This guy saved my bacon." He stuck out a hand and introduced himself. "Andy Gerardo."

I shook his hand. "Mike Russell." I'd always used my real name during my undercover career, having built a reputation as a rogue former cop.

The lightbulb went on. I had just rescued one of the ranking captains in the Genovese crime family.

I hadn't recognized Gerardo right from the start because of his car. Newark wiseguys all drove either black or dark blue Cadillacs. It was unheard of to stray from the gangster's main choice of transportation; the Caddy was the status symbol for the broken-nose set. It was big, bodacious, and reeked of power. But mostly they drove Caddys because they were American-made, and mobsters, despite their criminal ways, were a patriotic bunch. That Gerardo drove a different car, a *German* car no less, showed me that he was an innovator and smart. This was no dumb greaseball gangster.

Gerardo was one of the more polished mob guys I'd encountered. He was gracious and invited me to lunch. For a little hole-in-the-wall diner, the food was incredible. Even with my lack of tasting ability, the eggs and peppers were great, as was the polenta that came on the side.

We made small talk for a while, Gerardo thanking me several times for saving his ass. I wasn't pushy, didn't ask any questions, and answered all those asked of me.

"You're pretty good with your hands," Gerardo said. "You fight?"

"Had a few pro fights, needed to make some dough to support my wife and three kids. Had to let it go, there were guys better." I sipped my espresso. Turned out Gerardo had paid for the espresso machine, and no one could use it except him and his guests. I remembered from my intelligence briefings he had an electrical business around the corner called Lectricians. Gerardo made millions from the business, which was mostly legitimate, although I recall his getting New York and New Jersey highway-lighting contracts that were supposedly influenced by bribes. Regardless, Gerardo was the type of person that no matter how rich he got legitimately, he loved the lure of easy money that mob life ensured.

"So what do you do now?" Gerardo asked. He was wearing a gray pinstripe suit that, while a bit smudged from his recent visit to the sidewalk, still looked all of the three grand it must have cost.

I told him about my fledging oil business, my former job as a New Jersey state trooper ("I beat the shit out of one too many citizens"), and my hustling to make extra money removing old furnaces from buildings. "I need the money." I also told him I worked at King's Court for a while. He'd know that meant I was mobbed up, at least I had been. I wasn't supposed to know his status with the mob, but I knew he would check up on my past and find out I was a stand-up guy.

Gerardo thought for a while, then said, "You done the right thing. You could've gotten hurt, maybe worse. I repay people who risk their ass for me." He reached into his jacket and came out with a shiny alligator billfold.

I shook my head, waved my hand. "Oh, no, there's no need for that, Mr. Gerardo. My pleasure to bust those cocksuckers up."

He pulled out five bills from the billfold, all hundreds. "No, I insist. Here, buy your wife and kids something."

We went back and forth for a few minutes, and after a while Gerardo put the money away. I could tell he was impressed.

"Okay, tell you what," he said, "I've got some people might need some oil delivered. I'll throw some business your way."

"Thanks, Mr. Gerardo." I imagined he'd be making calls to some legitimate businesses and coercing them into using me.

"You come around for lunch whenever you want; your money's no good here. Maybe in a few days I might have some work for you. Your friends call you Mike, Mickey, what?"

"My friends call me Mikey Ga-Ga."

He smirked. "Well, okay, Mikey Ga-Ga, see you around."

Gerardo liked me, and I was going to milk that for everything it was worth.

What I had set into motion would be New Jersey's most in-depth investigation into organized crime since the inception of the State Police; the road would take me into the confidence of the ranking members of the Mafia to become one of the most trusted associates in the Genovese crime family.

I had gotten my wish; I was right in the middle of the action.

4

Balancing Act

I began frequenting Joe's Diner. I didn't make a pig of myself because I couldn't pay for anything. Gerardo made sure of that, and I didn't want anyone to think I was a freeloader, least of all Gerardo. Mostly I stopped in when I saw Gerardo's Bimmer out front. He was always pleased to see me, and he'd wave me over to sit with him and break bread. In Mafia circles it's considered an honor to be recognized by a boss of Gerardo's stature and be invited to share a meal. Food is a big part of the Mafia culture, as evidenced by the girth of most wiseguys.

I'd also stop into Joe's when I knew Gerardo *wasn't* there. I didn't want to appear obvious; if I was going to court this guy, I had to be subtle. If he found out that I was only going to the diner when he was there, as he surely would have, his antennae would have gone up. Then I'd either be an ass-kisser or a rat cooperating with the cops. If that happened, I'd either be shunned or worse, and one bullet in my noggin was enough, thank you. You didn't get to where Gerardo was in the mob by being a pushover.

When I dropped by alone, I'd leave a tip that covered the price of the meal and then some, which was a gesture of respect. When I shared a meal with Gerardo, I couldn't go into my pocket; to do so would be an insult to him. A lot of mob custom is steeped in tradition, and I wasn't about to tread on a hundred years of wiseguy decorum no matter how complicated the rules got at times. New associates would fare a lot better if Emily Post published a book of mob etiquette for the fledging wiseguy.

Gerardo seemed genuinely interested in helping me with my business. He asked about my customers, home-heating-oil prices, and profit margins to help increase my bottom line. I'd done a little research on my own about the oil-delivery business, but I was far from an expert, so I did what I was best at doing: I made shit up. But I knew I couldn't scam this guy forever.

What I needed was some street credibility. No matter how good a bullshitter I was, I figured that in time Gerardo would figure out I didn't know what the hell I was talking about, or someone would get clever and wonder why Premium Oil—a heating-oil-delivery company—never delivered any oil. Some wiseguy with an IQ that matched his waistline might also wonder why my company name wasn't stenciled on any of the trucks I drove, which I supposedly owned.

I came up with a plan to solidify my creds.

"I'm doing pretty good removing old oil furnaces," I told Gerardo over espresso thick enough to be mistaken for Saudi Arabian crude. I'd been doing furnace removal on the side and I could document the jobs.

"There's money in that?"

"Fuck, yeah. All those old buildings they're tearing down, the owners want the furnaces scrapped or relocated. Dirty business, but big bucks."

"I'll ask around, maybe I can steer you to some customers that want that done, too. You don't do this yourself, right?"

"Can't do this alone, I got two people give me a hand." Actually, I *was* doing it alone, but I wanted to make the business seem more viable. Now I needed to scrounge up a few guys who were dumb enough to think I ran a legit business and strong enough to heft a few tons of iron every day just in case Gerardo checked.

I figured it would be easy to locate a couple of mopes who wanted to make decent money in a depressed economy (Newark never had a thriving one) who would help me with the furnaces. First thing I'd do is take them to lunch at Joe's, which Gerardo would undoubtedly hear about.

Turns out I was wrong; finding guys willing to do backbreaking, filthy labor was damn near impossible. I asked everywhere with zero results, until I hit the bottom of the barrel: ex-cons.

While I didn't relish working with criminals, at least not the kind who didn't dress in $3,000 suits, I had little choice. Besides, hiring guys who just got out of the joint would show where my sympathies lay. I contacted a parole officer I knew, and he lined up two men who'd just gotten out of New Jersey's Rahway State Penitentiary after doing time for armed robbery.

The cons, Tommy and Jocko, turned out to be good workers. Tommy was built like an armored car, and Jocko made Tommy look anemic. Both could lift their weight in iron and were grateful for the work. They were loyal, never missed a day, and didn't talk much. I paid them more than they'd make sticking up convenience stores, and I liked that they didn't take themselves seriously, having left any attitude in Rahway. They might've been badasses on the street and in the joint, but they were grateful for legitimate work and that I never threw their pasts in their faces. Both were out on parole and knew even being convicted of a minor crime could get them a one-way trip back to the joint. For me they were the perfect employees.

I began contacting real estate agents and plumbers, broadcasting that my crew and I were willing to get down and dirty if they had furnaces that needed to be removed. Gerardo threw me some work, too, and I introduced him to my crew. The work flowed in, and I found myself making three times as much as I was earning as a cop. While this didn't help me in my alleged oil-delivery business, it showed I was a working stiff and was expanding my Premium Oil "empire," which only existed on paper.

While I was waiting for Gerardo to make me an offer I couldn't refuse—any menial mob job for him that would get my foot in the door—I was proactive by cruising past known mob hangouts and writing down license-plate numbers, then passing them on to my handlers to run for identification.

I made sure to make it home every night and kept my wife in the dark regarding my undercover assignment. I'd get a comment every so often about the grime under my fingernails despite my best efforts to scrub myself squeaky-clean in a shower at the gym I belonged to, but I'd offer a lame explanation and Angela would accept it. I think she didn't want to probe too deeply for fear she'd find out what I was really doing. Psychologically she didn't want to know, a classic case of denial.

* * *

After taking my new crew to Joe's for lunch a few times and a month of hauling filthy furnaces out of filthier buildings, I was no closer to working my way into Gerardo's crew. He was still buying me lunches and we got along famously, but there was no request to help him out with any mob-related business. I would have done anything, no matter how menial, but I needed him to bring it up to get in the door.

Finally it hit me: Gerardo viewed me as a legit guy—a "civilian"—no matter what my former association was with the Lucchese family. My take was that he thought the bullet I took to the head had scared me away from "the life." I had to change his opinion.

I reached out to Howie Martin, a police chief who ran several businesses on the side. Howie was a career cop and had been chief of police in a town in the area for five years, but he had an entrepreneurial streak. In addition to operating a civil-service promotional school for ambitious cops, he ran what he called a "security" business, which catered mainly to clubs, restaurants, and bars. He supplied bouncers and cash-pickup services to establishments in the rougher neighborhoods in Newark and Jersey City. He also wasn't above squeezing a few bucks out of local businessmen to spread around to the local cops to keep things running smoothly.

Business was booming and Howie had called me on a few occasions in the past wanting to hire me for protection when he made his cash stops. While Howie was a cop, he wasn't the confrontational type, unless he was facing an arrogant bank teller. He was a nebbish who knew the political side of policing and built a successful career on it. In the past I'd turned him down because I didn't want a hired-muscle reputation, but now that was exactly what I needed. Word of what I was doing would get around, and it might help me get a similar position in Gerardo's crew. That I was working for a police chief didn't make a difference, such was the reputation of New Jersey cops. The mind-set of the mob was that most cops were crooked, and the type of business Howie ran wouldn't detract from that supposition, even though as far as crooked cops went, Howie was only slightly bent. Howie's greed, however, would eventually be his downfall. He engineered a scam where he asked twenty cops who were taking a one-hundred-question promotional exam to write down five questions each, with Howie assigning the question numbers. In our portion of New Jersey, police promotional tests reused the same questions over and over. They came from a pool of about a thousand questions that never changed. Eventually, Howie had all the questions, and he used them as "sample" questions in his promotional school. He successfully advertised his school as having the highest percentage of officers who passed civil-service promotional exams. He was caught after a few years and did eighteen months in prison, losing his chief's job and his pension. But at that time Howie was riding a wave of business success and was off everyone's radar. I called him and his offer was still stood.

"What made you change your mind?" he asked.

"I looked in my wallet and there was nothing there."

"Two hundred a night. All you have to do is look mean and watch my back."

I assured him I could do that.

"Great, you start tomorrow night. Pick you up at eight."

My biggest problem now would be inventing another bullshit story to tell Angela about my new night job.

* * *

I'd been lifting weights all of my adult life and was pretty big. Carrying tons of furnace iron packed more muscle on an already imposing frame. To add to the image I made my rounds with Howie dressed in formfitting shirts, a black leather jacket, and mirrored Ray-Bans. Getting used to the sunglasses was the hardest part; I kept walking into furniture in darkened bars before my night vision kicked in.

All of the clubs we picked up money from were mob-connected. This usually came in the form of paying tribute—read *cash*—to the local wiseguy crew to keep them from burning the joints down. Owners paid protection money to the mob to protect them from the protectors. In addition to the legitimate money we collected for bank drops and the bouncers' payroll, Howie finessed a little more for the local precinct, most of which he pocketed. He knew how not to make waves; he gave enough to the uniforms to keep them happy. While he was a greedy bastard, Howie was well aware of Rule #1 in the shakedown business: make a show of being generous to those who keep you in business.

Things went smoothly for weeks, and every few nights I'd stop by Joe's with Howie for dinner. While Gerardo was never there past 5:00 p.m., I knew the counter crew and any wiseguy or associate present would make Howie immediately, and the word would get to Gerardo. My rep as a strong-arm guy was being molded.

After about six weeks of playing tough guy I stopped into Joe's for breakfast by myself. The counterman, an ex-con named Augie, placed a platter of sausage and eggs down, leaned into me, and slid a folded piece of paper across the counter.

"Mr. Gerardo wants you to see a guy."

Bingo.

The address on the paper was a mom-and-pop Italian restaurant on North Sixth Street in Newark, located in a heavily Italian neighborhood of close-knit families that had taken the overflow from the Little Italy section of Manhattan at the turn of the last century. On this quiet night, a bit chilly for the middle of May, the outdoor café was deserted. I was thirty minutes early for my meeting, but early in my business was the way to go. If something unexpected was to be encountered, you wanted to arrive before the surprise did.

The restaurant was small, brightly lit, and empty, not surprising for a weekday night at nine o'clock. I sat at a table for four in the back, watching the door. On top of a checkered tablecloth a candle was burning in an empty, wax-encrusted Chianti bottle, with a soft operatic aria playing in the background to complete the mood. I was beginning to feel guilty for being Irish. One lone bottle-blond barmaid with a tight sweater ignored me, and no waiters were in sight. I waited.

Five minutes later an ancient waiter, who looked as if the restaurant were built around him, materialized and took my drink order.

"I'm waiting for someone," I said.

He gave me a disinterested stare, grunted, and shuffled off, returning with my drink and a basket of thick-crusted bread.

I continued to wait, but at least now I had Scotch to keep me company.

I was still the only patron in the joint when the door opened and a wiseguy I'd seen around the neighborhood since I was a kid, Joe

Zarra, waddled in. Zarra was a soldier in the Genovese family and worked in Andy Gerardo's crew. He had been in the life since his teens. Because of his seniority, Zarra answered directly to Gerardo, who trusted him.

Where Gerardo was distinguished and polished, Zarra appeared extinguished and tarnished. He was in his sixties, short, very overweight, and bald. He liked to dress in velour sweat suits and had a cigar jammed in his face at all times. Rumor was he slept with it. Appearances aside, he had survived in the Mafia all his adult life without ever taking a serious bust, so stupid he wasn't.

Zarra spotted me in the back and made his way over, sitting down opposite me with a grunt.

"You Mikey?" he wheezed.

I nodded. "That's me."

He extended a hand. "Joe Zarra. Andy Gerardo said we should talk."

We shook, his hand reminding me of Silly Putty.

"Mr. Gerardo coming?

Zarra waved his arm. "No need." He looked around and raised an eyebrow. Within seconds, the lone waiter appeared. I'd have bet he hadn't moved that fast since the cops had chased him during Prohibition.

Zarra rattled off rapid Italian, and the waiter took off before I had a chance to order.

Zarra smiled, the ubiquitous cigar clenched, unlit, between his teeth. "I ordered for you. You'll like it, trust me."

We made small talk until the food arrived. Small talk is a staple in the mob. Before business is discussed, you have to go through the litany of wiseguy protocol: Tell me about your family. Fucking cold (hot, wet), ain't it? That fucking barmaid (tightrope walker, mother superior) has some tits, no? And on it went until the food arrived and we got down to business.

"Listen," Zarra said, "Andy tells me you're good with your hands."

I shoveled a piece of paper-thin veal into my mouth. It looked good, must've tasted great, but of course I wouldn't know. "I do okay."

"Andy says you're a stand-up guy, good enough for me." He dug into his pocket, came out with a folded index card, and handed it to me. "You know Greenwich Village?"

I looked at the card, read an address on West Street, and the name of a club: the Crisco Disco. "Sure." West Street was on the fringes of the Village in the meatpacking district, which was famous for gay clubs, leather bars, and private clubs that featured sadomasochistic themes. Anything went in the neighborhood, and the cops generally stayed away. Every so often a homicide would occur as the result of a mugging gone bad or the Fist Fuckers of America got carried away at one of their monthly meetings.

"The Crisco Disco?" I said. "You're kidding, right?"

Zarra shrugged. "What can I tell you? Faggot comes to town from fucking Omaha, wants his asshole reamed, he's only gotta get ahold of the friggin' yellow pages. Anyways, guy that owns that club, some guy named Rokop, gives us an envelope every week. Been okay for two years, now the envelope's light. Says business is slow and he can't afford the full nut no more." Zarra jammed what seemed like a half loaf of bread in his mouth. I waited.

"So, we want you should go talk to the guy." Zarra gave me the once-over. "You look badass enough to scare the shit outta him."

"And if he don't scare?"

"Fuck him up a little, but not too much. He's gotta learn a lesson, not stop breathin'. We still need to get paid. Maybe break a finger or whatever. There's five hundred in it for you. I'll be in Vegas for a few days, I'll call you when I get back."

I had a two-part dilemma. The first part was ethical: I couldn't hurt this Rokop guy, me being a cop and all; followed by the second part: I also couldn't turn down the job. Do that and I'd be persona non grata. A mob boss asks you for a favor once, you don't do it, they don't want to know you.

"Yeah, sure," I said, "no problem."

I met with Sergeant Nick and Big Jim Sweeney at the Joyce Kilmer rest stop on the New Jersey Turnpike to discuss what to do with the recalcitrant Rokop. We shared tepid coffee at eight in the morning while commuters inched toward the city at what seemed like negative miles per hour.

"You can't lay a hand on the guy," Nick said. "That's committing a crime."

"Fuck 'em, shove him around a little," Big Jim said. "It's gotta look real."

Obviously a difference of opinion.

"C'mon, you're my ethics board, I need direction," I said. "Make a goddamn decision."

For the next half hour I sat back and observed while my handlers discussed strategy. At one point my bladder gave me the only direction I was getting so far that day; I went to the bathroom.

When I got back, both voices of reason were quiet. Big Jim, speaking for both himself and Nick, had made their decision.

"Fuck it, Mikey, just go with the flow."

Their leadership and advice knew no intellectual or ethical bounds.

I was on my own.

My mind was swimming as I exited the Holland Tunnel on the Manhattan side. I had no idea how I was going to handle the situation, but I knew I had to come up with an equitable arrangement that would make everyone happy, most of all Joe Zarra. Conversely, I didn't want Rokop running to the police and destroying a good start to my undercover operation. In addition, it would be embarrassing if I screwed up and Rokop wound up in the trunk of his car in long-term parking at JFK Airport.

I found a legal parking spot on the street near the club, a good omen I thought, and maybe an indication of smooth sailing through what might be the best acting job of my career.

I walked the two blocks to the Crisco Disco, past groups of leather-clad bikers and cruising gay men who were virtually indistinguishable. I saw joints with names like the Anvil, the Slippery Fist, Gracie's Mansion (owned by former mayor John Lindsay's brother, who apparently had a pretty good sense of humor), and like-named places that existed for the leather and bondage crowd.

The Crisco Disco stood by itself between two abandoned buildings across from where the West Side Highway once stood. To enter the club I walked down four steps, both physically and socially.

The dimly lit room was smaller than I'd imagined, and crammed with men on the dance floor and huddled in corners. The music was deafening. Smoke hung heavy, and I coughed as I made my way through the crowd to the bar. Every form of humanity was there, from the aforementioned leather men to transvestites, transsexuals, businessmen in suits, construction guys still in their work clothes, young, preppy types, and the occasional off-duty priest (just guessing). I was reminded of the bar scene in the first *Star Wars* movie. I looked around for the Village People, but they were probably at someplace tamer.

The bartender was either one of the most beautiful women I'd ever seen or the most-well-put-together transsexual ever to undergo surgery. She (he?) was close to six feet tall with long auburn hair, tastefully applied makeup, and a body that made Marilyn Monroe look like Marilyn Manson. I bellied up to the packed bar next to two guys dressed in charcoal-gray suits.

"Rokop around?" I yelled to the barmaid.

"Who wants to know?" she said in a voice that was three octaves lower than James Earl Jones's. My bubble burst; definitely a guy, or former guy.

"Friend of Joe Zarra," I screamed back.

She (whatever) went to a phone, pressed two buttons, said a few words, and came back to me. "Straight in the back, office on your left."

I made my way through the crowd to the office and knocked. I heard a muffled voice, which I took for permission to enter.

The office was small but mercifully soundproofed. Behind a desk littered with papers and a half-empty bottle of vodka was a small guy, maybe forty-five, with a buzz cut, wearing a black sweater, and hoisting a martini glass. He didn't look happy.

"Look," he said, "Mr. . . . ?"

"Mike, just Mike."

"Well, Just Mike, if Joe's looking for what I owe him, he's gonna have to wait. Maybe forever." He took a healthy swig of the drink. He was fucked-up. I hated dealing with drunks.

I took three steps to the desk and towered over him. In my best threatening voice I said, "Mr. Zarra doesn't like to wait."

"And I don't want him to wait; I just don't have the cash."

I jerked a thumb over my shoulder. "The fucking place is packed. What's the problem?"

He opened a desk drawer and reached in. I went under my jacket for my pistol.

He jerked his hand from the drawer. "Whoa! Just gonna show you some paper."

I kept my hand on my gun. "Okay . . . slowly."

He produced two forms, both rent receipts, one old, one new. He slid them across the desk.

"My fucking landlord doubled my rent. Went from twenty large to forty. I'm struggling here. I can give Zarra money, but I gotta cut back twenty percent or I'm outta business."

And so the negotiations began. There had to be a way to make everyone happy; I needed an out not to have to lay a hand on him. After half an hour of back-and-forth I decided that my new best friend, Manny, wasn't a bad guy. He was a family man with a wife and two kids in Scarsdale trying to make it big in the bad city. In New York, money tribute to the mob was a normal operating expense in the nightclub business, and Manny knew it. He was willing to pay, but wanted the nut to be reasonable.

Problem was he couldn't budge on the price if he wanted to; his budget was tighter than a crab's ass that's waterproof. I believed him when he told me there was no way he could stretch one more dollar, but I wasn't in a position to be a nice guy. I was going to have to leave with money, or I'd have to apply force.

"Okay," I said, "enough of this bullshit. I need what you owe Mr. Zarra and I need it now." I got out of my chair and came around the desk. I had no idea what I was going to do.

"Ah, shit. Sally Boy was right, fucking Zarra has no compassion." Rokop braced for the first punch.

I stopped dead in my tracks. "Sally Boy?"

Rokop looked at me strangely. "Yeah, Sally Boy Randazzo. He told me Zarra didn't give a fuck about anyone but himself. What about Sally?" He pushed back his chair as far as the rollers would take him before he was stopped by a wall.

Sally Boy Randazzo was a capo with the Columbo family. He was an old-time mafioso who had been around since Vito Genovese came to power in the 1940s and was rumored to have made his bones by participating in the assassination of mob boss Albert Anastasia, who was infamously cut down while enjoying a haircut and shave in the Park Sheraton Hotel in 1957. Sally Boy was supposedly retired, but these guys never really got out of the life. They became elder statesmen who were called upon to settle disputes and were revered for their longevity, wisdom, and staying power. Something like former president Jimmy Carter's role after he left office, only unlike Carter, Randazzo was highly respected.

"How do you know Randazzo?" I was sensing an out here.

Rokop shrugged. "I dunno, friend of the family? Him and my dad grew up together. My dad's dead five years, but Uncle Sally comes around all the time."

"Uncle Sally?" Rokop may have just found the solution to his problem without knowing it.

"Yeah, well, we call him that. He's like an uncle but not really."

I sat on the desk. "Zarra know about your relationship with Randazzo?"

Rokop shrugged. "Never mentioned it. Should I have?"

I rolled my eyes. "Yeah, Manny, you should have."

Four nights later I was in El Caminetto, an upscale Italian restaurant on First Avenue in Manhattan. I was at a table across from Joe Zarra, tanned and fatter than ever, fresh back from his Vegas trip. He was taking in what I had to say about my visit to the Crisco Disco. Tonight Zarra was in a white leisure suit that made him look like John Travolta if he had taken nutrition tips from Elvis Presley. When I finished my story, Zarra just stared at me. He didn't utter a sound for at least a minute, undoubtedly the longest minute of my life.

"So, lemme see if I got this right. You took it upon yourself to let this fruit, Rokop—"

"He's a family man, Mr. Zarra, he's not gay," I said, immediately sorry for interrupting him.

Zarra did a slow burn, but maintained his composure. We weren't in a social club in Newark; the restaurant was crowded with citizens and he couldn't make a scene. He leaned toward me. "I don't give a fuck if he likes farm animals. What you're telling me is you let him slide not only for what he already owes me, but he gets a pass on twenty percent forever because his rent went up?"

"No, Mr. Zarra, not forever. And his rent doubled. His business improves, you get more money. He wants to cooperate. He'll open his books. And he got the pass because of Sally Boy. I figured you didn't need trouble with Brooklyn."

"Who gave you the right to make a decision? You were there to make a point, not make policy."

"You were gone in Vegas, and I didn't know where you were there. If I leaned on him and fucked him up and he went to the cops, you'd have been fucked. I was thinking of your welfare. And then there was the Sally Boy thing. I bounce Rokop around and he mentions it to Sally Boy . . ." I let the reasoning trail off. Zarra knew damn well it could've started a war.

His eyes bore through me while he thought. Suddenly, he pushed his chair back and said, "Wait here, I gotta make a call." He scooped his cigar from the ashtray, heaved himself upright, and made for the door.

I took a strong pull on my Scotch and drained the glass. I'm not much of a drinker, but I'd have liked another. I didn't act on my impulse. I'd need my wits about me if things went bad. I knew Zarra answered to someone, and he was making a call to pass along what I'd just told him. He was gone maybe fifteen minutes, but it seemed more like an hour. When he got back, he was all smiles. He clapped me on the shoulder before sitting down.

"You done good, Mikey, you done real good. We like that you showed initiative, that's a good thing, and you made the right decision."

We like what I did? Whoever he called liked what I did, and Zarra undoubtedly took the credit for my judgment. While I may have made Zarra look good, I also made him look foolish from his perspective. And I was the only person breathing who knew that. While he was all grins and accolades, I knew how these guys thought. To show who the boss was, he could have me clipped, then invent a story about my "lack of respect," and our secret about how

I saved his ass from a possible gang war would go with me to my grave. I decided to build his self-esteem and hope that defused any murderous thoughts he might be harboring.

"I knew that's what you'd have wanted me to do, Mr. Zarra. Without your guidance I'd've been lost over there."

His pudgy mouth broke into a grin, but his eyes were impassive, a sign of disingenuousness. "What we don't need is Sally Boy bitching about the crew—"

Didn't I just say that?

"—and the few bucks we don't make off that club is worth the goodwill with another family. Wouldn't want the jerkoff going to the cops either was what I was thinking, too."

"Right, Mr. Zarra."

Zarra ordered another bottle of wine, but the rest of our evening seemed strained, and the conversation was forced. He left before I did because I got stuck with the bill; new guys always buy dinner, and I was the new guy.

I went home that night thinking my decision at the Crisco Disco was either the smartest or dumbest move I could've made. Time would tell which.

5

Striking Oil

Two weeks passed. I was back to driving an empty oil truck in wise-guy territory, but I was getting some recognition by the way of head nods from wiseguys in the various bars and restaurants I'd stop into. The word had gotten out about my visit to the Crisco Disco despite Joe Zarra's attempt to downplay what I'd accomplished. I had averted a possible gang war, and everyone knew it. My years living in New-ark and being exposed to the mob had taught me many things, not the least being that despite their Runyonesque reputation, mobsters were yentas. Backstabbing had caused the demise of more gangsters than any form of treachery or violation of omertà. Some of these guys were like a bunch of old ladies, and they wouldn't pass up the opportunity to make another family member, particularly a crude asshole such as Zarra, look weak.

While Zarra may have felt I'd overstepped my bounds, he had to know I saved his ass by avoiding a confrontation with the Lucchese family, the largest of the five Mafia families in New York. Since my trip to Greenwich Village, I'd spotted Zarra on the street while I cruised the neighborhood in my oil rig. I'd honk, he'd wave, but I caught him in the rearview mirror more than a few times staring at my truck until he was out of sight.

I didn't trust him, not that I trusted any gangster, but him especially. You don't upstage these guys, and he knew that everyone on the street knew I'd done exactly that. While my role as an ex-cop shouldn't have endeared me to him, or for that matter the rest of the northern–New Jersey Mafia, there was some precedent for tolerating, in fact embracing, cops. Northern New Jersey had more corrupt cops across many police departments than anywhere else in the United States, as evidenced by the numerous cops who went to prison over the years for being outright criminals. And these were small departments; per capita we had the market cornered on crooked cops.

Bobby Louis Manna, third in line for the throne of the Genovese family, had Hoboken police lieutenant Frank "Dipsy" Daniello as his right-hand man. Both were later convicted in the 1989 plot to kill John Gotti at the behest of Vincent "the Chin" Gigante, after Gigante had taken umbrage when Gotti ordered the hit on Paul Castellano, boss of the Gambino family, without Commission authorization. Both Manna and Daniello got two consecutive life sentences. Bayonne cop George Weingartner, a contract killer and right-hand man to notorious psychopath capo John DiGilio, committed suicide rather than go to prison after the feds got him cold on a few murders. To make sure cops didn't screw up the investigation into his death, Weingartner videotaped the entire thing using a remote switch. Countless other cops served in lesser capacities in Mafia families.

Zarra ran a private club on Davenport Avenue, a few blocks from the Italian restaurant where I'd met with him to discuss the Crisco Disco matter. It served as headquarters for Gerardo's crew, and my goal was to be trusted enough to get inside and have an opportunity to plant listening devices. I had the makings of a solid reputation and now just made myself visible until I got my invite. My plan was to not be pushy, which was a fast way to raise suspicion.

I'd have stood a better chance with Gerardo, but he was on parole when I met him, and if he got caught consorting with known criminals, he'd go back to prison, so he avoided his crew and the club. Gerardo had told me he had no problem going to Joe's Diner because it wasn't on the feds' radar, and he only went there for breakfast or an early lunch, too early for the FBI to be out and about.

Now with the warmer weather, I'd stop by outside the club and schmooze with the wiseguys hanging out in front, who were commenting on passing women and telling each other how smart they were. After a short time I was on a first-name basis with most everyone in the crew. When I wasn't there, I'd drive to the Belmont Tavern on Bloomfield Avenue a few blocks away, a Gambino family hangout, to see what intelligence I could soak up while I stuffed my face with chicken Savoy, their signature dish. Joe Paterno was the capo running the restaurant, which doubled as family headquarters. Paterno and I had known each other for ten years, from my days as a street cop in Newark, a job I held before going to the state cops. Like all wiseguys, Paterno thought all cops were crooked, and I didn't dispel that notion.

I made it known to Paterno and the rest of the broken-nose set that I was involved in several crooked deals, giving the impression that I was a good earner. It showed ambition, lack of fear, and helped the bosses' bottom line. Whatever form of criminal activity a soldier or associate was involved in, he was obligated to kick a percentage of his scores up to the bosses. A good earner made money for the bosses, and that's what the mob was all about. Most mob movies speak of respect and honor, when in reality it was all about who made the most money. Many infractions by a good earner were overlooked, while a marginal worker could get whacked for getting caught in traffic and being late for a meeting.

I was doing some security work for a few clubs in the area, getting bouncer positions due to my size. These clubs were frequented by younger wiseguys, and the word filtered back to the bosses that I was muscle for hire, plus I invented a bogus stolen-property business that enhanced my budding criminal reputation.

Word got back to me that Gerardo's crew, particularly Joe Zarra, thought I was ambitious and had good earning potential. I figured I'd hear from Zarra again, not because he was impressed with my loyalty, but because he was a greedy bastard and would want to capitalize on my earning possibilities or my muscle.

I didn't have to wait long. About a month after the Crisco Disco thing, I stopped into Joe's Diner for a late lunch. The place was empty except for the counterman, Augie, who dropped what he was doing and made for the pay phone as soon as he saw me walk in. Ten minutes later Zarra strolled in as if he had just happened to be in the neighborhood. He was wearing a sweat suit and had a cigar jutting from his pudgy mouth.

"Hey, Mikey," he said, waving and all smiles as he plopped down on the stool next to me at the counter. "How you doin'?"

I looked at him nonchalantly. "Hey, Mr. Zarra." I went back to my sausage sandwich.

Zarra leaned in a little closer to me. "Listen, Mikey, I have a something you could maybe help me out with. You interested?"

"Always interested in making a few extra bucks, Mr. Zarra. And of course helping you out goes without saying." I smiled. If he knew I was jerking him around, he didn't let on. "What've you got?"

"Petey Fish, the dumb fuck, took off a Gambino truck in the Bronx last week, and we're gettin' shit over it. Tommy's beating the war drums and we need to settle this before it gets out of hand."

Petey Fish was Peter Bottaglio. He was called Fish because he had worked in the Fulton Fish Market back in the days when it was controlled by the mob, before the feds took it over. My opinion was they called him Fish because he had the brains of a carp. Anyway, the asshole apparently hijacked a truckload of men's suits owned by Consolidated Carriers, a legitimate company run by the Gambinos. Tommy was Tommy Gambino, son of the late Carlo Gambino, the so-called Boss of Bosses who, in the 1930s, was one of the founding fathers of the American Mafia as we know it today.

Tommy ran the trucking and garment-industry rackets in New York and was powerful. He wasn't the typical Hollywood mob boss. He was soft-spoken, slight of build, dressed impeccably, and kept out of the public eye. Unlike John Gotti, Tommy Gambino, like his father before him, believed the Mafia was supposed to be a secret society and kept an extremely low profile. But he didn't get to where he was in the hierarchy of the mob by being a pussy, and he was the last guy anyone wanted to piss off. Zarra had been dispatched by Andy Gerardo to straighten out the mess before bodies starting dropping. Naturally, the suits had been returned and the driver wasn't harmed, but a lot of fence-mending needed to be done to make the situation right.

"Sure, Mr. Zarra, whatever you need."

"I've got a sit-down in the city tomorrow over this in the Garment District and I need some guys with me. Not that anything's gonna happen, but it's good to show up with some guys, you know what I'm sayin'?" He didn't wait for me to answer. "Shows who we are. So, tomorrow we take a ride, you, me, and maybe another guy."

My antennae went up. I was never a fan of the term *take a ride*, because when it came to wiseguys, the "ride" often turned out to be a one-way trip. I knew Zarra was no fan of mine, and he could have been brooding about the Crisco Disco thing; maybe taken some ribbing and decided I had to go so he could save face. Italians, particularly mobsters, can hold grudges for years. Even the most minor of slights can lead to violence of huge proportions.

I'm reminded of the story of two wiseguys in Newark who were in a bar playing cards when one of them said he was going to the corner fruit stand to get some oranges, and did his buddy want anything? The other mobster asks him to get him a dozen tomatoes because his wife was going to make gravy (Italians call sauce "gravy").

The guy comes back twenty minutes later with his oranges, but minus the tomatoes. He apologizes, says he forgot, and his buddy says it's okay, he'll get the tomatoes on the way home. Fast-forward twenty years and these same guys get into a drunken beef over a football game and words become heated. The wiseguy who had to do his own tomato shopping whips out a gun and begins blasting, riddling his friend with bullets. Over the din of gunfire, the shooter was heard to yell, "You're a fucking asshole, and here's for the fucking tomatoes you never got me!"

While this might be an extreme example, it wasn't a stretch to imagine Zarra taking me out because I'd solved a problem in the Village he should've handled.

I had no choice, however. I had to go with Zarra on the road trip. If I panicked every time I thought something bad could happen to me, I should've chosen another line of work. I lived and breathed undercover work, and I was good at it. Having survived an assassination attempt once, I also had the feeling of indestructibility.

Zarra and I firmed up a meeting place for the following day, and he turned on his stool and hit the tiles. Halfway to the door he stopped, turned back, and climbed on the same stool. He leaned into me and said, "And come light, New York's got a three-year mandatory on a gun rap. If one of us is caught with a piece in the car, we all go for the time. No one's packin', including me." He clapped me on the shoulder. "Got it?"

"Yeah, no sweat." Something told me I was going to be the only one unarmed.

My heart was pounding like a jackhammer. Zarra was a made guy with enough time in the mob to make Al Capone look like an intern, and he was afraid of a gun bust? I didn't think so. My survival mode was kicking in; I had a problem.

I called Big Jim Sweeney at home from a pay phone on the turnpike and told him of my dilemma.

"I don't want you to go, Mike," Sweeney said quickly.

"Jimmy, I don't go and we can kiss this operation good-bye." It was my responsibility to make the case against Gerardo and his crew, and I took that responsibility seriously.

"Well, good-bye it is then. Too dangerous, Mike. This guy Zarra is an egomaniac. You upstaged him and it looks like he's setting you up to get clipped. You survived one bullet to the head, don't press your luck."

I gave this some thought. While I sought Sweeney's advice, I didn't like what I was hearing. I expected him to say, "Fuck it, go for it," similar to the counsel he'd given me when he and Sergeant Nick batted around my Crisco Disco dilemma. That was why I called Sweeney instead of Nick. I was doing the same thing shyster lawyers do when they're defending a guilty client: judge shopping. I know Nick would have told me to back off, but I never expected the same reaction from Sweeney. Subconsciously I wanted to proceed and meet Zarra for the trip to the sit-down.

Sweeney and I went back and forth for a few minutes until he finally caught on. I wasn't going to listen to his sage counsel; he was spinning his wheels.

"I can order you not to go, you know," Sweeney said.

"You can. Are you doing that?"

After a long pause he said, "Mike, you've got kids. Think of them." He didn't mention my wife, but cops rarely do. A widow could always remarry; kids only get one dad.

I knew if things turned to shit with Zarra, I could handle it. I'm an undercover cop, this is what I do. I didn't think for a minute that I might be depriving my kids of a father because whatever Zarra had in store for me, I would countermand it. I had no doubt—well, very little—that I'd be home the next night for dinner.

"So you're not saying not to go?"

"I tell you not to go," Sweeney said, "you're gonna make like this conversation never happened, right? You'll go anyway."

I chuckled. "What conversation?"

I heard Sweeney exhale loudly. "Do you know where this sit-down is?"

"In the Garment District, probably Tommy's office where the trucking business is."

"We're gonna be all over the block."

I knew if I was going to get clipped, it would be on the way to or coming back from the meeting. No way was Zarra going to disrespect Gambino family territory by killing anyone on their turf. But I didn't say anything. I didn't want a tail. Zarra was a street-hardened gangster and he'd take precautions to shake any surveillance. But I played along.

"Okay, that's good."

We debated my wearing a wire for a few minutes, but I decided against it. I wasn't trusted enough by Zarra to be wired up. I might get tossed at any time just for general principles. A recording device is most effective when it's worn on a trusted man, a turncoat, a rat, who has time in the mob. I was still trying to gain trust, so no wire. I had a plan to plant recording devices in Zarra's club, when and if I ever got invited inside, where I had a shot at being disassociated from any electronic eavesdropping equipment should any be found.

I'm a good sleeper, not what you would expect of someone who does what I do. Somebody wants to take me out, they could best accomplish the deed while I slept, even if they tripped over the dog, woke the kids, and started a fire on the way to my bedroom. I'd sleep through it all. The night before the Zarra meet, however, I stared at the ceiling until the sun broke through the smog that blanketed Newark. I was worried despite my bravado, and it played on my psyche.

I climbed out of bed noiselessly at six, showered, shaved, shoveled down bacon, three eggs, and a mountain of leftover hash browns. Even the thought of death couldn't affect my appetite. I put on a suit, white silk shirt, no tie, and highly polished black dress boots. You attend a sit-down, you dress the part. We were representing Andy Gerardo, and we needed to look respectable. I'd also found out a while ago that the properly outfitted wiseguy never wore a sport jacket; it was always a suit, tie optional.

It was Saturday and Angela and the girls still slept while I quietly slipped out of the house to my destiny. There were no forehead kisses for my girls, and I didn't wake my wife to tell her I loved her. No potential farewells because nothing was going to happen to me. I had to think positive.

I had slipped a four-inch, fixed-blade knife in my boot and a .32 Seecamp semiautomatic pistol in a wallet holster into my back pocket. I doubted I was going to be tossed because that would give away my fate and the battle for my life would be on. If I was searched, however, chances are the pistol would be overlooked in the well-camouflaged wallet rig, and they might stop looking after they found the knife.

Wiseguys kill when the victim is calm and comfortable. You never see it coming. If I was marked for death, it would happen when Zarra, the driver, the third guy, and I would be engaged in normal conversation. The attack would come with lightning speed, probably with a knife to the heart if we were in a legitimate car, or with a gun if the car was stolen. A heart wound is almost instantly fatal and most bleeding is internal, therefore no stains on the upholstery; a gunshot could be sloppy, but if it was a stolen car, who gave a fuck?

I met Zarra a few blocks from the New Jersey entrance to the Holland Tunnel on a deserted, warehouse-lined street. His personal car, an Oldsmobile 98, the size of an aircraft carrier, was idling curbside, with Zarra outside leaning against the door, wearing an ill-fitting suit he probably wore to his high school graduation. I'd probably get stabbed if they were going to take me off in the car; Zarra wouldn't allow a mess in his Olds.

I didn't recognize the driver, but a third guy I did recognize got out of the backseat as I pulled up to the curb. His name was Pauly Nash, short for a long Italian name no one could pronounce, and a hitter of legendary reputation. He was in his early fifties and was said to have taken out twenty-two men, mostly with a garrote or a knife. A killer who prefers to get up close and personal with his victim is a psycho in my book, someone who enjoys killing. I was beginning to question my career choice.

Pleasantries were exchanged between Zarra and me: Nash just stared at me. The driver, a dim-witted gofer whom Zarra referred to as Ralph, grunted, his hands never leaving the steering wheel.

I got in the backseat with Nash without having to be told the seating arrangement. It was Zarra's car; he'd be in the front shotgun seat. We pulled out and headed for the tunnel. No one spoke until we reached the Manhattan side.

"Kinda late to ask," Zarra said, "but no one's carryin', right?" He turned to look at me.

I shook my head. "Not me."

Nash said, "Nah." A man of few words.

Zarra put his hand on Ralph's shoulder. "Do some of that evasive shit you do."

Ralph nodded. "You got it."

For the next ten minutes we circled blocks, parked, entered traffic again, parked a second time, and went the wrong way up a one-way street. While Zarra checked his side mirror and Nash turned to peruse what was behind us, I crossed my legs and put my hand on the top of my boot directly over the knife. I'd have a harder time getting to the gun, but the blade would be out in a flash.

Zarra said to Ralph, "Okay, we're good. Head uptown."

If I was going to get it, now would be a good time. Nothing happened. We continued northbound with Zarra giving orders.

"I go into this office, you guys wait outside with whoever Tommy's gonna have there. Make nice while I talk to Tommy. The agreement was talk, no trouble. Even if we don't straighten this thing out, we leave in one piece. That's the deal."

By now I'm feeling a little more secure. I knew I'd make it to the meeting; coming back from it was another story. Zarra had me as a show of power, why not utilize me? If he was planning to whack me, the return trip would serve just fine.

Ralph pulled into a garage on West Thirty-fifth Street, the heart of the Garment District. We walked two blocks south on Seventh Avenue. All the while I tried to hang back and have the three of them in front of me, but every time I did that, Nash was always a step slower and right behind me. I didn't want to be obvious so I stayed in step with Zarra. No one said anything. I looked around a few times for Sweeney and his band of merry men, but I couldn't spot them, and I could spot a cop with a bag over my head. They were either so well camouflaged that even I couldn't find them, or they got hung up somewhere and never made it. It didn't really matter to me; no one was going to dispatch me in the middle of midtown Manhattan at high noon with a few thousand witnesses present.

Zarra stopped in front of a soot-covered building and said, "Here."

We took the elevator to the third floor and entered a narrow hallway. Three huge guys were in front of a frosted-glass office door that had DYNAMIC DELIVERY stenciled on it, which I found out later was the parent company of Consolidated Carriers. I assumed Tommy Gambino was inside waiting for Zarra and his litany of excuses for why one of his men hijacked a Gambino truck and what he was going to do to make it right.

When we reached the door, Zarra said to us, "Wait here."

Nash, Ralph, and I stopped in our tracks and shared what little space there was in that hallway with our goon counterparts from the Gambino family while Zarra went inside. Like passengers on a New York City subway, we avoided eye contact and no one said a word until Zarra emerged from the office twenty minutes later. He was expressionless and didn't share what went on between him and whomever he spoke to—I assumed it was Tommy Gambino— on our walk back to retrieve the car.

We changed positions in the Olds for the return trip. Nash now sat in the front passenger seat, while I shared space with Zarra in the back, no explanation given for the new seating arrangement. Zarra was lost in thought and quiet, not uttering a word. Whatever was on his mind, it was bothering him, but I hoped it didn't involve killing me. Naturally I didn't ask questions.

"Ralph, drop off Mikey first," Zarra finally said, snapping out of his reverie when we entered New Jersey from the Holland Tunnel.

Ralph nodded and made a sharp right in the direction of my car. I deflated, feeling a load of stress leave me like air from a popped balloon. If I was going to get clipped on the return trip, it would've been in Manhattan—where I would've been dumped—or an area far from Genovese territory on the Jersey side. My car was parked two blocks from a Gerardo wire room, an unlikely location for a hit.

If this trip was a test, I'd passed it. If I was being paranoid and our journey to the big city was exactly what it appeared to be, I had been chosen because I was becoming trusted. Either way it was forward movement and that was a plus. I got a grunt from Zarra as the car pulled to the curb and I got out. As I watched the car head back to the club, I let out the breath I felt I'd been holding since the trip began.

I drove home in a much better frame of mind than when I'd left. I took the girls and Angela out to dinner. On this rare night out, we had a good time, although I felt guilty for having to continually deceive my wife about my job. I also felt almost giddy for having survived the day and gotten a step closer to embedding myself in Gerardo's crew. Zarra, I thought, should be pretty pleased with himself, too. It appeared he'd avoided a confrontation with the Gambinos. If things had gone bad, he would've stopped at the nearest pay phone and called Gerardo. The Gambinos would also consider the avoidance of violence a good payoff, and whatever compensation was offered from our end for the hijacking of one of their trucks was amenable to them.

Everyone apparently made out except Petey Fish. A week after the sit-down he left his house to get a pack of smokes and was never heard from again. Petey, apparently, was the compensation.

I was becoming more accepted with Gerardo's crew. I also built up my résumé by working a deal with a guy who owned a legitimate heating company. He subcontracted me to pump out oil tanks for customers who were switching from oil to natural gas. Every so often I'd run into a connected guy while on a pumping job.

We were at the beginning of the summer and I started to spend more time in front of Gerardo's headquarters club on Davenport Avenue schmoozing with the wiseguys, but I still hadn't been invited inside. I didn't press it. I'd park my rig, pull up one of the chairs that littered the sidewalk in front of the club, and attack my lunch, which was usually a foot-long hero sandwich that I took my time eating. Most everyone was friendly, and some even took to calling me Mike the Cop. In the beginning I'm sure some of the crew may have thought I was an active cop, albeit a crooked one, but still on the payroll and using my oil business as an additional source of income. The bottom line was no one gave a good goddamn if I was the commissioner.

Newark had the reputation of being one of the most corrupt cities in the country. Every mayor since World War II had gone to prison for corrupt activities, the most infamous being Hugh Addonizio, who served as mayor from 1962 to 1970 and was convicted of corruption after leaving office. According to former U.S. district judge Herbert J. Stern, Addonizio "literally delivered the city into the hands of organized crime." Angelo "Gyp" DeCarlo, a boss with the Genovese family and politically connected in New Jersey, was pardoned by President Richard Nixon in 1972 after being convicted of murder and sentenced to life in prison. He served just eighteen months.

So Mike the Cop was just a small fish in an ocean of corrupt individuals that led all the way up to the White House. Welcome to Newark, New Jersey, business as usual. If someone asked, I'd tell them my cover story, and before long I was accepted as a former cop who was fired for being too "hands-on."

Made members of the crew had to make an appearance at the club at least twice a week. Bobby "Kabert" Bisaccia, an associate because he wasn't Italian on both sides of his family, would occasionally drop by. He was a true psychopath whom I'd known since I was a kid. He wasn't what you would call muscle; he just killed people, mostly in New York. His chosen profession aside, we got along pretty well.

I'd trade pleasantries with Thomas "Peewee" DePhillips, a book-maker, loan shark, and labor racketeer who was a highly respected earner who at any given time had a hundred workers on the street.

The biggest money earner, however, was Sal Cetrulo, a capo in his midforties with the power of an underboss because of the money he generated. He was cunning, although polite and respectful. Cetrulo liked to brag that he'd never served a day in jail, a boast I hoped to disprove shortly. He invested the mob's dirty money in legitimate businesses, such as building condominiums along the Hudson River from Hoboken to Fort Lee. But a gangster is a gang-ster, and I would soon see Cetrulo's true persona when the rivalry between crews became violent.

Seven or eight other guys I identified would later become collateral targets of the investigation, including members from other families such as Michael Perna (Lucchese family) and James Randazzo (Colombo family). In addition, three or four wiseguys from Philadelphia would stop by, one the infamous Nicky "Little Nicky" Scarfo, who never met a guy he didn't want to kill. He had a well-deserved reputation of being an out-of-control psychopath, but I never saw that side of him. When he came around the club, he must have been on medication because he had a great sense of humor and got along with everyone.

Numerous cops of all ranks from neighboring departments, both on and off duty, stopped by, as did politicians. For me, standing on that corner proved to be a veritable gold mine of intelligence. I went home every night and transcribed my hastily scribbled notes into something readable. It seemed my biggest worry was getting writer's cramp.

I kept track of who came and went. I identified James Palmieri, a soldier who handled loan-sharking and gambling. I also chatted up Ralph Vicaro, a capo who ran the club when Zarra wasn't around. These guys and most others were pleasant. A few, however, weren't. The aforementioned John "Johnny D" DiGilio was one of them.

DiGilio was a made guy and vice president of the International Longshoremen's Union. Because of his union position he had more power on the street than a capo in the family, and he liked to throw his weight around. A former boxer and genuine tough guy, he'd always come up to me in front of the club and ask me what I was doing there. I was my usual straightforward self and pointed to my sandwich. He'd give me the stink eye, mumble something about "stupid Irish muscle," and go into the club. It wasn't so much that he didn't trust me; he just didn't like non-Italians, whom he would refer to as *medagons,* i.e., "shit Americans." To him, if you weren't

Italian, you were sewer scum. This attitude didn't extend to his entourage, however, which consisted of two former Irish cops who were built like Rosie O'Donnell and acted as his drivers and bodyguards. In 1988, DiGilio's lack of social graces got him murdered, and I for one don't miss him.

A new guy started coming around. He was six feet four inches and had to be 275 pounds. I'd never seen him before, and I knew most of the wiseguys from living in Newark all my life, and those I didn't know I met in front of Zarra's club. When I ran his license plate, I identified him as Silvio DeVita. I gave his name to Sweeney and Nick, but they just shrugged and told me to forget about him. That reaction piqued my curiosity, and I checked further on my own. DeVita had just been released from prison after serving thirty years for killing a Newark police officer. My handlers chose not to tell me because they thought I'd go off on him and compromise the operation. After everything I'd been through, DeVita could have killed Mother Teresa and I would've given him a pass. I was focused on infiltrating the crew, not being the Masked Avenger, and I passed that on to my handlers for future reference. I wanted to be kept in the loop because it was my ass on the line out there, not theirs.

DeVita would have staying power. He only trusted Sicilians off the boat from the old country—"zips" as they were called in the Mafia—and dealt exclusively with them. Native-born Sicilians still believe in the Mafia tradition of omertà and wouldn't rat if you held their testicles to the fire. DeVita avoided me as if I were a leper. Today Silvio DeVita is eighty years old and in charge of the Essex County crew.

Family hit man Anthony DiVingo, another club regular, just didn't like me, and we were always trading verbal jabs. Four years prior to my appearance on the scene, he'd been cleared by a jury in the murder of Anthony "Little Pussy" Russo in Long Branch, New Jersey.

Even Zarra was coming around, and he was actually friendly. Some days we'd talk for a few minutes when he came to the club, usually around noon. I knew enough about wiseguys to know that they become your friend for one of two reasons: They either wanted to put you at ease before they killed you, or they saw you as a way to make money or save money. Wiseguys are some of the cheapest people you'll ever meet. I figured if Zarra wanted me dead, by this time I'd be dead. Therefore, the money angle interested him, and it didn't take long to get an offer I couldn't refuse.

On Saturday during the July Fourth weekend I was having breakfast with James Palmieri in a diner on Bloomfield Avenue when he came at me with a proposition I knew came from Joe Zarra.

"Mike, you should rent the store in front of the club for your oil company. It's vacant now, and it'll be a good cover for the club. You need a place, right?"

In case Zarra got nosy about where I conducted my business, I'd told him I gave up my office because I had gotten a large rent increase. I figured that to be a reasonable story, and Zarra believed it. I also mentioned I was looking for new office space, an alleged quest that would go on forever, or at least until the investigation ended. Zarra was apparently having Palmieri feel me out about relocating to the club's building. JP, as Palmieri was known, wasn't a made guy, and he couldn't offer the storefront to me without Zarra's permission. While JP was a bright guy, he was a street-level bookmaker who made a lot of money and never wanted to be made because the money he'd have to kick up to the bosses would increase. His official position was that of associate, but unofficially he was known as Zarra's gofer.

This storefront was a partitioned section of one big building, the largest portion being utilized by the club. The storefront and the club shared a common wall, but had separate entrances. I felt as if I'd died and went to mobster undercover heaven. All forms of electronic eavesdropping devices could be placed in the building by breaching the wall. I tried not to salivate.

I made as if I were thinking about the prospect. "What kind of number we talking about for rent?"

"Lemme make a call." JP excused himself and went to a pay phone. Three minutes later he was back.

"Four-fifty a month."

The monthly nut wouldn't be a problem, but I'd have to clear it with my handlers before I took the deal. I couldn't see Sweeney and Nick not going for the offer; we'd get a mountain of intelligence from court-ordered phone taps and video. The only problem I foresaw was the ethical dilemma in paying an organized-crime crew rent money. That money would probably be used to perpetuate more criminal activities.

"Tell you what; I'll check my books, see if it's doable," I said. "Give me a day or so and I'll get back to you, okay?"

"Sure," JP said, "no problem."

I had to go through the entire State Police chain of command on a holiday weekend to get permission to rent the store. A request like this was unprecedented, and a colonel had to give it the okay. I got it the next day and called JP.

"Yeah, looks good," I told him.

Like all gangsters looking for a future payback, JP said, "You know we're doing you a favor giving you the store at that price, and you're getting it because me and Joe trust you."

"I know, and I appreciate it. Tell you what, you're being good to me, I'll be good to you. The club's heating oil will be half-price. Pass that along to Mr. Zarra."

"Thanks, Mike, he'll appreciate your generosity."

This was a magnanimous gesture I'd have to back up. The state cops would have to buy heating oil every so often to make my word good. We were not only feeding organized crime rent money, we were keeping them comfy, too.

"What'll I do first?" I asked JP.

"Meet me in the club tomorrow so I can show you around."

A double bonus. In addition to getting the store, I now had permission to enter the club. Once I was in, I could come and go as I pleased.

6

We're Talking
Real Money Here

JP gave me the tour of the building the next day. We began with the club. It was a typical wiseguy hangout: lots of mismatched (read *stolen*) furniture of every imaginable color, a battered bar, a fully equipped kitchen, a pool table, a craps table, a TV suspended from the ceiling, and a big baccarat table where they ran monte games. The house took 25 percent of the monte winnings, and this was one of their big moneymakers with pots as high as $40,000.

A few guys were playing cards, others were sipping espresso and watching TV. Framed prints of Italian street scenes and vistas were on the wall. I saw one landline phone as I sized up the room for cameras and audio. It looked to be about two thousand square feet with poor acoustics. We'd make do when the time came.

I was greeted as if I belonged there. The cardplayers barely looked up from their game, and the guys watching TV grunted hellos. I was fitting in.

Next door, my new office was about a third of the club's size, and the wall that separated it from the club was ordinary plasterboard. I was already plotting how I was going to install the cameras.

I began to move furniture in that week but had to scramble to get a typewriter. I settled on an old Royal I had used to write reports when I booked prisoners. It was in poor shape, mostly from interrupting my typing chores to utilize the machine as a club to control unruly criminals. I used off-duty state cops as movers. They knew nothing of the operation, they were just doing as they were told.

It took me about two weeks to make the place look presentable with some paint and a gallon of Windex to remove crud from the windows. While I was busy with the chores, John DiGilio would stop by and try to recruit me for muscle work or any of the myriad scams he was working on the docks. As part of his pitch he'd tell me what a great guy he was because as vice president of the Longshoremen's Union he was giving jobs to cops' kids. I knew this allegedly magnanimous gesture was a backdoor approach to keeping local cops on the pad; instead of paying them directly, their kids got the money.

I passed on DiGilio's offer. I was there to nail Gerardo's crew, and if I took Digilio up on his proposal, it would be a slap at Joe Zarra after getting me in with his crew. I saw that Zarra was getting a little worried that I'd go with DiGilio. He'd always ask me what DiGilio wanted after he left the club. Both wiseguys saw me as having great earning potential, and Zarra didn't want to lose what he already had. I intimated to Zarra that I wasn't going anywhere, but he still wasn't satisfied.

"That fucking DiGilio is nuts," Zarra said. "He comes around you anymore, you make sure I know about it."

Nice to be appreciated.

I hired a guy named Wally, a local firefighter, to letter my truck and windows with the business name and supposed services I provided. Finally I had a truck that had my nonexistent-company name on it. Wally worked for a decent hourly wage and a daily pint of Southern Comfort. By the time he left work every day he was so drunk I felt compelled to check his the spelling of his lettering.

After conferring with Jim Sweeney, who was now my main handler, we decided on four separate phone lines to handle the number of anticipated wiretaps. When the phone-company installer showed up, he commented that I could save money by getting one phone line on one instrument with four buttons.

"This place is too small for all them phone lines," he said.

I put on my best wiseguy act. "No one wants your opinion; just put in the four fucking lines."

It looked as if a lightbulb went off in the installer's head. "Oh, okay, I get it."

I'd succeeded in giving him the impression I was setting up a wire room for taking bets. It was no secret that the adjacent club was a mob hangout. I was just glad that Zarra or another member wasn't around to see the installer put in the multiple lines. No way a business my size needed more than one dedicated line. To make the place look real, I brought in a load of tools and put them on the floor where anyone who entered the office could see them. I also parked my beat-up 1960 Chevy truck on the street in front of the club after I filled it with some useless scrap to make it appear I was busy.

A nice-size hole was in the wall that separated my office from the club, and it would've made a great spot to plant a camera, but Zarra wanted the hole plugged and I complied. Shortly thereafter I sawed in a slit so I could view what was going on in the club.

I wasn't in my phony business a week when JP stopped in to ask a favor.

"Mikey, my kid, he needs a job. You got something for him?"

The last thing I needed was JP's son working for me and screwing up my investigation. But I couldn't turn Palmieri down because this was one of the paybacks for getting me the office space. With wiseguys the debt is never repaid, and I'd be doing favors for JP and Zarra forever.

"Sure, I can use him to help my crew with furnace removals. I've got one tomorrow, bring him around." I had plans for his son and was sure he wouldn't last a day.

The kid showed up the next morning. He was about seventeen and so skinny that if he turned sideways and stuck out his tongue, he'd look like a zipper. He had trouble picking up twenty pounds, and by the end of the first hour he was almost in tears from the heavy lifting and dirty labor. My regular guys, Tommy and Jocko, sent him home before lunch. I called JP.

"Didn't work out, too much heavy lifting. Sorry, man," I said.

"Ah, that's okay, the kid's mother made him soft."

One crisis averted, but another was about to crop up.

* * *

Anthony Noce, the guy in the legitimate oil-delivery business who lent me the trucks I used in my pseudobusiness, called me at home and asked for his truck back. I had been using several of his trucks, switching vehicles as his need for the trucks changed, but now he needed the one remaining truck I had. Without a truck I had zero credibility.

"Is this necessary, Anthony?" I asked. "You have a fleet of the fuckers."

Noce, whom I'd known for years, ran a thriving business he'd inherited from his father. He had lent me his excess trucks with no questions asked and I appreciated it, but I needed at least one of his vehicles to maintain my cover.

"I need it, Mike. Business is booming. Either I take your truck back or I have to lease one. You wanna pay for that?"

"Not really. When do you need it?" I was already formulating a backup plan.

"Yesterday."

"How about the end of the week?" That would give me three days to come up with another truck.

He didn't respond for a few seconds. "Okay. I gotta have it back in the yard no later than Friday morning. Deal?"

"Deal."

Now I had to get a replacement truck.

A wannabe gangster named Artie Rush owned Reliable Fuel, a downsized version of the same kind of company Noce owned. Artie talked the wiseguy talk, but that was about as far as it went. He was a degenerate gambler whose main association with the mob was that on any given day he owed Gerardo's crew thousands of dollars in street loans or gambling losses. He had several trucks but only used half of them because he was too busy losing his money to run his business. He was a fixture at the club, but only because he made frequent trips there to pay off his debts.

I was desperate for a rig to maintain my cover and decided to take a chance on Artie. I stopped by his lot the next afternoon and found him in his office scrutinizing a racing form.

"Hey, Artie, how're you doing?"

He looked up from his calculations, annoyed, until he saw it was me. Artie would kiss any wiseguy's ass to curry favor. Artie saw me as a respected associate because he'd seen me talking with Joe Zarra on many occasions, and I'm sure he'd heard about my new office adjacent to the club.

"Hey, Mikey! C'mon in, sit down."

I sat in a folding chair. Artie found a half-full bottle of bourbon in his desk and tipped two stiff ones in glasses so cloudy with remnants of past indulgences that the booze appeared to turn gray as he poured.

"Need a favor, Artie."

"Oh, yeah, Mikey, sure. Anything for you."

A gangster buff, such as Artie, would do just about anything to be considered an insider. What's good about a buff is that they take omertà more seriously than do the real wiseguys, the result, I suppose, of seeing too many gangster movies. I knew I could trust him to keep his mouth shut and ask few questions, if any.

"We need to borrow one of your trucks." I used the plural *we* to make my request appear to be part of a larger criminal conspiracy. If he acquiesced, he would be pleasing the entire crew, not just me.

"Sure, Mikey, how long you need it for?" As soon as he asked, I knew he was sorry he had.

"Hey, Artie, we just need it, don't know for how long." I leaned in closer to him. "Think you can accommodate? I mean, you need it back, all you gotta do is ask. We'll take good care of it." The way he ran his business, I knew he'd never need the truck. He should be grateful it would be on the road and not mothballed with the battery draining and the tires deflating.

He forced a laugh. "Sure, Mikey, got a good one for you." He rattled around a desk drawer for a while and came up with a labeled set of keys. He tossed them to me. "Bring it back when you're ready."

Every day for the next two weeks I drove Artie's rig to my office and parked it in front of the club. Clearly stenciled on the side was RELIABLE FUEL, which was obviously not my company. The wiseguys had to trip over the truck to get into the club. No one said anything about the switched trucks, and it was business—or a lack thereof—as usual.

I hadn't seen Andy Gerardo in almost a month and I wanted to reestablish contact with him. While I assumed we'd get him on the wiretaps and video, it wouldn't hurt to touch base and thank him for getting me some work. I didn't want him to think I wasn't grateful for the opportunity he'd given me through Joe Zarra.

These wiseguys are a touchy bunch. If Gerardo thought I was ignoring or avoiding him, it would be taken as a sign of disrespect, and he could have me banished as quickly as he had allowed me into his crew's inner circle.

I drove past Joe's Diner for two days until I spotted his BMW one morning at 9:00 a.m. He was in his usual booth, dressed in an expensive suit, facing the door. He was alone.

I waved when I entered and he beckoned me over.

"Hey, Mikey Ga-Ga, long time no see. Sit down." He looked relaxed, with a good tan and a ready smile.

We made the obligatory small talk for a while until I changed the subject after Augie brought my breakfast.

"I was hoping to catch you here, Mr. Gerardo. Wanted to thank you for giving me the opportunity to do some work for you. Comes at a good time. And for the office, too."

"My pleasure, Mike. Zarra's been telling me you're doing good. There's more than enough work for you, you keep doing what you're doing. I may have given you the okay, but you're proving your worth. There'll be more for you in the future."

I decided to play dumb. "You don't come to the club anymore? I been in my new office a month, haven't seen you." I knew damn well he couldn't be seen consorting with known criminals while he was on parole.

"Busy, Mike. But I'll be coming around soon enough."

That could only mean he'd been a good boy and his parole officer was going to cut some time off what he owed.

"That's great. I'd like to show you what I've done with the office. Fixed it up really nice."

He took a last hit on his coffee and got up to leave. I stood up, too. He waved me down.

"You sit, enjoy your breakfast; I gotta be going. You listen to

Zarra. Any problems, let him know and I'll straighten them out. I'll stop around to check out your office." He clapped me on the shoulder. "Be good."

I'm thinking, I'll be good all right. Good for me, bad for you.

The morning after my breakfast with Gerardo, Joe Zarra caught me in front of the club at nine thirty as I was getting out of my truck. Being at the club, or anywhere else for that matter, at that time of the morning was uncharacteristic for Zarra. He usually got up at the crack of noon. He was carrying two containers of coffee and looked disheveled, even more so than usual, but I attributed that to the early hour. But the cigar was there; ever present between his fish lips.

"Come inside with me a minute," he said, and held the door open to the club. I got the impression he had been waiting for me to show up. The club was empty. Most wiseguys, like Zarra, were not early risers.

Zarra heaved himself onto a plastic chair in front of a minuscule, Formica-topped table, placed both coffees down, and said, "Sit, I wanna run something by you. We're talkin' big money here." He pushed a container toward me. "This coffee's for you."

He got right down to business. "Can you pump oil from electrical-pole transformers?"

I thought about it. I knew what transformers looked like: cylindrical, like kitchen garbage cans, about three feet high, mounted on top of power-line poles, and I knew they contained thin oil that was loaded with PCBs, which were dangerous to work with due to their toxicity. Why Zarra would be interested in them was a mystery, but it had to have something to do with some kind of scam. I also surmised that Zarra didn't know an electrical-pole transformer from a golf ball, and whatever he was going to propose was coming from Andy Gerardo, who owned an electrical-contracting company.

I was straight with him. "I don't know. I'd need to take a look at one close up and see if I have the equipment to do it."

Zarra stood up and pushed back his chair. "Great, drink up, we're going for a ride."

This time the term *going for a ride* didn't upset me. I was curious to know what was spinning in the devious mind of Andy Gerardo.

We went in Zarra's Olds to an abandoned factory in Lodi, which held over three hundred electrical-pole transformers that needed to be drained before they could be sold for scrap.

"Okay," Zarra said, "do your thing."

I examined the transformers and concluded that the pumping equipment in Rush's truck wasn't equipped to do the job and told Zarra this.

"You sure?"

"Very." I decided to test the waters. "Mr. Gerardo probably has the pumps that can do it. His company probably has all kinds of equipment I don't have. There's PCBs in this oil. That's dangerous shit."

Zarra scratched the stubble on his face and stared at me. I knew he was contemplating telling me what the scam was and deciding if I could be trusted with the information.

He put his hand on my shoulder and began leading me out of the building. "Listen, I really don't think he'd want to get involved in this. My idea was we drain this useless shit oil, mix it with number four heating oil, and sell it as pure heating oil. We'd make a fucking fortune."

Right away I knew this had to be Gerardo's idea. Zarra was an old-time mafioso; he was comfortable with traditional crime, and this was new territory. But I had to hand it to Gerardo; the idea was brilliant. Number four heating oil is tarlike, thick, and could be diluted and still do its job. The thin oil in the transformers was a good choice because it was cheap—or free, depending on where they got it—and unlike using water as a diluting agent, the transformer oil would mix well and go undiscovered. The downside was the transformer oil was dangerous to handle due to the PCBs, and the customers who had it in their furnaces might be subject to an untold number of illnesses. But the mob never cared about anyone else; it was all about how much money they could make and how fast they could make it.

We drove back to the club in silence, and I never heard anything about the scam again. I'm almost positive they found someone else to do the pump job; the profits were too good to pass up. What I found interesting was that this crime wasn't traditional Mafia fare; I'd never heard of anyone doing something similar. Gerardo was breaking into unchartered territory, and I felt similar scams would be forthcoming. I didn't have too long to wait.

Zarra came back at me less than a week later with a comparable idea. Once again, I was sure Gerardo was behind it. This was a scam to evade federal taxes on diesel fuel. A heating-oil truck would be two-thirds filled with number-two heating oil and the remainder with kerosene. This combination produced premium diesel fuel, which would be used to fill trucks in mob-connected businesses. These businesses would beat the federal taxes they would have to pay if they were filling up with real diesel fuel pumped from government-regulated pumps.

Since no special equipment was needed and no potential hazardous material was involved, I got the go-ahead from Sweeney to participate. I made eight trips to Jersey Carting, a mob-connected waste-disposal business, and filled their trucks with our homemade brew. I also made a few deliveries to New York to drop loads at a carting business owned by Angelo Ponte, who also owned Ponte's Restaurant on Manhattan's West Side. Artie Rush agreed to the use of his trucks to make the deliveries. His profits were deducted from his sports-betting debt and the usurious interest that was accruing at warp speed.

The scam proved so profitable that variations of it were extended to major office buildings in the metropolitan area, including the Empire State Building.

A new source of income for the Mafia had emerged, and before I was finished with my investigation, I would see a major case develop in the area of environmental crime.

I was gathering important evidence even before we planted our first wire.

My undercover operation would not have been possible without the cooperation of the State Police. Except for decisions I was forced to make in the field, I had to run everything by Sweeney. He, in turn, needed to get clearance from his bosses, and those bosses went to their bosses and so on. This chain of command—from the lowest rung of the ladder to the highest—was a mirror of the military model. There was always accountability when using the chain of command.

The system works well in theory, but rarely in practice in police work. The majority of high-ranking bosses in police organizations didn't get to their lofty positions by being active street cops; they got their rank by studying for civil-service exams, and once they attained a maximum civil-service rank, it was whom they knew that allowed them to advance even further. Civil-service promotional tests are difficult to pass and require devotion to studying. Depending on the department, on average, only one out of eight cops ever makes sergeant or above. Street police work gets in the way of civil-service advancement because of the numerous hours spent in catching bad guys, arrest processing, and court time. Therefore most high-ranking bosses have little idea of what goes on in the street and make their decisions accordingly.

Another problem is politics. Any rank over captain is attained via political appointment, and these positions come with a quid pro quo, i.e., the politician or boss of higher rank who helped get someone promoted will ask for payback sooner or later, mostly many times over. In that way they're similar to the Mafia: The debt is never repaid. It's the gift that never stops giving.

Most upper-level police bosses don't like to make critical decisions, fearing the wrong one will result in their demotion back to their highest civil-service rank, usually captain. Exceptions to this rule exist, but it only takes one shaky boss in the chain of command to stop the system cold when an important decision has to be made. It's joked, with some degree of truth, that appointment to a rank above captain requires the candidate to undergo castration before being sworn in. I once saw a box strategically placed at the entrance to an auditorium where a ceremony was about to be conducted to elevate an assistant chief to the rank of chief. Printed crudely across the box was DEPOSIT TESTICLES HERE BEFORE BEING PROMOTED.

With each promotion, bosses become more isolated and distrustful. A top-management boss loses touch with the rank and file, resulting in the distrust of street cops, those actually fighting crime. This is the area where I experienced problems.

For the most part, I was rolling the dice. I was under deep cover and obviously couldn't consult with top-level bosses if a serious problem arose, particularly if immediate action was required. Such is the nature of undercover work. However, when a minor problem occurred or advice was needed that wasn't time sensitive, or I had an idea I wanted to implement, I ran it past Jim Sweeney. He would then run it up the chain of command for approval. Herein was the problem.

I'd come to the New Jersey State Police after a stint with the Newark Police Department. The state cops had more respect for the wiseguys than they did for Newark cops, and I couldn't blame them. That the department was corrupt was not in dispute. But not all Newark cops were crooks, and I was one of the honest ones, as evidenced by my desire to go with the State Police.

My Newark PD background, however, subjected me to suspicion from State Police management. They were constantly bombarding Sweeney with questions: Was the easy money I was always around influencing me in any way? How did they know I wasn't feeding them disinformation? Had I crossed over to the other side? How did they know I could be trusted? Had they really found one of the few cops from the Newark PD who didn't take money from the wiseguys?

Sweeney backed me up 100 percent, and that made my life easier. We'd meet twice a week at a location and time of his choosing. Meetings took place at Newark Airport, at rest stops on the turnpike, on PATH trains that ran from Hoboken to the World Trade Center, in an aisle in Home Depot, and any other location deemed safe for me. Meeting locations would constantly change, and I'd always be notified at the last minute where they would take place.

Meetings generally lasted about thirty minutes. Sweeney would growl like Kojak and smack me in the back of the head to make a point. It was a playful gesture, but he was built like a football player and had hands the size of manhole covers. More than once I left these meetings with scrambled brains. Sometimes Nick Orilio was there, too. He was the serious one, running strategy past me and making sure logistics were correct. They were both concerned about my well-being, not forgetting that a few short months ago I was left for dead in an alley.

In the end, our friendship and mutual trust made the operation the smashing success it became. However, when it came time to take credit, the three of us would be brushed aside, with the bosses taking the bows, but we didn't expect any less. We were professionals and would slip into the background and obscurity, knowing it was part of the political process. For us, the results counted, not the accolades.

Zarra stopped in my office to offer me a job.

"You'll collect money from our video-poker machines. You wanna do that?"

"Sure. What do I do?"

"Twice a week you go to the addresses in this book"—he handed me a small, spiral-bound notepad—"and empty the machines. JP'll explain how to do that. You give twenty percent to the store guy and you're done. You keep five percent of what's left." Zarra told me his crew had about ninety machines in mom-and-pop candy stores, bodegas, bars, and liquor stores spread out in Essex and Passaic Counties.

This was a huge moneymaking operation. I knew these machines were rigged, giving unrealistic odds to the house. Every establishment had two to four machines. JP later told me that to make it appear that they paid off, one machine could be electronically controlled by the owner via a switch located out of sight of the player. When activated, the machine would hit for a player, and the gamblers on the other machines would figure that their machines were due to score and they'd pour more money into them. Of course they wouldn't hit. Winning machines were alternated to give the impression they were all easy marks. Everything was rigged to give a large percentage to the house. A player couldn't walk away a legitimate winner if his machine got struck by lightning. Zarra controlled every machine.

I was also told of a spindle in the back of the machines that I could reset when I collected the money to make the count lower, thereby screwing the owner of the store out of money.

My education completed, I began my pickups.

Things went smoothly for a week. I'd skim about 20 percent by resetting the spindles on the machines and shortchanging the store owners. They appeared to be none the wiser, and if any of them had an idea they were being ripped off, they never said anything. The vast majority of these store owners were decent, law-abiding people who were just trying to make a few extra bucks. They were thankful for whatever I gave them and never complained.

One day I was leaving a candy store by the railroad yards in Paterson after making a collection when I ran into Bobby "Kabert" Bisaccia, whom I'd known from the club and been fairly friendly with while I was growing up in Newark. Kabert served one purpose: to kill people. Today he didn't look happy and that didn't make me feel secure. He was with Charles "Buddy" Muccigrasso, an associate who was as wide as he was tall. He was strictly muscle and could hit you all day long and not hurt. Somehow I doubted this was a chance meeting. They were blocking the sidewalk, which forced me to stop in front of them.

"Mikey," Kabert said, "we're going to have to rob you." He had his hands in his pockets. Buddy just stood there.

I was dumbstruck, but I recovered. "What the fuck are you talking about?"

"These machines you're picking up from? This is my territory. Who told you you can put machines here?"

I knew Zarra's reach didn't extend this far into Paterson, but I'd assumed he'd worked out a deal with Kabert and his boss, Louis Gatto, an old-time Mafia capo who had made his bones in the 1930s and had a stranglehold on all mob-run gambling operations in most of the Paterson-Lodi area.

I knew I had to stand up to these guys; to not do so would be considered a sign of weakness. "I'm doing this for Joe Zarra, take it up with him. I don't know nothin'." I took a step around them. Buddy moved and blocked my way.

Kabert laughed and said to Buddy, "You believe this fucking

mick prick? He takes one to the head and he still didn't learn nothin'." Buddy started to laugh, probably because Bobby was laughing. Buddy wasn't known for his ability to think.

These jerks were yucking it up, so I decided to join in and began to laugh with them. I was anything but amused, but I made a good show of it. I was armed but I couldn't see me explaining my way out of a gun battle without seriously damaging the investigation. I also couldn't see me making some lame excuse to leave and looking to my handlers for guidance. I was a street cop, and by definition we make decisions on the spot. Hopefully my judgment would be right.

"Listen, asshole," I said to Kabert, "I've known you since I've been eighteen, so don't be bullshitting me about holding me up. You need to take this up with Zarra, not me." It was bravado, playing on our street relationship, which spanned two decades.

Kabert may have been a lunatic, but he was smart. He would create a world of problems robbing a man from another crew at gunpoint regardless of being on the righteous side of a territorial dispute. Conversely, he couldn't bring himself to back down, so what he basically did was come up with my suggestion.

"I think Louis needs to take this up with Zarra," Kabert said.

"Good idea," I said, "now you're thinking. If it don't work out between them, you can always call me and make an appointment to rob me." I clapped Kabert on the shoulder. "See you around, I hope just not around here."

The three of us had a laugh over that remark, and I got the hell out of the neighborhood as quickly as possible.

I learned later that Zarra bitched and moaned about the confrontation and vowed he wouldn't give up the machines in Gatto's territory. His blustering didn't last long, and within a week he pulled his machines out of that section of Paterson.

I continued to do the collections in our own territory without a hitch. Zarra was pleased with my work, and I found myself becoming more entrenched in the crew.

It was time to take the next step.

7

Gathering Dirt

Joe Zarra was on a roll. If it's true that wiseguys are happiest when they're cheating and stealing, then Zarra was in broken-nose heaven with the money rolling in from the various heating-oil scams he had going. About this time, he began calling the club the Cage because he reasoned the club was inhabited by a bunch of caged animals. The new name spread throughout the neighborhood quickly and stuck.

With his new influx of cash Zarra began backing floating craps games. These games were constantly moved to stay one step ahead of the state vice cops, and inclusion was strictly by invitation only. He got a percentage of every pot, which came to considerable money.

Sweeney was pleased by the intelligence and the evidence I was gathering. We had yet to place our first wire, and we already had numerous wiseguys involved in state and federal felonies, and the best was yet to come.

The investigation was exploding. My information was going up the chain of command, and over fifty detectives were assigned surveillance duties on Gerardo's crew. These one-man units followed individual crew members from the time they left their homes until lights out at night, whatever time that might be. A huge chunk of the State Police investigatory budget was being expended on this investigation, but whoever in Trenton controlled the purse strings knew it was worth it.

The State Police structured the investigation with Jim Sweeney and me at the inception stage. We would initiate an investigation, and once the crimes we were uncovering were clearly revealed as organized crime, the New Jersey State Police Organized Crime Bureau would get involved. This meant a whole new set of bosses who saw potential glory down the road and who would make a grab for total control as time went on. This I could deal with when the time came, but it was the FBI that concerned me. If the Bureau saw headlines in an investigation, they were infamous for snatching cases from the locals after most of the work was already done. While I intended to cross that bridge when and if the time came, I didn't realize at that time how soon the FBI would come a-knockin' at my door.

While top cops jockeyed for position in the higher echelons of the New Jersey State Police, I was still doing my grunt work on the street. If I wasn't collecting money from the slot machines Zarra had spread over two counties, I was hauling bogus heating oil all over the tristate area.

Every time Zarra took me aside for a private chat, I thought for sure he'd gotten wise to my bogus heating-oil business, but he never did. His greed overtook good sense. Somewhere in the recesses of that corrupt brain of his he had to know something wasn't right with me, but he never questioned it. Dollar signs did his thinking for him. Historically, if a wiseguy was going to get busted, it was usually due to one of two things: greed or his inability to keep his mouth shut. In New York, John Gotti had done a doubleheader—getting indicted because of his big mouth and his insatiable thirst for more money—and Zarra's terminal greed would eventually mean his downfall.

"We gotta talk," Jim Sweeney told me in a phone call to my home one evening. Coming from my wife, those words would've sent chills down my spine, but hearing Sweeney utter them meant nothing more than a boss stating a certain degree of urgency. In this investigation most everything we talked about involved something serious or urgent, so I wasn't too concerned.

"Sure. Where and when?"

"My house, dinner, Friday. Say six o'clock."

My antennae went up. This was out of character for Sweeney, who, like most cops, kept his police life separate from his private life. To bring work home was way out of character for him.

"Dinner? Do I bring a covered dish?" I asked in a weak attempt to break his balls. He either ignored the remark or just didn't care.

"Not my idea, Mike. Orders from the boss. There'll be two captains and two lieutenants from Organized Crime there. Oh, yeah, and your new partner."

I didn't know if I heard him right. "My new what?"

"Partner, Mike. It came from the top. This is too big for one guy."

I felt my face reddening. "What the fuck, I'm not doing a good enough job by myself or what?"

"Take it easy, it's not us, it's the OC guys. They're running the show now and they want you to partner up."

I'd been in law enforcement long enough to know that Sweeney had no control over whoever made the decision to give me a partner, so it was no use bitching to him about it. I wasn't happy, and I'd make sure everyone within earshot Friday night at Sweeney's house knew about it, too.

I was accustomed to working alone, and I'd started this case from scratch. I knew all the players and they trusted me. To introduce a new partner into the mix would surely put me at a disadvantage. This new guy, whoever he was, would be an outsider with Gerardo's crew and as such wouldn't be trusted for a while, if ever. I'd also have to keep my eye on him to make sure he didn't make any mistakes that could jeopardize the operation and our lives. How much experience did this guy have? Did he look the part, talk the talk, walk the walk? Worse, if he turned out to be a cowboy and took unnecessary chances, I'd be spending most of my time containing him. Undercover work attracts risk takers, and sometimes risk takers have death wishes. We're a complicated lot and a shrink's wet dream, but I had a handle on my bravado; for me it was about the case, not a dick-measuring contest. Would this new guy have the same attitude as me?

Conversely, because so much traffic was going in and out of the club, with many wide-ranging scams and other crimes, I saw the Organized Crime Bureau boss's point of view. On the surface it seemed impossible for one lone undercover to handle everything. My main goal at the meeting at Sweeney's house would be to convince those in attendance that I could handle the undercover work on my own, but I wanted to make sure I didn't come across as an arrogant asshole.

*   *   *

I got caught in Friday rush-hour traffic on the turnpike and arrived at Sweeney's house a few minutes late. Cops are never late, it's in our DNA, and I felt like a jerk for being the last person to arrive at the meeting.

I was greeted at Sweeney's modest ranch-style home by Big Jim and Nick; two older men, who were introduced to me by their rank, both captains; and two younger lieutenants, who introduced them-selves. Another man, William Newsome, stood off to the side and nodded. I assumed he was my new partner. Sweeney's wife and kids were not at home.

Sweeney loved Italian food, and not surprisingly the dinner was a massive Italian buffet catered by a local restaurant and laid out on double tables in his finished basement. There were hot and cold dishes as well as several varieties of antipasti and plenty of beer. Sweeney must've read my mind because he whispered to me, "The job's picking up the tab."

The meeting was informal. We got our plates loaded up and sat around in a lopsided circle and talked. Newsome and I had our first meeting of the minds. Without communicating, we apparently both thought the same thing: Stay out of the business end of the conver-sation until the bosses asked our opinions. I lost most of my bluster when I realized the OC people wanted what we wanted, a successful conclusion to the case. I also had good vibes from Newsome; call it a cop's intuition.

Billy Newsome was about six feet tall and Irish-looking: red hair, freckles, pale complexion, the works. I thought this to be a plus. My looks were working for me by going against type as to what a wiseguy should look like, and it would probably work for him, too. Newsome was in good shape. He had competed in triathlons and was slender but muscular. He lived in south Jersey so no one would know him in the Newark area. While the bosses talked among themselves, Billy and I drifted off to another part of the room.

"Hey, Mike, I just want to let you know I realize this is your case and I'm not going to make an end run around you to grab the glory. I'm here to help. You tell me what needs to be done and I'll do it."

We ruminated about wiseguys for a while until Nick summoned me over to where he and the OC bosses were sitting.

"Give them a summary of the case so far, Mike. Me and Jim told them what we could, but they want to hear it from the guy with his boots on the ground."

For the next hour I ran down everything I'd done during the investigation. I got few questions; everyone was listening intently to what I had to say. I summed up with what I considered to be a nonnegotiable demand.

"With all due respect," I began, "we all want this case to be a screaming success. In my opinion, for us to get there, I need Sweeney to stay on as my immediate supervisor. He knows me, he knows the wiseguys, and he knows the case. I feel safer with him where he is right now." I nodded at my new partner. "And so will Billy."

Sweeney looked uncomfortable. I knew that once the Organized Crime Bureau took over responsibility for the investigation, they would want to put their own midlevel supervisors into the mix, guys whom they worked with every day and trusted.

One of the captains finally said, "That's a tough request."

"Well, sir, if you don't keep Jim on, I'd have to seriously consider quitting the case and going back to patrol."

I was met with stony silence. Sweeney looked as if he wanted to crawl into a hole. What I said was a bluff. I'd sooner drink toxic waste than go back on patrol. I had too much invested in the case. I lived and breathed it every day. I could work with anyone the OC guys gave me because I basically did whatever I wanted to do anyway. But I also knew my handler, and he was as wrapped up in the investigation as I was, and the job owed it to him to let him continue. To let Sweeney go after he had contributed so much was unfair and uncalled for. The Organized Crime people knew if I walked now, they'd have to start from scratch. You can't order someone to work undercover, it was strictly voluntary, an option I would use to my advantage at another time as the case progressed. Without talking it over, one of the captains said, "Done." The other three bosses nodded in agreement.

I made sure I didn't look at Sweeney because I would've broken out in a big grin. I love it when I tell bosses what to do; it so rarely happens.

I met with Billy, my new partner, every day for a week, until I felt he was up to speed enough in oil-business jargon to seamlessly integrate into the operation without arousing suspicion. He was like a sponge, soaking up everything to the point where he knew as much as I did (or didn't) about the business I owned (or didn't).

I had laid the groundwork for Billy's appearance on the scene by mentioning to Zarra on a few occasions that I'd need someone to man the phones in the office because I was spending so much time helping the crew with my increasing responsibilities on their behalf. On the average day I'd be collecting from the slots or delivering sham heating oil at least four hours a day. How was a conscientious businessman such as myself going to keep a legit concern operating without some help? Zarra had no objection except to ask that I hire someone who could be trusted.

"Don't pick the first mook who comes along," he said. "Do a little checking; make sure you ain't hiring a fucking FBI agent or something."

"You can trust whoever I get like you can trust me," I said.

The State Police set up a command post in a trailer behind their headquarters at the State Police Barracks on the Garden State Parkway. The investigation into the northern New Jersey mob was headed by Lieutenant Colonel Louis Toronto, a no-nonsense and highly respected career boss with many years of organized-crime investigations on his résumé.

The trailer was off-limits to all but those working the case. Cops are a curious bunch, and the presence of the trailer on department property must have sent rumors flying, but a need-to-know policy was in effect because of potential intelligence leaks. When compared to Newark, the State Police thought themselves squeaky-clean, yet they, too, had stray cops, two of whom were discovered when it came time to make arrests in this case. When the arrest and search warrants were being served, two troopers from the alleged incorruptible State Police Organized Crime Bureau stole $100,000 from the $1 million in cash that Sal Cetrulo had stashed in his house. They were caught, convicted, and sent to prison. Cops are human, and corruption crossed department lines.

The troopers assigned to the trailer would be monitoring court-ordered wiretaps and video-surveillance tape. Real-time monitors were installed to capture criminal activity as it went down, accompanied by audio to record the voices of the wiseguys as they talked themselves into prison. An assistant district attorney was on call around the clock to settle matters of law and expedite warrants. As the investigation grew, the amount of manpower increased, almost daily. Within a short time we'd have the cameras and audio in place in the club and we'd be up and running.

The club that I now had access to was proving to be *the* spot to be in north Jersey if you were a wiseguy. On any given day, at least twenty made guys, including bosses and associates, came and went from the club. Members of other crime families, primarily the Gambinos, also stopped by frequently, as did mobsters from Philadelphia. Writing down license plate numbers of everyone who frequented the club was a logistical nightmare because these guys would park all over the neighborhood, generally grabbing the first illegal spot they found. A cop on surveillance would have to tag along—usually on foot—after a wiseguy as he left the club until he got to his car, then radio a surveillance vehicle to follow the target. This left plenty of room for miscommunication and lost targets, not to mention if the foot cop was a stranger in a neighborhood where everybody knew everybody else. I came up with a simple solution I hoped would solve the problem.

I approached Ralph Vicaro one afternoon in front of the club. Vicaro was a respected capo about Zarra's age and had been in the crew since the 1960s and was easy to talk to. I felt if I came up with a good idea, he'd implement it.

It was a sunny, warm day, not humid, and several of the wiseguys were in front of the club sunning themselves. Vicaro was in a folding lawn chair reading a newspaper.

"Mr. Vicaro, how're you doing?"

Without looking up he said, "These fucking obituaries would make better reading if they told you how the person died, you know?"

"Huh? Oh, yeah. Someone you know died?"

He looked at me. "You get to be my age, kid, this is the first place you go when you open up a paper. Like the sports pages when you're younger. You wanna see who you outlived."

How do I respond to that? "Just wanted to ask you something, got a minute?"

"Sure, kid, shoot."

"Parking is a fucking nightmare around here, guys are bitching." Actually, no one had said anything about the parking problem. "If it's okay with you, I'll spread the word in the neighborhood that this block is off-limits to everyone except us. You know, like VIP parking."

Vicaro gave my idea less than five seconds of contemplation. "Good idea, kid. Go around the neighborhood and pass the word. Tell 'em, it's coming from me."

Within two days Davenport was ours. Some of the neighborhood residents bitched and moaned about the crew's commandeering Ninth Street, but they didn't have much say in the matter. The wiseguys loved it, and I let Vicaro take the credit. I considered starting a valet parking service, but that may have been a bit much. With the crew and their guests now parked in one central location, I could take down license plate numbers without leaving my office, plus it freed up the surveillance cops to actually conduct surveillances.

* * *

JP and I went to a warehouse in south Jersey to pick up a shipment of video-poker machines and stored them in a warehouse close to the club. The following day we drove to Essex County to recruit new store owners to let us install the machines in their businesses. These new stores would replace the ones Zarra had lost in Paterson as a result of his poaching Louis Gatto's territory.

JP handled the sales pitch. If the store owner nixed the idea, JP would say, "You really have no choice. We'll be back at the end of the week with the machines." Dale Carnegie had nothing on JP, but of course Dale never had a gun for a sales tool.

The floating craps and poker games were so big by this time that Zarra started utilizing four empty storefronts as permanent rotating locations for the invitation-only games. These games alone were netting Zarra more than enough to make him wealthy. But of course this wasn't enough; Zarra wanted more. "What's yours is mine" was his motto.

And of course the scams continued.

I introduced Billy around as my new employee to anyone who would stand still long enough to listen. Most of the crew wouldn't have given a damn if I'd brought in a one-eyed, transvestite dwarf; everyone was making money and that's all they cared about. JP, on the other hand, had questions. He was sprawled out on a lawn chair on the sidewalk in front of the club with a foil reflector under his chin catching the last few rays of a dwindling summer sun.

"Who's this fucking new guy, Mikey? Where do you know him from?"

"Relax, he's from the old neighborhood in Jersey City. He's

stand-up, I vouch for him." Jersey City has a big Irish community, and I knew JP, much less anyone else in the crew, would not be familiar with anyone who lived there. With these guys, if you weren't Italian, the only thing you were good for was getting ripped off.

JP still wasn't convinced. "So you know him, right?"

"I know people who know him. He's okay, relax. I just need him for the winter season, then he'll be gone." The case would probably be over by then.

JP went back to baking his skin to a nice leather texture. "Okay, just gotta check. I figured he was okay. I can smell a cop a mile away."

Right.

Billy knew a lot about horse racing, and that made his transition from an outsider to one of the guys happen pretty quickly. It's a rare wiseguy who doesn't play the horses and love to talk about it.

As summer gradually morphed into fall, I got busier than ever. While Billy copied license plate numbers and mapped out possible locations for phone taps and cameras, I was almost exclusively on the road delivering fake heating oil and slot machines. I'd pick up the machines in a warehouse in Point Pleasant that was managed by an associate named Pat Sporino. A few times I had no idea what I was carrying. I knew better than to ask though and kept my curiosity in check. If Zarra wanted to share something with me, he'd do it. We'd find out eventually through subpoenas anyway.

One day I delivered a truckload of five-gallon buckets labeled DRIVEWAY SEALER to a building-supply company in tony Scarsdale, New York. The loads came from a truck roll-off box in lower

Manhattan, where I picked up four pallets of the alleged sealer before depositing them in an unmarked warehouse in the Meadowlands in New Jersey, then made the Scarsdale delivery the following day. I had no idea what was in the buckets, but there was no paperwork and minimal conversation when I dropped the load in Scarsdale. I can only assume the buckets contained cheap toxic material that was being passed off as driveway sealer. I put the supposedly legitimate building-supply company on my search-warrant list.

In a new scam, we would steal heating oil from federal HUD housing complexes and sell it at a discount through newspaper ads, cash only. We had no shortage of buyers or, as I liked to refer to them, future defendants.

I also helped in the demolition of the old Colgate factory in Jersey City. The structure was huge, about the size of the Port Authority Bus Terminal in New York, and while the demolition work was legitimate, what I was doing wasn't.

The demolition was handled by Interboro Carting, which was owned by Angelo Ponte, who also owned Ponte's Restaurant in Manhattan. He was in his late forties, had been connected to organized crime for a while, and was a made member. Eventually he would run afoul of Rudy Giuliani, who was a federal prosecutor before he became mayor of New York and would send Ponte away on a federal antitrust conviction. Ponte had been involved in a few heating-oil scams with Gerardo's crew in the past and was now directing the illegal dumping of tons of toxic waste that we were pulling out of the building.

Every day I'd load my truck with fifty-five-gallon drums of toxic chemicals and deliver them to BASF Company in Kearny, New Jersey, which in turn illegally dumped the chemicals. No paperwork was involved in these transactions; I'd make the delivery and the drums would vanish. Eventually this stuff had to make its way into New Jersey drinking water.

During my daily trips to the demolition site, I'd catch Ponte staring at me. I ignored it until he approached me one day as I was about to leave with a load for BASF.

He looked me right in the eye and said, "You're a fucking cop, aren't you?"

Now the normal reaction from an undercover cop would be to vehemently deny the charge, or to stutter and stammer through a weak response, but I chose to go in the opposite direction.

"Yeah, you're right, I'm a fucking cop. I'm working undercover and all you motherfuckers will be in jail by this time next year."

What ensued would be a Mafia version of a Mexican standoff. We starred at each other without saying a word for what had to be the longest thirty seconds of my life. I kept looking directly into his eyes, knowing if I broke away, Ponte might think his suspicion was accurate.

Instead Ponte broke the stalemate and started laughing. "You're a funny motherfucker, Mikey."

"Listen, I *was* a cop, got fired two years ago. Everyone knows that, so stop with this cop bullshit, okay, Ang?"

"Just busting your chops, Mikey. Go, go do your run, see you later."

But he wasn't just busting my balls; he was serious. While good street cops have a second sense regarding criminals, sharp wiseguys have a sense of who's a cop, and the stare down had been a test. I had passed, but as soon as I had driven outside the gates, my hands trembled and my throat went dry. I had to remind myself that no matter how smoothly things might be going, it could all turn to shit in the blink of an eye.

Sal Cetrulo came into my office a few days later and asked me to take a ride with him to help with a "thing" in Edgewater.

"You got a problem?" I asked. A *thing* was usually a mob euphemism for an illegal act that was better left unsaid, at least for the moment. I hoped I wasn't about to be asked to participate in a hit.

"No, no, not me. A friend of mine. Owns a joint."

A friend of mine refers to a civilian, a nonmember of the Mafia; *a friend of ours* refers to a made guy or an associate. Obviously, from Cetrulo's brevity, he didn't wish to elaborate, so I stopped asking questions and went with him. He wasn't talkative on the way to Edgewater either, keeping the conversation to generalities.

We wound up on the *Binghamton,* a ferryboat that had been used to transport commuters from Hoboken to downtown Manhattan before the PATH trains were put into service in 1962. It was now a restaurant and bar docked on the New Jersey side of the Hudson River in Edgewater with sweeping views of New York City. Nelson Gross, a connected politician with a checkered past, was the owner and Cetrulo's buddy with the problem.

Gross had been the chairman of the New Jersey Republican State Committee in the 1960s and was appointed by President Richard Nixon as the special assistant to the Office of Narcotics Control under the US secretary of state, a no-show job rewarding him for his support of Nixon over Nelson Rockefeller in the 1968 run for the White House. Gross had also served federal time for tax fraud and conspiracy and was involved in other crimes and shady dealings.

He was married to Noel Love, heiress to the Guggenheim fortune. The day Cetrulo and I went to see Gross, he was riding high as the owner of the successful *Binghamton* restaurant and was still a power in northern New Jersey politics.

Gross was waiting for us on the top deck in a lounge area, seated in a booth with a great view of lower Manhattan. The restaurant hadn't opened for the day as yet, and aside from a few workers stocking the bar and setting tables, we had the place to ourselves.

Gross stood up and greeted Cetrulo warmly. I waited silently until they finished with the ginzo cheek kisses and hugs. When Cetrulo introduced us, I shook Gross's hand and hoped he wouldn't kiss me. He didn't. Gross was in his fifties with well-coiffed gray hair, a little over six feet tall, and well built.

"You guys want something to drink? Eat?" he asked.

"I'm good," Cetrulo said, and looked at me.

I said, "No thanks," but could have polished off one of the lobsters I'd seen being unloaded by the case when we had arrived. But I figured I was there for muscle and flash, not to stuff my face.

After a few minutes of weather talk, Gross got to the point.

"I've got security problems, Sal. I'm being robbed blind by the help, a lot of coke use by the customers, and bullshit problems on the door. The coke bullshit can cause problems with my liquor license, and the shitheads who work for me are stealing everything from what's in the registers to cases of food. There're fights on the door almost every night. Drunk assholes want to get in and won't take no for an answer. I can't get a handle on any of it. This place is too fucking big."

Cetrulo said, "Mike here is our security expert, Nelson. Used to be a cop." Cetrulo looked at me. "Mike, handle this."

It doesn't take a genius to solve problems like Gross's; most security difficulties can be resolved using common sense. I started asking questions and making suggestions. Apparently Gross liked my ideas because he hired me on the spot to clean up his joint.

I was going to use off-duty cops as undercovers. They'd be hired as waiters and bartenders and would weed out the thieves. I also knew a woman who did mystery shopping whom I could put in from time to time. Mystery shoppers buy goods or services and watch to see if the proper figures are rung up. The current security people on the door would be replaced by some head breakers from the Cage. I'd be paid in cash, most of it going to Cetrulo and on up the ladder.

When we left the boat and started on the ride back to Newark, Cetrulo said, "You did good in there, Mike."

"Right, thanks."

"Do a good job here, it's important."

"I always do a good job, Sal."

"Here especially." Then he opened up with his master plan. "You do good here, we offer to drop Gross's weekly nut for a piece of the place. We're gonna bust the joint out."

"Busting out" a business is a classic mob scam. The wiseguys work their way into a business by ingratiating themselves with the owner and become silent partners. Once in, they begin ordering more supplies than the business requires, all on credit, with no intention of paying the creditors. The excess supplies are then sold on the black market for 50 percent of wholesale with 100 percent of the profits going to the mob. Wiseguys can work this scam on any retail business, but they particularly like clothing stores and restaurants because the goods are easy to move. With restaurants it's food and booze. When the business's credit is shot all to hell and the mob can't squeeze out another credit order, they burn the joint down for the insurance money and walk away. Busting out a business is a slow process and doesn't usually begin until the mob has been entrenched in the business for a while. During that time every wiseguy that's not anorexic eats for free.

If the owner gives his new partners shit, he's dealt with accordingly. Gross would eventually be found stabbed and bludgeoned to death in September 1997 on Manhattan's West Side. Two of Gross's busboys on the *Binghamton* were later charged with and convicted of his murder. But for now Gross wasn't through asking for favors, and we would soon enough find out what he wanted next.

8

Here's Looking at You, Mikey

Family life was agreeing with me. I was hanging out in the club and doing mob business during the day, giving me my evenings free to be with my family, something I wasn't used to doing throughout my police career. The more I hung out at the club, the more I appreciated a stable home life.

What bothered me the most was seeing the sons of the wiseguys trying to emulate their fathers' attitudes and callousness. During the summer these kids would come down to the Cage, looking like younger versions of their dads. They swore, bullied kids in the neighborhood, dressed like their fathers, and many wanted to do what Daddy did when—and if—they grew up. It made me realize what a powerful influence I had on my three little girls, and they needed me around as much as possible.

I understood how hedonistic I'd been for most of my marriage, and while I still needed my daily adrenaline rush, I also needed to play with my kids. My wife, Angela, was thrilled because I was around the house more, and by the time September rolled around, I had no doubt that she knew I wasn't on patrol as I had claimed to be. She chose to overlook all the inconsistencies and relish my new role as a good husband and father.

I was coming home every day with dirty hands. After a few months of delivering (and stealing) oil products, it was becoming increasingly difficult to get the grime out from under my fingernails. The stuff also became embedded in my skin, and no amount of scrubbing in a turnpike rest area could remove it all. Angela was a neat freak and had to notice. Plus, after a while I stopped bringing home my uniforms, which I explained away by saying the barracks had a washing machine, and the dry cleaner's was next door. Pure laziness on my part, but I saw that she would overlook anything as long as I came home safe and didn't whine about being a daddy and a husband. I had changed and was happy and she saw that. My home was my escape after dealing with truly bad people every day.

The time had come to begin installing the phone lines we needed to tap the Cage. It had been agreed that we'd wait a few months until I was a fixture in the club and trusted by the crew, and I was now one of the guys. The trailer with the monitoring equipment had already been in place in the parking lot of the State Police Barracks for a month.

Jim Sweeney chose a trooper from the Electronic Surveillance Unit, Pat Riley, to assist me with the installation. Yet another Irishman, he was a whiz with all things electronic and found no problem risking his ass to help me record the crew right under their noses.

"Why they pay me the big money, Mike," he told me.

Pat was a bull, six foot three inches and at least 240 pounds of solid muscle, and easy to get along with, perhaps because he was me in a bigger suit. Nothing fazed him and he had a great sense of humor. I'm sure Sweeney chose him because he reminded Sweeney of me and there would probably be no personality conflict. We had to be a well-disciplined team and couldn't afford to make a mistake.

Pat and I thought it best to do our work just before sunrise. Wiseguys are night people, and we figured 5:00 a.m. to be the best time to avoid being seen by anyone in the crew. The club was empty and locked up by 2:00 a.m. most nights with the wiseguys in their jammies and in their beds with their wives or girlfriends.

I picked up Pat in a Garden State Parkway rest area at 4:30 a.m. that first day. He had a load of equipment, and it took two trips to transfer it all into my truck.

"All this shit to lay some wire?" I asked.

"Most of it is countermeasure equipment." He saw my puzzlement. "I want to sweep the place for bugs first. Your buddies might be bugging your office."

Made sense. I had been trapping the front door and windows with transparent tape when I left every day, but the wiseguys could have found the rudimentary silent alarm system. I used a simple piece of tape that extended from the door/window to the sill/jamb. If anyone entered, the tape would break free, and the next day when I opened up, I'd know someone had been in my office. But if the tape was found they could easily have planted a bug and resealed the tape on their way out.

It took Pat about forty-five minutes to sweep the entire office. He did it twice, once with the equipment and once visually.

"You're clean," he said. After that either Pat or another trooper would sweep my office three times a week until the case ended. I even took to trapping the windows and only door when I went to lunch. I was taking no chances, no shortcuts. If I made one mistake now, the entire operation could be compromised.

"Okay, what do we do first?"

Pat looked at the dropped ceiling and extended a ladder. He removed one of the panels and poked around for a few minutes before coming down.

"You know all that BX cable you got running through the ceiling?"

I shrugged. "I'll take your word for it."

"It contains the wiring for the building. We're gonna gut the cables and replace the wiring with the phone lines we're gonna use for the taps. This way, if someone gets nosy and looks up there, all they're gonna see is BX cable."

We worked on a short length of BX cable at a time and placed it right back where we found it. It took us five days. In the meantime, the requests for wiretap warrants were submitted to a judge. We waited until the last-possible minute to submit the paperwork so as to diminish the possibility of a leak.

While the prep work was in progress, I heard that Gerardo's wire room, where his sports-book and horse-racing bets were collated, by the Holland Tunnel had been relocated to New York. A new law made it a felony to operate a bookmaking establishment in New Jersey, but in New York it was still a misdemeanor. With the football season starting, I placed a few bets with Zarra, who shared with me that the new book was in Staten Island. He saved me a lot of time by telling me the address. The new location went on the search-warrant list.

Meetings with Sweeney continued per our agreement with the OC people. Things were running so smoothly that the OC bosses were congratulating themselves for allowing Sweeney to be the supervisor liaison between them and me. Although Sweeney was only a master sergeant, he was wielding the power and control of a deputy chief. Whatever he asked for, he got. All this could change in the bat of an eye if I screwed something up, but for now we were golden.

I was required to submit daily reports over and above what I verbally told Sweeney at our weekly summits. Every night I would go to the Meadowlands Racetrack and randomly choose one pay phone from the bank of fifty pay phones just outside the track. State law prohibited pay phones inside the racetrack proper. I would report to a detective and a lawyer from the attorney general's office the nature of the crimes committed that day, license plate numbers, and any intelligence I deemed valuable. Little by little we were compiling a list of crimes that we hoped would put the entire crew away for a long time. After the phone call I would immediately destroy my notes and enter the track to place a wager or two. This was my "unwind" time.

A few days later I received a phone call at my office from Dennis Marchalonis, special agent in charge (SAC) of the FBI's Lucchese Squad in Newark. Dennis was an acquaintance of about five years and was always looking to pick my brain for information on Lucchese capo Michael Taccetta and his crew. We tagged him "Agent Bullshit" for his penchant of promising the State Police anything in exchange for information on the Luccheses. I hadn't had any contact with him since Taccetta's crew tried to clip me with a bullet to the head. My bullshit meter went off the charts when he told me on the phone he was Dennis March.

"Hey, Mikey, how you doing?"

I recognized his annoying nasal twang immediately. I had to be careful how I responded. "Same shit, Dennis, different day."

"What are you doing with that oil company in front of the club on Davenport?"

This wasn't good. Marchalonis was apparently involved in an operation that was zeroing in on Gerardo's crew. I felt that they had either gotten wind of what I was doing and wanted to snatch the investigation out from under us after the State Police had done all the work or, by sheer coincidence, had initiated a case in the same location. I was going with the former.

I said, "Can't talk right now, I'll get back to you later," and hung up on him. I raced out of the office like my ass was on fire and ran smack into JP, almost knocking him over.

"Whoa, cowboy, where you going in such a fucking hurry?" he said when he regained his balance.

I was moving quickly because I wanted to get in touch with Sweeney so he could terminate any conflict with the FBI. Calling from the office didn't seem like a good option.

"Going up to Jimmy Buff's for something to eat," I said, referring to a street lunch wagon about three blocks away that made great Italian hot dogs.

"Jesus Christ, you must be pretty fucking hungry."

I gave him a wan smile. "Well, you know me and food. Want something?"

"Yeah, gimme a half dozen hot dogs with everything." Of course he never went into his pocket. Cheap bastard.

"Not a problem," I said, and was gone.

I drove two miles before I found a pay phone that worked, but got Sweeney on the first ring. After I told him about Marchalonis's phone call he said, "They'll always be office boys with fucking guns." Sweeney, like most street cops, was no big fan of the FBI. He agreed with me about Marchalonis's jockeying to steal the case.

"So what do we do?" I asked.

"Mike, I live to fuck with the FBI. Let me take care of Agent Bullshit. Don't worry about it."

I knew it might take awhile for Sweeney's politicking to produce results, so I forgot about it, thinking it would all work out. I went back to the Cage feeling better and got a warm welcome from JP when I handed him six steaming hot dogs.

My relationship with Ralph Vicaro, the acting capo in the club, and Sal Cetrulo was moving forward as I became more trusted. Vicaro would give me $50 just to sit next to him when he had a potential problem with one of the crew. Capos collected money, they hated to give it away; so while the $50 wasn't any big deal, it was symbolic of the faith Vicaro had in me. And if a capo trusted you, you were a stand-up guy.

Cetrulo would ask me to go with him when he met with civilians about putting slot machines in their businesses. He taught me some Italian phrases that he would use if we were meeting with non-Italians to alert me to a possible problem: *sigillare le labbra* (seal the lips), *non pensarci più* (forget about it), and *fare questa cosa* (do this thing, or follow my lead). The Italian curses I already knew. This stuff they don't teach you in Berlitz. After a while we were hanging out in front of the club and bullshitting about everything from sports to mob business. We were also going to the *Binghamton* every Thursday to pick up the weekly nut for the security work we were doing for Nelson Gross.

Gross always met us in the restaurant with an envelope stuffed with cash. He'd hand it to me and I'd pass it to Cetrulo, neither of us counting it. Another bit of mob etiquette dictated that you never counted money given to you for a business transaction, legal or illegal, because it showed a lack of respect to the payee. It also went without saying that it would be foolhardy for anyone to short wiseguys.

Cetrulo and I would generally hang out for a few minutes, maybe have drinks, before we made an excuse and split, but one night Gross insisted we stay and have dinner.

"Anything you guys want . . . on the house," he said.

Gross's security and theft problems had been solved within two weeks, and he was thrilled with the service, although I could tell he would have liked a break in the bill. We were banging him pretty hard, but that was part of the come-on. I assumed Gross wanted to renegotiate the amount he was paying us, and he was softening us up with a lavish dinner. If I was correct, Cetrulo would offer our services for free for a small percentage of the business, and Gross would leap on it. In addition to providing security, Gross knew Cetrulo could make problems with the police go away and apply pressure to politicians to extend favors to the business. Knowing Gross's background, I expected he also wouldn't object to the crew running a few poker games on the premises for a small cut, and I do mean small.

Cetrulo and I glanced at each other. It wasn't my place to accept the dinner offer because the made guys did all the talking unless otherwise directed, but I knew what Cetrulo was thinking: We've got him now.

"Sure, Nelson, we'd like that. Wouldn't we, Mikey?"

I smiled. "We'd like nothing better." Cetrulo was about to make a score, and an extortion charge would eventually be added to the ever-growing list of crimes the crew was accumulating. Instead of talking about money, however, Gross hit us with something totally unexpected.

"My wife's fucking around on me with her tennis pro," he said after we ordered our food.

Cetrulo and I stared at Gross, but I kept my mouth shut.

"I'm not Dear fucking Abby, Nelson. This shit happens," Cetrulo said. "What do you want us to do about it?" This was a rhetorical question, but Gross didn't see it that way.

"I want the cocksucker clipped," Gross said. "He's fucking my wife, for crissakes!"

All of a sudden I took center stage because Cetrulo wasn't about to respond to Gross's request. Cetrulo had to assume that since we weren't dealing with a "friend of ours," it had to be presumed that Gross was setting us up to get pinched. Anyone from outside the circle of trust that was the Mafia was immediately suspect as either a rat or too weak willed to withstand grilling by the cops should the hit, or whatever crime in which the civilian was complicit, go bad.

Maybe Gross had got caught up in an FBI sting doing something illegal and was offering up the crew to get out of trouble.

I was getting vibes from Cetrulo: nip this fucking thing in the bud before we get subpoenaed before a grand jury. I had to be careful about what I said. I was a cop; I couldn't entrap anyone. Legally, the term *entrapment* meant I couldn't influence anyone to do something they wouldn't normally do. I also had to assume we were being recorded, by whom, who the hell knew. My concern was getting caught up in another agency's investigation, thereby jeopardizing our own. Cetrulo knew that if he was recorded saying *anything* about a murder, even nixing the idea, it couldn't be construed as entrapment because that's what the mob did; they murdered people. This is what they *normally* do. Cetrulo wanted me to do the talking because I wasn't a made guy, didn't have a history with the mob, and had no criminal record. I had to get Gross to change his mind about killing his wife's lover, thereby legally nullifying any conspiracy that might be forming.

"Mr. Gross—" I began.

"Nelson," he corrected me.

"Nelson . . . we don't do what you're suggesting."

Gross looked at me as if I had two heads. "Waddaya mean you don't do what I'm suggesting? You're the fucking mob; you whack people. I want this fucking guy dead. He's fucking her three times a week. I don't even get to do that." His face was turning red and his jugular was throbbing. I thought it possible he might stroke out and we'd have nothing to worry about.

I smiled. "You're misinformed. We're a corporation now; we don't do none of that stuff you're talking about. That shit went out with tommy guns and spats."

"What, am I in the fucking twilight zone or something?" Gross said. "A corporation? General Motors is a corporation; they make fucking cars. You make people dead."

It appeared as if my approach wasn't working.

"Is it the money?" Gross asked. "How much is this gonna cost me? Ten thousand?"

I saw an out. "Add a zero onto that." He'd never go for a hundred grand; I don't care if his wife was banging the entire Seventh Fleet.

He went quiet for a moment. "That's too fucking much."

"Listen, Nelson, you're not going to find anyone to do it for less, more than likely more. Let it alone or divorce the bitch."

Gross sighed, rubbed his forehead. "Yeah, well, maybe you're right."

"Of course I'm right," I said. "You're pissed now. When did you find out about her with this tennis guy?"

"I dunno. Last week?"

"Calm down. Think. This guy gets dead and who are they gonna come to?"

He took a sip of his drink. He sighed. "Yeah, yeah, you're right."

Cetrulo nudged me under the table: time to go. I gave him a look. I wasn't going anywhere until I was sure I'd talked Gross out of murder. I didn't want him hiring someone else. There was no shortage of people in New Jersey who would kill for you for a lot less than ten grand. If Gross looked, he'd find someone. All I needed was to read about some poor schmuck in tennis whites turning up floating facedown in the Hudson.

After twenty more minutes of cajoling, I had Gross convinced it was a bad idea. Now it was my turn to nudge Cetrulo. We left.

We were in the car for ten minutes before Cetrulo said a word.

"This fucking guy is bad news, Mike."

"No shit."

"I'm gonna push up the clock," Cetrulo said. "We gotta start making inroads in taking over his joint and get him out."

"You gotta do what you gotta do." I knew what *I* had to do: put everything that just went down on paper and get it to my handler as quickly as possible, just in case Gross had a change of heart and committed the murder himself. His wife's boyfriend needed a subtle heads-up, too. A visit from the State Police would see to that.

After this meeting, Cetrulo handled picking up the money by himself, while I moved on to other mob business. Before the crew could take over the *Binghamton,* our case culminated with the arrest of most of Gerardo's crew. Nelson Gross got to keep his floating restaurant thanks to the New Jersey State Police.

Pat and Billy continued to lay wire in the ceiling of the club's building while I made my criminal rounds. The surveillance on the individual crew members continued with troopers racking up significant overtime following the wiseguys. Most of them weren't tucked into bed before 3:00 a.m., and their day usually started around noon. Billy was mapping the Cage by peeking through the hole in the office wall to see where the members were hanging out. People are creatures of habit, and wiseguys are no exception. Everyone had his favorite area inside the Cage where he would socialize and talk business. We needed to know those locations to aim the cameras and place the recording devices accurately. Pat and Billy were now coming and going from the office in broad daylight, and no one questioned them, although they would both offer some bullshit cover story if challenged. Within weeks they were going into the club and placing bets with Joe Zarra. No one in the crew suspected anything; they were clueless. I was shocked. Either we were very good, or the wiseguys were very stupid. I went with the former. We were amped up and ready for whatever came next.

We also began monitoring the uniformed cops in the zone cars who worked the late tours (midnight to 8:00 a.m.) in the north district where the Cage was located. We needed to make certain that the cops weren't supplementing their incomes by moonlighting for the crew in some way. Most guys who worked the graveyard shift were volunteers because they needed to work those hours to tend to businesses they had during the day. Supervision was sparse, and once a zone car went on patrol after midnight, the cops were mostly on their own. Within a few weeks we knew which units were spending the tours with their girlfriends, where they hid the cars to catch some sleep, and where they hung out when they were supposed to be doing police work. We also had to ascertain which patrol teams were sharpest and if our cover might be blown by observant cops. The good news: no one was working for the crew. The bad news: a few zone teams actually patrolled, and the surveillance troopers had to be careful they weren't made.

I hadn't seen Andy Gerardo in a few weeks, and I was getting pressure from Sweeney to reestablish contact. I wouldn't do it; there was no reason to from Gerardo's perspective. He was the boss; when he wanted to see me, he'd issue the edict. It had to happen eventually; I was trusted by Gerardo, and I knew he'd reach out to me sooner or later. He was still staying away from the Cage because of his parole status, but being the boss of a crew was like owning a bar: if you weren't around constantly to supervise your employees, they would rob you blind. I bided my time awaiting the inevitable summons.

A week later it came in the form of a personal visit from Augie, the counterman at Joe's Diner. Wiseguys are not fans of telephones and don't use them if there's a reasonable alternative. Augie stopped by my office and got me away from Billy, who was sitting on a silent phone and looking bored.

"Mr. Gerardo wants to see you."

"Same place?" I assumed this meeting, like all the other meetings, would be at the diner.

Augie shook his head and gave me the name of the Tadol Italian Bakery on Bloomfield and Clifton Avenues. "For breakfast, eight a.m., tomorrow. Okay?"

"Yeah, sure," I said, and Augie was gone.

I got to the bakery fifteen minutes early the next morning. The mom-and-pop retail store had a few tables to accommodate customers who wanted to eat in, hang out, and schmooze. Gerardo was already there. He was dressed casually in a black silk shirt, neatly pressed gray slacks, and a black zipper sweater. The bakery was empty of customers, and we sat at a table in the back. I was greeted warmly.

"Mikey Ga-Ga, how're you doing?"

"Great, Mr. Gerardo. Good to see you."

Gerardo ordered breakfast for us and we made the obligatory small talk until the food arrived and the server vanished.

"Mikey, what we talk about today stays between us, *capisce*?"

"Sure, Mr. Gerardo, goes without saying."

He got down to business. "How many stores Zarra got with the video-poker machines?"

"Eleven locations. We had more, but then after that Gatto bullshit in Paterson—"

"Yeah, I know about that. What's the weekly nut?"

I shook my head. "I don't really know. I don't count the money, just bring it back to Zarra. His instructions." I knew exactly what the count was because it went in my weekly report to my handlers, but wanted to appear to be a good soldier by following orders.

"I want you to start counting the money and give him the weekly count."

"Sure, no problem," I said.

"He's gonna know it came from me and that I'm up on his operation. Mikey, you manage a bunch of thugs, you get what you deserve if you don't stay on top of them. I can't be seen at the club so I'm relying on you to do this for me."

"I appreciate your trust in me, Mr. Gerardo. I won't let you down."

"I know that, Mikey, I know. Anything going on down there I should know about?"

Gerardo was testing me to see if I'd talk behind Zarra's back. He knew scores and other scams were going on he didn't know about—and didn't get a cut of—but any boss would write off small loses to keep his crew happy. He wanted to know that I wasn't a rat. If I'd rat for him, I'd rat on him.

I told him what he wanted to hear: "Nothing, Mr. Gerardo, everything's going good."

* * *

A week later Augie paid me another visit at the office.

"Same place and time. Tomorrow." Then he was gone. A man of few words, Augie.

The next day it was déjà vu, just new duds worn by Gerardo. The food arrived and he got down to it.

"You still have connections on the force, Mikey?"

I made a show of thinking. "I got a cousin, Sully, on the Newark PD. He's the only guy I can trust." I had several cousins, none of whom were named Sully, and none cops. "Waddaya need?"

"From time to time I'll need someone to do record checks, see if any of my guys've been popped by the cops or feds, see if they have incentive to flip and become informers. Can this be done?"

"No problem. I'll throw Sully a yard per name. That okay?"

"Sure, fine. Another hundred for you for your trouble."

"Thank you, Mr. Gerardo. Very generous of you." Gerardo knew the score. For a cop to run a criminal-record check, he'd have to enter his own PIN into the National Crime Information Center (NCIC) federal computer database. If someone checked, the search would come back to the cop who'd entered the search criteria, and without a valid reason for the search the cop could find himself in a world of trouble. It was risky and Gerardo knew it. Two hundred dollars was a bargain for such information.

Gerardo pulled a piece of paper from his pocket. "You're first assignment. Check on this guy." He handed me the paper.

The name was Silvio DeVita, the guy who'd recently been released from prison after serving thirty years for killing a police officer. He was on lifetime parole, and even a minor bust could send him away forever. Gerardo wanted me to check for any recent arrests.

It was a smart move. DeVita would most certainly flip when faced with the rest of his life in the can.

"And do it once a month," Gerardo added.

My reputation was growing. I was doing everything Zarra asked of me, didn't bitch and moan, was honest with my collections, and could be counted on to keep my mouth shut. I didn't know how appreciated I was until Zarra came up to me one day when I entered the Cage.

"How you doin', Mikey?"

"Great, Mr. Zarra. How you doing?"

Zarra waved a beefy mitt. "I'm doing fine. Hey, from now on call me Joe."

I had arrived. While Zarra wasn't part of the mob's hierarchy, he was a made guy. With my enhanced rep came more responsibility. A few days after we officially became buddies, Zarra dispatched Sal Cetrulo and me to a bar on Route 1 in Hudson County to make a loan collection. I was now privy to Zarra's loan-sharking operation.

The bar was closed, but the owner, a small-time hood named Lou Malavacca, was there and was expecting us. He let us in, and he and I went to the bar to discuss business, while Cetrulo went opposite the bar to play Pac-Man. To allow me to conduct business was another sign of my new standing in the crew.

The joint was a real dive and reeked of stale beer and cigarettes. Malavacca looked right at home; he was slovenly in old jeans and a stained sweatshirt. His face hadn't seen a razor in days. Malavacca was a degenerate gambler and was into Zarra for thousands.

He was in a foul mood, didn't offer us a drink, but was throwing down straight Absolut vodka from a bottle, which he poured almost nonstop into a shot glass in front of him.

He was argumentative from the start: "I ain't paying you guys shit."

I tried to be the diplomat. "Lou, you made a deal. You want us to go back to Zarra and tell him you ain't paying?"

He inhaled another shot of vodka. "That fucking Zarra knows me for years and he's hitting me up for 156 percent interest a week? Citizens pay that rate. What fucking balls on that guy. Suck my dick for the money."

With the Pac-Man game pinging in the background, I leaned into him. I knew I couldn't hurt the guy, but nothing in the rule book said I couldn't intimidate him.

"Lou, don't be an asshole. There're two of us here." Meanwhile Cetrulo wasn't saying a word. All I heard was that friggin' game binging and banging. Where the fuck was Sal to back me up? I didn't dare turn around to look for him, thinking Malavacca might sucker punch me off my barstool.

"And waddaya gonna do, fuck me up?" Another blast of vodka. "Fuck you, too. You're nothin' but a fucking four-hundred-dollar-a-week ex-cop turned leg breaker. You're a fuckin' asshole. They send a fucking asshole to talk to me? Fuck you." He poured himself another drink.

Finally, I heard Cetrulo's voice behind me. Nice and calm he says, "Mikey, c'mere for a second."

We huddled by the video game while Malavacca steamed and drank.

"Let him cool off for a while. Go take a piss or something while I go to the corner and call Zarra."

Capital idea. We needed to defuse the situation.

I walked through the dimly lit room to the men's bathroom, which smelled even worse than the bar. I did my thing and began to wash my hands, then I heard a gunshot so loud I thought I was the target of yet another assassination attempt. That notion dispelled, and with my ears still ringing, I barged through the bathroom door to find Malavacca sprawled face-up on the floor next to his stool with a pool of blood rapidly forming around his head. Sal Cetrulo was standing over him. I didn't see a gun.

I was incredulous. "What the fuck happened?!"

Cetrulo turned to me. "I dunno. Some nigger came in here and shot poor Lou in the head. I was outside looking for a phone to call Zarra. Prick ran down the block. Fucking neighborhood's going to shit." His eyes were bugged but he looked calm.

I gaped at Cetrulo for a good ten seconds. What the fuck do I do now? I knelt down next to Malavacca. Very dead. A small entrance wound was in the back of his head, but the exiting of the round blew off the front part of his skull. One eye was gone, the other was wide-open and staring at me. I felt Cetrulo come up behind me. For a second I felt icy fear, as if he were going to clip me right there and eliminate a potential witness. That fear was dispelled when he leaned on the bar and said, "Hey, Mikey, check this out."

The bottle from which Malavacca had been drinking had had its top sheared off by the exiting round that had pierced his skull. Floating in what remained of the vodka was Malavacca's missing eye.

"Here's looking at you, Mikey," Cetrulo said with a sideways grin.

* * *

The ride back to Newark was uncomfortable. Cetrulo was driving as if he didn't have a care in the world. A thousand thoughts were racing through my mind. I had to get to a phone to report what I'd just witnessed, or didn't witness, if I had to be precise. I was also trying to figure out what I was going to tell my new best friend, Joe Zarra. He was going to be apoplectic. Cetrulo, for his part, was relaxed and downright cheerful.

"Fucking nigger did us a favor. Asshole deserved to be whacked. Lou disrespected you, Mikey."

"That he did, Sal, that he did." What kind of a fucked-up world did I inhabit?

Obviously, Cetrulo wasn't about to confess, and I wondered what he did with the gun. He probably still had it on him. I was unarmed. I dismissed the thought from my mind as we pulled up in front of the Cage.

Cetrulo hit the sidewalk and said, "We gotta go see Joe. I'll go in first. You wait in your office."

I took a chance by calling Sweeney from my office. At my request, he conferenced a lawyer in from the attorney general's office before I began my narrative.

"Jesus motherfucking Christ!" Sweeney screamed after I'd finished.

The lawyer was cooler, contemplative. "You didn't witness the shooting, right?"

"Didn't see shit."

Silence on the line for the longest ten seconds of my life. I knew the lawyer was thinking of the case we were building and what impact Malavacca's murder would have on it. Sweeney was mute, I supposed, because he couldn't find the words to express his rage, not necessarily at me, but at the entire screwed-up situation.

"Okay," the lawyer finally said, "obviously you can't testify to seeing anything. Fuck it, let the local cops handle it."

Sweeney said, "That's it?"

"That's it," the lawyer said.

Sweeney said, "We just make like we weren't there?"

"Right," the lawyer said.

I tried to lighten the moment. "Hey, Jim, four years of law school. Listen to the guy."

"Mike," Sweeney said, "please shut the fuck up."

"Done." So much for levity. After a few seconds I said, "I gotta go. Zarra's gonna wonder where I am." I hung up.

"Tell me what you saw." Zarra was surprisingly calm, his rage undoubtedly spent on Cetrulo. We were knee to knee on folding chairs in the corner of the Cage.

I told him, emphasizing the point that I didn't see Cetrulo shoot anyone.

Zarra leaned back and folded his arms across his chest. "Motherfucker," he mumbled. "How the fuck am I gonna get paid from a dead guy?"

Joe Zarra, humanitarian. I treated his question as rhetorical and kept my mouth shut.

"Mikey, I sent you there because you're the guy with a fucking brain. Sal's a fucking idiot. This shit's not supposed to happen when you're there. You get paid to think."

"I'm sorry, Joe."

"I gotta think." He cradled his head in his hands, rubbing his temples. Aside from the lost revenue, I'm sure he was anticipating the talk he was going to have with Andy Gerardo about what happened. "Okay, go home, forget what happened. Maybe put out an APB on the black guy." He forced a grin.

Hard to believe, but the incident had an upside. I was now totally trusted by Zarra and Gerardo because I never mentioned anything about the killing to anyone, not even guys in the crew. The murder never even made the paper, and I'm assuming it's gone unsolved as just another robbery.

The decision by the attorney general's office not to pursue the murder case hinged on my not having witnessed the killing, and, as Cetrulo said, a lone black guy could have wandered into the bar and blown Malavacca away while I was in the men's room and Sal was outside. To have me involved in a murder investigation would have compromised the biggest underworld sting in New Jersey's history and would have seen Cetrulo probably walk for the crime anyway.

Justice was served, for everyone except Lou Malavacca.

9

On the Wire

I spent the weekend after the Malavacca debacle with my family. It was a welcome respite from the insanity of the Cage and the volatility of the crew. Things were still going well at home and I wanted to keep it that way, but Angela was beginning to ask subtle questions about my secretive ways and ever-increasing absences from home. I was still supposed to be working days in uniform. With the tour ending at 4:00 p.m., I should've been home shortly thereafter. She knew the vagaries of the job, and I could always make excuses for being a few hours late, the best fiction being late arrests that necessitated time-consuming processing and arraignments.

Angela, however, was pretty sharp, and I wasn't keeping track of the numerous arrests I said I was making. After coming home late for the fiftieth time, I found Angela seated in the kitchen, drumming her manicured nails on the Formica table. It sounded like the drumroll in the execution scene in the movie *Paths of Glory*.

"Another arrest?" she asked, doubt evident in her voice.

"Yeah, sweetie, it's Newark, you know? Never a dull moment." I avoided eye contact.

"Well, I've been keeping track of your arrests. You're locking up more people than Batman."

"And I do it all without a cape and a pimped-out car," I said, unable to keep a sheepish grin off my face. Time to change the subject. "What's for dinner?"

So it went. Angela was probably thinking I had a girlfriend on the side, but I thought it best to avoid any conversations that dealt with my extended hours. She would find out what was really going on soon enough.

That Monday I got my second call from Special Agent Dennis Marchalonis—Agent Bullshit—of the FBI. He gave me a phone number and hung up. I drove two miles to a pay phone and called him back.

"To what do I owe the honor of another call?" I asked.

"I want to apologize." I was momentarily speechless. The FBI *never* apologizes. "For what?"

"My call the other day. I don't want to give the impression I was poaching your case."

Obviously Jim Sweeney had worked his magic and gotten Marchalonis to back off whatever he was doing on Davenport Avenue.

"So what *were* you doing?" I asked. "Sounded like Grand Theft Wiseguy to me."

"Following up on some intel regarding the Franconero hit.

Remember that one from a few years back? We just got word from a snitch that Tommy Ricardi was responsible. What do you hear?"

George Franconero, singer Connie Francis's older brother, was murdered in the driveway of his home in North Caldwell, New Jersey, on March 6, 1981, by two men who cut him down in a volley of gunfire. Franconero was an attorney (which some might say was reason enough to shoot him) who had run afoul of factions in the Genovese and Lucchese crime families. He began as a lawyer for the board of education but wound up complicit in a scheme with both crime families to defraud banks. Four banks closed as a result, and the feds were all over the weakest link in the plot: Franconero. He was allegedly cooperating with the feds when he was murdered.

I had to laugh. "Tommy Ricardi? Who's your snitch, Mother Teresa? Tommy Ricardi couldn't find his ass with both hands. Don't you guys ever work the street? Ricardi is a fucking idiot." Ricardi and a bunch of other jerks were all made by boss Tony "Ducks" Corallo in the early 1980s when he opened up the books to any asshole that wanted to be inducted into the family. Charles "Lucky" Luciano, who put the word *organized* in organized crime, must have done flip-flops in his grave.

The Franconero hit was carefully planned. North Caldwell had one police officer on patrol the day of the murder, and someone called in a phony car crash miles away from Franconero's house. While the lone cop was responding to the diversion, the target was being bumped off in his snow-covered driveway.

"Dennis," I said, "Ricardi couldn't plan a good shit, let alone the way Franconero was clipped. He once beat a guy to death with a golf club; that's the extent of his planning ability."

"You know so much, who did it, then?"

"Now I'm doing your job for you? You know the shoeshine guy hangs out in front of the Cage sometimes?"

"That half-blind retard? He did it?"

"No, dumbass, but like everyone else, I bet he knows that Louis Gatto pressed the button. You guys gotta get out more. I've got better sources in Chuck E. Cheese for crissakes." I loved breaking the FBI's balls. It was a hobby of mine.

Marchalonis couldn't get off the phone fast enough; the FBI can't handle the truth. As far as I know, the FBI didn't pursue the Tommy Ricardi angle any further. Ricardi was disliked by everyone, and he eventually pissed off Vic Amuso and Anthony "Gaspipe" Casso, two powerful New York hoods who were so violent they scared other mobsters. John Gotti even turned down a request by Gambino boss Paul Castellano to whack Casso because Casso scared the shit out of Gotti. When Ricardi got word that both Amuso and Casso were going to come across the river to kidnap and torture him to death, Ricardi rolled over quicker than a circus seal. He ratted out everyone, including a number of his cousins. Result: he entered the federal Witness Security Program (WITSEC) and is today roaming the streets a free man. Sleep well, America.

We got some good news the following day: the wiretap warrants were approved and signed by a state judge. The warrants were good for ninety days, the standard length for wiretap warrants. Either we obtained indictable information in that time or the warrants would expire. If the case was hot with good intel coming in, the judge could extend the life of the warrants in ninety-day increments. We had no doubt that this would be the case.

* * *

I needed access to the club to plant the bugs, but the front door was secured with three sturdy locks. My first thought was to pick the locks in the middle of the night, but picking takes time. I couldn't afford to be seen on my knees in front of the door by a passerby, and besides, contrary to what you see in the movies, lockpicking is an art that takes constant practice. While I could fumble my way through it, I hadn't picked a lock in a while, and now wasn't the time for on-the-job training.

I came up with a novel idea and passed it on to Sweeney. I'd get my lower arm fitted with a cast and sling, then hide in the sling a puttylike substance I'd gotten from a locksmith that is used to make impressions of locks for key replication. Since I spent most of my day in the Cage anyway, no one would pay any attention to me when I made imprints of the locks.

"Brilliant, no?" I said to Sweeney.

He stared at me for a while. Finally he said, "Who are you, Harry fucking Houdini? There're three locks on the door. You mean to tell me no one's going to see you do this?"

I shook my head. "These guys are either playing cards, eating, watching TV, or all three at the same time. All I have to do is press the putty stuff against a lock as I pass the door, then stuff it between the cast and the sling. Takes a few seconds. I'll make three passes—go out to lunch, come back, whatever. I got a locksmith'll make the keys."

"I don't think so," Sweeney said. "Why can't you do this at night when the club's closed?"

"Because it adds an extra nighttime trip: make the impressions, come back to see if the keys work, then a third to plant the equipment. This way I make the impressions during the day, come back with the keys the same day to test them, then only one trip at night to do the job. Reduces the odds of getting caught in front of the club at night."

Sweeney thought about it. "Let me run it past the bosses."

I got the go-ahead the following day. That same afternoon I went to Columbus Hospital and arranged to be fitted for the cast and sling by a nurse I knew. By Thursday of that week I had wiseguys signing my cast after telling them I broke my arm during a furnace installation. No one seemed to care what allegedly happened to me. Most wiseguys have no empathy with anyone and only care about themselves. I think this lack of compassion is endemic in sociopathic personalities. Most of my encounters with members of the crew went something like this:

WISEGUY: "Hey, Mikey, what happened to your arm?"

ME: "I dropped a two-thousand-pound furnace on it."

WISEGUY: "No shit? Hey, want some ravioli?"

There were no problems, no suspicions. I wish I could say the same thing for the reception I received at home when I showed up with the cast.

"You tripped getting out of a radio car?" Angela asked, suspicion dripping off every word after I tried to explain away the cast.

"Well, actually I'd already gotten out of the car and was going into a Chinese restaurant and I tripped on a loose floor tile by the door." I found that the more elaborate the lie, the more believable it was. At least with everyone but my wife.

Her left eyebrow went up, a sure sign of doubt. "Uh-huh."

A few days later Angela was examining the signatures on my

cast. "Who's Sally Donuts?" she asked, scrutinizing the names like a *CSI* technician.

"That's Salvatore, guy that works in the adjoining zone. Eats a lot of jelly doughnuts. Hey, what's for dinner?"

Her gaze was glued on my cast. "And Vinny Gorgeous?"

"Cop owns a beauty parlor with his sister. Boy, am I hungry."

She looked up at me. "Louie the Thief?"

"Another cop, wants to be a lawyer. C'mon, Angela, what's with the third degree?" The wiseguys were signing their street names. Good thing Alphonse the Psycho was in the can after an assault arrest.

"They sound like gangsters to me, not cops."

"There's a fine line between cops and gangsters, sweetie."

She gave me the who-are-you-bullshitting? look, turned, and walked away. Another bullet dodged.

The next day I made my three passes at the door locks in the Cage with nary a glance from the crew. By that afternoon I had the keys to the kingdom.

We decided to wait three days until early Monday morning to begin installing the cameras and taps. Sunday is a day of rest for wiseguys. It's traditional for Italians to have a massive family dinner at around 2:00 p.m. (the rest of the world would call that lunch), and while the women gossiped the rest of the day away, the men would curse at the television while watching football or whatever sport was in season. By early evening the guys would be so ripped on homemade red wine they couldn't get off the couch with a forklift. By 10:00 p.m. they were in wiseguy dreamland. We figured 4:00 a.m.

Monday morning would be a good time to plant the bugs. The closest any of the crew would be to the Cage at that time would be a trip
to the bathroom for their third swollen-prostate-induced piss of the
night, then back to bed until noon.

On Friday, three days before the scheduled break-in, Sal Cetrulo
came to me in the club with a request.

"Mikey, we need a favor." The *we* told me whatever he was going
to ask came from the top, probably Andy Gerardo.

"What do you need, Sal?" Whatever it was, I hoped it didn't involve guns, knives, or blunt instruments.

"You know Demus pretty good, right?"

Joseph "Demus" Covello was a successful bookmaker around
my age whom I'd known for many years. He was a made guy but
eschewed violence and had gotten inducted for his math skills; he
was a genius when it came to numbers, and his book was always
profitable. He put nothing on paper, kept everything in his head.
We had remained friendly over the years, but I'd lost touch with
him when he suddenly relocated his operation when the heat from
the feds began to sear his tightie-whities. He was now running a
successful book plus a legitimate dance club called the Limelight in
Hollywood, Florida. His club had the only chrome dance floor in
the country, and when the cocaine craze took hold, patrons took to
doing lines off the floor.

"Yeah, I know him," I said. "Haven't talked to him since he went
South, though."

"That's okay, just as long as you're on good terms. You are,
right?"

"Yeah, sure."

"We need you to talk to him."

"About what?"

Cetrulo told me that Zarra and the other bookies in the crew had been hit by the perfect storm of winners over the last two weeks and were having trouble keeping enough cash available to pay future winners.

"We need to lay off bets for a while, and Demus is always flush with cash."

To "lay off" bets, bookies placed bets with other bookies when there was too much action on a specific team, horse, or whatever else gamblers bet on. If the heavily bet favorite won, it could break a bookie's bank, and he'd be hard-pressed to pay winners. The winners *had* to get paid; there's no crying poverty or IOUs in bookmaking. No payoff or a late payoff meant the clients would go elsewhere in the future to place their wagers. A bookie that was heavily leveraged and might take a beating would "lay off" a portion of the bets with a cooperating bookie in case disaster struck and thus make it easier to take a loss. Laying off bets involved invoking favors and capitalizing on friendships. Bookies being asked to take layoff bets were under no obligation to do so. This is where I came in.

Demus and I went way back to the old neighborhood, and if I asked him to take the layoff bets, he'd undoubtedly comply, but asking such a favor usually involved a personal request; it was a matter of respect. To ask a bookie to take a possible money hit for you, you ask for the favor in a face-to-face meeting. With my tenuous situation at home, I didn't want to go to Florida.

"Sure, Demus would do it for me, Sal, but I'm going to have to ask for a pass on this one."

"Why's that, Mikey? This shit's important."

"My family life's going pretty good, and me going to Florida would create problems with my wife. It's just bad timing, Sal."

Cetrulo locked eyes with me for what seemed like a minute. I knew he was running my past performance and reliability through his head, plus that I hadn't mentioned a word to anyone about the Malavacca incident. Keeping one's mouth shut in the Mafia was becoming a lost art, and I knew he appreciated my silence.

Finally he said, "Okay, Mikey. Just make a call for us and set up a meet, okay? JP'll go down there. You're doing good for us. You got your pass."

The next night, and two days before the breach, Sweeney decided to drum up some bonus evidence by wiring me with a recorder and having me show up at the regular high-roller, Saturday-night craps game in the Cage.

Putting a recorder on me was vetoed at the inception of the operation because I was a FNG (fucking new guy), would immediately be suspect, and could be searched at any time. Now that I was a trusted associate and considered one of the guys, wearing a wire would be safer.

I met Sweeney and a tech in the headquarters trailer behind the State Police barracks to be wired for sound. The miniature spool-to-spool recorder, called a Kel set, was taped to my crotch, an antenna wire was run down the side of my leg, and the microphone taped to my chest. The equipment is outdated by today's technological standards, but back then it was state-of-the-art.

I showed up at the Cage around eight o'clock. The place was

packed with players and onlookers. The din in the room made me wonder how any discernible intel could be gathered, but this had been anticipated, and I was assured that the tape could be cleaned up electronically so individual voices could clearly be heard.

I wasn't there ten minutes when my microphone began picking up Cousin Brucie Morrow, a popular oldies DJ on WCBS-FM radio broadcasting from New York City. Initially, I thought someone was playing a radio in the room, then I realized that the Kel set had become a transmitter and my chest was playing the Rolling Stones singing "(I Can't Get No) Satisfaction." One of the players, a degenerate gambler from another crew, heard the music, too.

"Where the fuck's that coming from?" he said, indignant that his concentration was being interrupted.

"Where's what coming from?" I asked innocently.

"The music, numb nuts. You don't hear it?"

I looked around. "I don't hear anything. Excuse me, gotta make a visit." I beat feet to the men's room and pounded my chest until I killed Cousin Brucie, after which I got the hell out of there. A noble experiment gone wrong. If it weren't for the background racket the gamblers were making, I might've been exposed. I wasn't about to wear any more wires, at least not that evening.

Monday, 3:00 a.m. I was jammed in the HQ trailer behind the State Police Barracks along with twenty-five other cops in various forms of dress. In addition, fifteen surveillance units were roaming the area around the Cage monitoring police calls and pedestrian traffic, which was minimal at that hour. In a corner of the trailer were three huge guys all dressed in black with partially deployed ski masks on their heads.

"Who are those guys?" I asked Jim Sweeney, who was in command.

Sweeney looked up from a mountain of paperwork. "They're the mugging team." He went back to reading.

"Oh, yeah?" Nothing surprised me about this operation. "Who're they supposed to mug?"

Sweeney stopped reading. "If any of the crew stops by the Cage while you're in there, these guys"—he pointed to the three gorillas—"will jump out of the alley and mug them." He shrugged. "Hey, this is Newark, muggings happen all the time."

They had planned for any contingency, but I doubted any of the crew would visit the club so early, but better safe than sorry.

I entered the club alone at 4:05 a.m., went quickly to the door to my adjoining office, which was bolted from my side, and let Pat, the tech guy, in. It took us five minutes just to drag in all the equipment he had with him. The first thing we did was to drape the glass-block windows with sheets so we could turn the lights on. Pat also had a handheld fluorescent light covered with dark-colored cellophane he used for close-up work.

Since we had previously stuffed the BX cable in the ceiling with telephone wires, all we had to do was run the cable down the wall that divided my office from the club and drill a tiny hole for the camera. We put the microphones in strategic areas around the club and began conducting equipment tests with the HQ trailer. Back in

my office we camouflaged the camera among other equipment resting against the communal wall.

As the installation continued, I kept an open phone line from
my office to Sweeney in case something went wrong. As a backup,
in the event of a power failure, I also had a police radio. Even with
these two contingency measures I had one final backup: an Ithaca,
a sawed-off shotgun in a shoulder holster. Shows you how much
faith I had in technology.

Pat was doing the tech work and I helped as much as possible,
but he was the expert and I let him do his thing. Two and a half
hours later the installation and testing were complete and we were
good to go for ninety days.

This would be an easy wire to work because I could look through
the peephole in my office wall to ascertain if anything was going
on I could legally record. State law dictated that we could only stay
on a wire for twenty minutes, and if nothing of a criminal nature
was occurring, the wire had to go down for twenty minutes before
it could go up again. Because of the peephole I could spend minimal time on the wire—only when something worth recording was
happening—and be down for most of the day with less of a chance
of getting caught by the wiseguys or someone else walking into
my office. We collected great evidence because of that hole in the
wall.

For the first week or so I felt my way around and got used to the
equipment. Pat would come in twice a week throughout the operation in a Checker taxicab he was operating—which was actually a
State Police decoy vehicle—to check on the camera, wires, and power
sources. He became such a familiar figure at the club that he began
picking up fares from the crew. We were now driving wiseguys to

sensitive locations we knew nothing about until Pat became their cabdriver of choice. You can't make this stuff up.

As we eased into the second week of the operation, Billy and I were now a well-oiled machine. He would watch the street from his desk and would alert me when any of the crew were entering the Cage, and I would go to the peephole and look for activity. If I saw an opportunity to record a conversation, I would tell Billy and he would call the trailer to go hot on the appropriate bug. The camera would roll, taping everything that transpired through a lens the size of the tip of a ballpoint pen. I felt like Steven Spielberg. Roll 'em!

Most serious mob business was conducted between noon and 3:00 p.m. I made sure my face was plastered to the peephole that entire time, looking for the next incriminating conversation. After three o'clock the crew liked to relax, gamble, and have a few cocktails. I kept Pat in proximity if anything went wrong with the equipment. He was reliable and loved the assignment. "We're gonna crucify those assholes," he said on more than one occasion.

I was getting a little concerned about the window that fronted my office. We had a panoramic view of Davenport Avenue and could watch the wiseguys coming and going from the Cage. The problem was that while we could see out of the window well, the wiseguys could see inside the office just as easily if they were so inclined. Normally, their only concern was getting inside the Cage to gamble, drink, and plan scams; they could care less about the Irish guy next door. But it would take only one curious mobster to glance inside my office and catch me with my face pressed up against the common wall between my office and the club to arouse suspicions. I had the window lettered with my fictitious business information, which helped, but I wanted to further reduce the odds of getting caught spying.

I told JP I wanted to install a tinted sunshade to block the rising sun in the east, which was distracting me during the morning hours.

"That okay?" I asked.

JP didn't know east from west. "Yeah, sure, who gives a fuck?"

I had the sunshade installed that afternoon. Once the tint was in place, I could see out, but no one could see inside the office from the street.

I had another meeting with Andy Gerardo in the Italian bakery a few days later. Gerardo was still being a good boy and was staying away from the club.

After the usual small talk was out of the way, he said, "Is everybody clean?"

"To the best of my knowledge," I said.

"You're doing a good job monitoring Zarra's collections. I appreciate that."

Like I had a choice. "No problem, Mr. Gerardo." My gut feeling was that Gerardo wanted something and all this was a preamble.

"Mikey, do you have any connections in state parole?"

There it was. "Maybe. I knew a few guys, have to see if they're still there. What do you need?"

He leaned across the table. "I'd like my file to disappear. Can you find someone to make that happen? I thought I was going to get an early release from parole, but that's not working out. I need to get back to business without looking over my shoulder. It's worth a lot to me."

I mulled the request. On one hand I was pleased that he trusted me with such an important favor. Bribing a parole officer was serious business, and for him to put his future in my hands was indicative of how much he trusted me. On the other hand I thought, *What balls this guy has!* Did he think that he could make any problem go away by throwing money at it? But the more I thought about it, I figured this was New Jersey; for a price someone could have the entire state moved to the West Coast, no questions asked.

"With all due respect," I said, "you're a major organized-crime figure. This could be a challenge, but I'll look into it."

"You do this for me, Mikey, and I'll move you out of that railroad tenement apartment you live in, in Lyndhurst, and buy you a fucking house."

The prick knew where I lived, and that didn't make me happy, but I had no reason to believe my family was in danger. I was too well trusted, and besides, the unwritten mob rule was that families were never touched no matter how egregious the infraction of a member or associate. But rules could be out the window if some hothead had his way. I had to be careful.

"Okay, let me make some calls. No promises." I had no intention of involving state parole in this operation. We could easily get their cooperation and have a parole officer pretend to take a bribe, but more people would then know about the investigation, which would increase the possibility of a leak. I planned on waiting a few days and reporting back to Gerardo that my contacts had dried up.

He raised a well-manicured hand. "All I can ask."

I assumed the meeting was at an end and slid my chair back to leave.

"Another thing before you go. Sperduto, keep an eye on him for me."

He was referring to Tommy Sperduto, a made guy in the crew who was a bit of a loner and arrogant. He didn't like me and the feeling was mutual.

"What am I looking for?" I asked.

"I think sometimes he thinks he's self-employed."

Gerardo thought Sperduto was skimming tribute money and wanted me to look into it. If you steal from a boss, you're dead, case closed. I felt like yelling at Gerardo, "I'm a cop, you asshole, I don't set people up to get clipped." Instead I played into him. "No problem, I'll keep my eye on him."

Before I left, he told me to continue to check on Silvio DeVita for recent arrests.

"I don't trust him as far as I can throw my Bimmer," he said.

That afternoon JP returned from Florida and his meeting with Demus Covello. When Billy alerted me that JP was entering the Cage, I went up on the wire and camera. Billy made his call to the trailer and we were hot.

I watched through the peephole as JP corralled Joe Zarra by the pool table.

"We're good to go," JP said. "Demus'll lay off up to forty large for the next month. I figured that was good enough. We'll be okay by then. Demus did the right thing by us, and he says we owe his cooperation to Mikey. Says Mikey's a stand-up guy."

"We already know that," Zarra said.

"Nah, but he went on about him for twenty minutes, couldn't stop talking about his boxing skills. Said when Mike was a cop he saw him kick ass all over Newark. Said he didn't carry no nightstick, no Mace, no blackjack. Just a gun and leather gloves. Loved to fight, Mikey did. Boxed semipro."

I was glad to know I was held in such high esteem, but then it hit me that with all the talk about my fighting skills, it would be just a matter of time until I was asked to break a leg or two, maybe even whack a guy. Something else to worry about.

Zarra changed the subject back to Demus's taking the layoff bets. He and JP got specific, talking about Demus's rates for taking the bets from them.

"A little fucking high, don't you think?" Zarra said.

JP shrugged. "Maybe a half point over, but he knew we were in a bind and it was short notice. He covered us, Joe."

"Yeah, well, fuck him, too," Zarra said. "C'mon, let's have a drink."

They wandered off to the bar, and the conversation went to women and sex. I turned off the wire.

I entered my empty office the next day to a ringing phone. It was Demus Covello.

"Hey, Mikey! Thought we should catch up."

And catch up we did, for about five minutes. While the call appeared to be social, I knew it would morph into business; it always did with these guys.

"You know, Mikey, you and Joe Paterno owe me big-time for what I did for you guys."

"I know, Demus. Zarra's saying good things about the way you handled the request," I lied. "It won't be forgotten."

After some dead air, he said, "Listen, Mikey—Paterno, Gerardo, all the bosses, think very highly of you. You're moving up pretty fast. Just be careful. You ain't in Kansas anymore; this is the bigtime. Hey, tell me, how many hits you done so far?"

I laughed. "Demus, two rules you know we have. We never talk business on the phone, and two, the most important one . . ."

"Yeah, what's that?"

"*Sigillare le labbra.* Seal the lips."

Now Demus was laughing. "You're right, Mikey. You got that Italian down pretty good."

"They made me an honorary Italian, been around here long enough." Next thing you know I'd be having dinner at two in the afternoon.

Two high-level made guys—Joe and Sal. *(Mike Russell)*

My fake oil business in Newark, New Jersey. *(Mike Russell)*

This is the Genovese club in Jersey City where the Hoffa hit was sanctioned.
(Mike Russell)

22 rounded up as lawmen move against the Genovese crime family

By P.L. WYCKOFF

Teams of federal and state agents swept up 22 reputed members of the Genovese crime family in New Jersey during pre-dawn raids yesterday, charging them with crimes ranging from racketeering to a plot to murder reputed New York City Gambino underworld boss John Gotti and his brother.

Officials said the arrests deal a crippling blow to the New Jersey faction of the Genovese crime family and set the stage for a new power struggle to fill the "void" that will be created. They said exposure of the Gotti murder plot also indirectly aids the reputed Gambino family leader.

U.S. Attorney Samuel Alito Jr. and other officials said the plot to kill Gotti reflected a power struggle between the Gambino and Genovese organizations over lucrative North Jersey loansharking and bookmaking operations. Those operations had been controlled by alleged South Jersey mob leader Nicodemo (Little Nicky) Scarfo until his arrest last year.

The houses of the 22 suspects were searched during the raids, the culmination of a year-long probe of Genovese activities, said John McGinley, FBI special agent in charge for New Jersey.

"The whole theory here is to take down an entire operation at one time," said State Police Superintendent Col.

Photo by Richard Raska

From top, Frank Daniello, Richard DeSciscio and Martin Casella are led by federal marshals to a van at the West Orange National Guard Armory

Clinton Pagano. The defendants were named in two federal indictments unsealed yesterday morning.

The arrests leave a "void" in crime circles that could lead to further power struggles among mob groups and

indirectly help Gotti, said Pagano and McGinley.

Gotti and his brother, Gene, were warned of the rubout plot by FBI

Please turn to Page 16

As a result of my undercover work—twenty-two arrests. (Star-Ledger)

Mob Boss
Andy Gerardo
being trans-
ported to jail.
(Mike Russell)

News media coverage of the arrests.

Photo by Richard Tashjian
Former State Police undercover agent Michael Russell examines papers on upcoming criminal cases

Reviewing court documents.
(Star-Ledger)

Genovese crime family members being arraigned in Newark. *(Mike Russell)*

Andy Gerardo *(right)* and his attorney were very upset because he was held without bail. *(Mike Russell)*

Made member Joseph Zarra and Mob Captain Ralph Vicaro at their bail hearing (they were brought to their knees). *(Mike Russell)*

Mike with police Hummer in Hollywood Beach, Florida. *(Mike Russell)*

On the set of AMC's "Mob Week," 2011. *(Mike Russell)*

On the set of AMC'S "Mob Week," 2011. *(Mike Russell)*

Chicago hit man Frank Cullotta taking aim at the Mob Cop. *(Mike Russell)*

On the set of AMC's " Mob Week," 2011. (*Mike Russell*)

This scar on the back of my head that took over sixty stitches to close is a result of a gunshot wound at the very beginning of my investigation. To this day I have no sense of taste or smell. (*Mike Russell*)

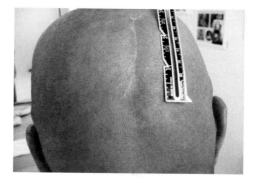

Jerry Smith and Mike discussing undercover police operations in the late '80s. (*Mike Russell*)

Mob Cop on the job.
(Mike Russell)

At a commendation ceremony, sometime in the early '70's when I was a rookie cop.
(Mike Russell)

Fox29 Philly News Team's Dave Schratwieser and cameraman Bryan Zilas filming Philly Mob Boss Joey Merlino, October 2012, in Boca Raton, Florida.
(Mike Russell)

10

One Man's Garbage . . .

Within days of becoming fully operational with the electronic surveillance equipment, we began to reap a mountain of quality incriminating information as well as new leads to crimes we hadn't been aware of. Not only were we recording the wiseguys, Billy and I were identifying them in real time by looking through the peephole as they were implicating themselves in major criminal activity. This made the case bulletproof when we got to court because the wiseguys couldn't say it wasn't them talking on the wire or appearing on the videotape. There was nothing to confuse a jury; they would have the eyewitness testimony of sworn police officers attesting to who said what to whom.

By now, 146 detectives and an assistant state's attorney were assigned to the case, by far the most far-reaching investigation into organized crime in New Jersey history. State Police bosses were beginning to complain that the entire Organized Crime Bureau was tied up on this one case. The scope and depth of the investigation was worth the expenditure of money and man-hours, however, and the bosses in Trenton knew it. Cops like to bitch and complain no matter what rank they are or how well things are going.

To make the case even more solid, Billy and I were betting up a storm with Zarra, JP, and the other crew bookies. If it ran or threw a ball, we bet on it. On Wednesdays, we either paid what we owed or collected what we had won. Each transaction was recorded for posterity on audio and video, each wager another nail in the crew's coffin. For the record, we came out ahead, making the cash winnings available as evidence.

I began driving Sal Cetrulo to New York's East Harlem on Thursdays to meet with Anthony "Fat Tony" Salerno, a gangster boss of legendary status. We would bring a shaving kit stuffed with cash as Salerno's tribute from the crew's weekly gambling earnings. Salerno was an old-time mafiosoi, having begun his career in the 1930s under Charley "Lucky" Luciano, in what would later become the Genovese family.

Salerno was called Fat Tony due to his size, and he embraced the nickname rather than eschewing it. He had run a numbers and sports-gambling empire in East Harlem since the 1940s that was said to net him $1 million yearly. He was also a background figure of great influence in the Teamsters Union and owned one of the largest concrete businesses in New York, one of many legitimate companies he operated.

Salerno was what was known as a "front boss." While law

enforcement thought him to be the head of the Genovese family, he was in reality fronting for Philip "Benny Squint" Lombardo, the heir to head the family after the death of Vito Genovese in 1969. In essence, Fat Tony took the heat off Lombardo—and later boss Vincent "the Chin" Gigante—by letting the cops think *he* was the boss. Make no mistake, he was up there in rank as an underboss, but Lombardo was the real power. Fat Tony, in true Mafia tradition, volunteered to fall on the law enforcement sword as the boss of the Genovese family should it come to that.

For the first several meetings I waited in Cetrulo's Cadillac Seville outside Salerno's base, the Palma Boys Social Club on East 115th Street. Salerno's club was the last stronghold in what was once a thriving Italian neighborhood. These days the neighborhood was largely Hispanic and Asian, but that never affected Salerno's income. The love of gambling crosses ethnic lines.

On a later visit to see Salerno, Cetrulo told me to come with him inside the club. If Salerno's club wasn't a clone of the Cage, it was damn close; with little left to the imagination I was back in Newark. I think Salerno shopped in the same mismatched-furniture store that services all wiseguy clubs.

Cetrulo introduced me to Salerno, who looked like everyone's grandfather. He was over seventy, rotund, bald, and casually dressed. He was fond of cigars, and in all my visits to East Harlem he was always smoking one. For a boss he was unpretentious and friendly.

"Hi, Mikey. Sal tells me good things about you." Salerno shook my hand and offered me an espresso, which I accepted.

His right-hand man, Vincent "Fish" Cafaro was there, too, and he and Cetrulo went off to a corner to confer. Cafaro would later turn government witness and wear a wire. He was instrumental in sending Salerno and other Mafia bosses to prison for a hundred years each in the infamous Commission Case in 1986. Ironically, Cafaro's son, also a made man, was offered the same deal as his dad to turn informant, but turned it down, renounced his father as a rat, and went to prison without flipping.

Salerno was friendly toward me right from the first handshake. While Cetrulo and Cafaro were discussing mob business, Salerno talked to me about everything but.

"I was born and raised right up the block, Mikey," Salerno said. "Neighborhood's changed but the people are still good. Can't get good guinea food no more, though—except maybe for Rao's." He was referring to a popular Italian restaurant two blocks away that was taking reservations three years in advance. I was sure Salerno didn't have to wait that long for a table.

"You get out of the neighborhood much, Mr. Salerno?" I asked. The espresso tasted like tar. I felt my heart racing from the infusion of industrial-strength caffeine. Didn't seem to bother the old man, though. He was sucking it down like water.

"Every chance I get. Got a hundred-acre horse farm up in Rhinebeck. Beautiful up there. Ever been?"

I told him I hadn't.

"Come up to see me. My guest."

I thanked him and said I'd make a point of doing that, and he went on to tell me about his brownstone in Gramercy Park farther downtown, and his condo in Miami Beach. I was beginning to think that crime paid after all; at least if you're a high-ranking Mafia don.

We made more small talk for another hour, and at one point I found myself liking the guy. I reminded myself of what this seemingly kindly old man had done to get where he was today, and my affection waned.

One such incident involved the Philadelphia mob. In 1980, longtime Philadelphia Genovese boss Angelo Bruno was murdered by his consigliere, Antonio "Tony Bananas" Caponigro, in a bid to take control of the family. He committed the murder without consulting with the bosses in New York who oversaw the Philadelphia faction of the family.

Fat Tony was incensed. The murder of a boss must be authorized by the Commission, which consisted of the heads of the five New York families. To disregard this edict meant certain death for the violator. Salerno reached out to notorious hit man Joseph "Mad Dog" Sullivan, whose claim to fame—in addition to murdering thirty men—was that he was the only inmate to ever escape from the Attica Correctional Facility, thought to be escape-proof.

Sullivan was summoned to the Palma Boys Social Club, where Fat Tony told him they had a "banana to peel." Tony Bananas was quickly dispatched by Sullivan in a tenement a short distance from Salerno's headquarters with the aid of a MAC-10 submachine gun. His body was dumped in the Bronx.

The void left by Tony Bananas was eventually filled *by* Nicodemus "Little Nicky" Scarfo, arguably the most violent Mafia boss in history. He secured power by killing over thirty rivals in three years and had a reputation as a certifiable psychopath. I knew Scarfo from his infrequent visits to the Cage. I saw him again on a trip to New York with Cetrulo when Scarfo came to pay his cash tribute to Salerno. He was probably having a visit to reality that day because I found him to be a personable guy with an infectious sense of humor. What struck me as odd, however, was his admission to me that he had personally killed nineteen people. Not something you tell someone you've known for less than an hour. Scarfo was eventually convicted of numerous murders and other crimes and is serving multiple life sentences.

Cetrulo and I went back to see Salerno for months, every Thursday like clockwork. When the old man wasn't available, we dealt with Cafaro, who was also friendly and affable. The old-time Mafia bosses were unlike the younger bosses of the current generation, most of whom had an attitude and lacked basic social graces.

On one trip I volunteered to hold the shaving kit that held Salerno's tribute cash, and Cetrulo told me he wouldn't trust me with a peanut-butter-and-jelly sandwich, let alone the old man's money.

"Thanks for your confidence in me," I said, but smiled as I said it.

"It's not personal, Mikey, it's just that we're all a bunch of thieves, you know?"

I just nodded and changed the subject. "Hey, Sal, we should switch cars next time, take mine instead."

Cetrulo gave me a look like I was an imbecile. "What're you, fucked-up? This is a brand-new Caddy Seville. You're driving around in a shitbox for crissakes."

He was right. I had a 1980 Chevy Malibu that had more rust on it than the *Titanic*, but I offered a logical reason for the switch. "This car sticks out, Sal. It's too fucking new and shiny. At least let's park it around the corner from the Palma."

He was quiet for a minute. "You know, you're right. Next trip we take your car."

I proposed to Sweeney that we bug my car, and while he liked the idea, the State Police bosses vetoed the plan. I never found out why. For the last few trips to see Salerno we took my heap, Cetrulo complaining every time. Eventually, Cetrulo passed the weekly trip to another crew member, and I never saw Salerno again. For a while I entertained the idea of going to his mansion in Rhinebeck, but I didn't want to open up another front in the investigation. My time was stretched to the limit.

Fat Tony Salerno would die in prison in 1992, convicted under the new federal RICO statute, which made it a crime to be a boss in an ongoing criminal enterprise. He was eighty. After Vincent "Fish" Cafaro finished testifying against Salerno and other mobsters, he vanished into WITSEC, only to leave voluntarily a few years later. He's still out there somewhere, looking over his shoulder and dodging the ghost of Fat Tony in his dreams.

While I'm on the subject of ghosts, the apparition of Lou Malavacca was haunting the crew, particularly Cetrulo and me. Unlike poor Lou, the incident just wouldn't die.

Bobby "Kabert" Bisaccia, the Gambino captain I had a run-in with over Zarra's slot machines in Paterson, cornered me in front of the Cage one day and ripped into me for five minutes about the shooting.

"Nice job, genius," he said. "You think anybody believes that story about the black guy? What're we, fucking morons?"

I couldn't let this sawed-off asshole disrespect me in front of the crew even though I knew Cetrulo's story about what happened was weak.

"You think I can see through walls, you fucking jerkoff? I was taking a leak. Sal says a black guy came in and did the shooting, then that's what happened."

We went back and forth for a few minutes with nothing resolved. Kabert left, but that wasn't the end of it. John DiGilio, the captain who controlled a lot of Hudson County, was calling for a sit-down because the shooting took place on his turf and he didn't want any blame for the killing hung on his crew. Everyone agreed to meet in the Stone Crab, a Gambino restaurant on the Newark/Belleville line on Belmont Avenue.

The restaurant hadn't opened for business yet when Cetrulo, Zarra, and I arrived. DiGilio was there with Kabert. We were all dressed casually. Had a family boss been present, suits and ties would have been mandated. A lone bartender was behind the stick looking bored. Sit-downs are historically nonviolent; guarantees of safety are the norm, although full-blown gang wars have developed because the issue that brought about the meeting went unresolved.

We sat at a round table near the door, and everyone made nice for ten minutes before DiGilio got down to the matter at hand. "Okay, let's talk about why we're here." He turned to me. "Mikey, you mean to tell me this *melanzana,* he comes into the bar, shoots one fucking bullet, and hits Lou right in the back of the fucking head and splits before you and Sal can do anything about it?"

"It is what it is. You gotta talk to Sal about that, I was in—"

"Yeah, yeah," DiGilio said. "I know, I know, you were in the bathroom."

"Right."

DiGilio was steaming. "I believe that like I need another asshole! You guys are out of control! That's my area! If you and these relics you're working for think you're going to take over my turf, you're fucking mistaken!"

Before the meeting turned nasty, Zarra called for a five-minute break. Cetrulo, DiGilio, and Kabert went to the bar, with Cetrulo staying as far away from the Gambinos as possible. Zarra corralled me by the door.

"You know this is your fucking fault, Mikey," Zarra said. "If you weren't in the shitter, Lou would still be around and he'd be payin' me."

I had to hold my tongue. Mob rules dictated that since Cetrulo was a made man, Zarra wouldn't say anything bad about him. I had to eat it while Zarra pinned the blame for the entire incident on me.

We sat back down and DiGilio led off with an apology. "I'm sorry I lost my cool. It won't happen again." Another mob rule is no one is supposed to raise his voice at sit-downs; things are supposed to be discussed without emotion, facts detailed in a civilized manner.

Zarra had me run through the events in the bar when Malavacca was shot. My narrative was followed by Cetrulo's. Neither DiGilio nor Kabert interrupted us. When Cetrulo was finished, DiGilio and Kabert excused themselves and went to a corner and talked in hushed tones. Five minutes later they were back at the table.

The Gambinos didn't believe for a second that some lone black male killed Malavacca. But then again, no one gave a shit about the victim. It was all going to boil down to money. Mobsters like to talk about respect, but its all bullshit from seeing too many *Godfather* movies. DiGilio was concerned about the shooting's being a prelude to Gerardo's crew muscling into his territory, thereby costing him money. The respect issue arose from the infringement of DiGilio's territory to begin with. It was a slap in his face. The bottom line was, the sit-down was a dick-measuring contest with DiGilio wanting our crew to know his space was not to be infringed upon.

With promises made by us and face saved by DiGilio, we all shook hands and made for the bar. As we left the table, DiGilio said, "Mikey, could you use your connections to see if there's any arrest warrants coming down?" Rumors had been flying for weeks that a grand jury had been impaneled to hear evidence relating to DiGilio's crew.

"With all due respect, Mr. Digilio, you should go to Daniello for that information. He's closer to that stuff than I am." Lieutenant Frank Daniello was still active in the Hoboken PD and was corrupt as a cop could get. He was in DiGilio's pocket and everyone knew it.

DiGilio nodded and, changing the subject, surprised me. "You ever want to make some real money, you might consider coming with me. You're going nowhere where you are now."

DiGilio was trying to entice me into switching crews. While this type of thing goes on all the time, it's considered a breach of mob etiquette, and if the person being approached is a particularly good earner, a serious conflict with the opposing crew could ensue if the request is pressed. This told me that my reputation as a reliable, loyal associate had spread outside the crew and my services were in demand. Of course, it could also have been a test, with Zarra behind the request, enlisting DiGilio to see if I would bolt, thereby testing my loyalty to the Gerardo crew.

"I appreciate you asking, but I'm good where I am," I said.

DiGilio nodded and smiled. "Okay, Mikey. You change your mind, give me a call."

* * *

My meetings with Gerardo became a scheduled weekly event, only the location changed to a different Italian bakery. I guess Gerardo liked his pastries. We met this time at 6:00 a.m., an effort I guessed to avoid the FBI, whose agents disliked coming to work early.

Gerardo was at a back table facing the door, not out of character for him. Wiseguys are like cops in this regard: they don't like surprises and will seat themselves in a public room with a good view of the door and who's approaching them.

For the first time since I'd known him, Gerardo didn't look pleased to see me. He didn't get up or extend his hand.

"Sit down," he said, its sounding more like a command than a request.

I sat.

He stared at me. "Look at me. Look me in the eye."

I did.

"This escalating violence is upsetting me. Not only is it bad for business, but it's an indication that I can't control my crew. Now, tell me about the Louie Malavacca thing."

I had explained what had happened so many times I could do it in my sleep, and I went through it again, leaving nothing out.

Gerardo stared at me during my presentation. Not unlike a cop, he was looking for "tells," which are facial expressions or body language that would give me up as a liar. I was nervous even though I knew I was telling the truth. What would happen if he thought I was lying? If this were a grand jury, I could get indicted for perjury, but in the court of wiseguys the penalty is much more severe. I was finding myself hoping Gerardo had sharp people skills. He let me sweat for a while after I had finished before he said anything.

"Listen, Mikey, I can suppose that the mysterious black guy is all bullshit. I didn't call you here because I wasn't sure. I called you here to see if you were lying about what you know." He took a sip of his coffee, knowing full well that the pregnant pause was making me sweat. "I'm convinced you're not lying. As for Cetrulo, I'll deal with him."

I knew Cetrulo was safe. It takes a lot to clip a made guy; to do so would require someone higher in the food chain than Gerardo to push the button. Assuming Cetrulo shot Malavacca—and no one knew for sure—it was no great offense. Malavacca wasn't a made man and was a bit of a pain in the ass. It might wind up costing Cetrulo a few grand to DiGilio as tribute because Malavacca was shot in his territory. DiGilio wouldn't be expecting anything; the matter was put to rest at our sit-down at the Stone Crab, and the money would be considered a gesture of respect. Case closed. Finally.

I squirmed a bit in my seat thinking the meeting was over, but Gerardo grabbed my arm, indicating otherwise.

"Don't go anywhere yet."

"Yeah, okay." While Gerardo had softened a bit since I sat down, I could tell he was still wound tight.

"I hear Peewee's operation is booming. I want you to go to his place and see what you hear."

Tommy "Peewee" DePhillips was a bookmaker/loan shark extraordinaire. At any time he had at least a hundred men on the street taking action and lending money. He was New Jersey's biggest sports bookmaker and a huge earner for Gerardo. Peewee owned the Finish Line restaurant, a successful eatery from where he ran his gambling operation. Gerardo obviously thought Tommy was skimming money.

"Okay, Mr. Gerardo, I'll give it a shot, but I'd feel a little out of place over there. Maybe I could—"

"Just fucking do it!" Gerardo bellowed, causing the bakery's only three patrons to turn and stare at him, but quickly turn away. Everyone knew Andy Gerardo; staring at him was like looking at the sun for too long—it was bound to cause pain.

"Sure, Mr. Gerardo. Not a problem."

Gerardo deflated a bit and shook my hand. "Okay, Mikey. Go do your thing."

My "thing" was going to land his ass in prison.

When I got back to my office, Billy was on a hot wire, listening to a conversation through headphones. When he saw me, he waved frantically. "Mike, we got time-sensitive shit here."

"What?"

He raised a finger. "Hold on." After a few minutes he broke off. "You know Jimmy Randazzo?"

Indeed I did. James Randazzo was a made man in the Colombo crime family. He was a big-time loan shark who operated freelance in north Jersey and was the only New York–based Colombo soldier working in our area. He was permitted to conduct business in Genovese/Gambino territory because he was a good earner and paid his tribute to the New Jersey crews. Randazzo also linked the three crime families by acting as a liaison with the Colombos. He was known as an "honest" gangster, paying what was owed to the bosses and not skimming from the proceeds.

Billy had monitored Randazzo talking to Sal Cetrulo about pulling off an armored-car robbery in Elizabeth, just south of Newark. Randazzo wanted Cetrulo's advice because he had a dilemma: how to launder the expected two hundred grand he expected to steal.

Cetrulo told Randazzo to take a road trip with the cash down to Florida, using cash for expenses and no credit cards. When he hit the Daytona area, he should stop in every bank he saw and get bank checks totaling less than $10,000 per bank to avoid bank reporting regulations. This was the 1980s, when South Florida was the cocaine capital of the world and many banks ran fast and loose with banking laws by helping drug dealers launder money.

Randazzo thought this was a great idea. He also told Cetrulo that he had two insiders in the armored-car company who would supply the route and the best location to rob the armored car. The heist was scheduled to go down in one week. Obviously, we had to move fast, and we began making the proper notifications.

The State Police quickly moved into action. They began around-the-clock surveillances of those involved in the robbery conspiracy. The crime was to occur in a pharmaceutical company's parking lot, where the truck would be hit during a cash transfer.

The troopers had the parking lot surrounded on the day of the robbery and swooped in on the stickup team before they had a chance to approach the armored car. No shots fired, no one hurt, bad guys collared. Randazzo wasn't at the scene of the robbery and avoided a conspiracy arrest by working a deal with the New Jersey State attorney general. The substance of the deal was never made public, but it's assumed Randazzo agreed to become an informer. His alleged new career as a rat lasted four years.

In 1993, Randazzo was murdered by Aurelio "Ray" Cagno on the orders of Carmine "the Snake" Persico, a New York boss.

In 1957, New York City took commercial garbage collections away from the Department of Sanitation on a trial basis and opened them up to bids from private carting companies. New York did this as a potential cost-saving measure, and other large municipalities across the country followed suit when the experiment proved successful. Thus began organized crime's involvement in one of the most lucrative ventures in Mafia history.

Infiltration of existing legitimate carting businesses and the establishment of their own companies began in New York, where the five families reigned supreme. These were the heady days before the Kefauver Committee, Joe Valachi, and Robert F. Kennedy's war on organized crime; even before J. Edgar Hoover admitted there *was* a Mafia. The private carting was one of the mob's first ventures into legitimate commerce.

It was an easy setup; go from business to business with a sales pitch, which went something like this:

> WISEGUY: "We're gonna pick up your garbage."
> RESTAURANT OWNER: "How much is this gonna cost me?"
> WISEGUY: "Less than a stay in the hospital."
> RESTAURANT OWNER: "Great. Sign me up."

Within a short time, most every commercial establishment in the five boroughs was getting its garbage collected by a company run by organized crime. Reluctant business owners who balked at getting involved got garbage delivered to them instead of having it picked up. Late with paying a bill? You got a six-foot-five-inch late notice.

The success of the private-carting business had mobsters looking for other legitimate businesses to muscle in on. Window washing came next. Storefront businesses were solicited by gangsters to have them wash their windows. Those who protested that they could wash their own windows soon found themselves without any windows to wash. Windows that weren't smashed to smithereens were egged in the middle of the night. Owners returning to open up the following day had to deal with dried eggs that had hardened to the consistency of cement. But I digress.

The northern–New Jersey faction of the Genovese crime family was heavily involved in the private carting, but they didn't normally start from the ground up; for the most part they forced their way into existing companies.

Joe Zarra told me to pay a visit to Charley Piscaty, who owned Piscaty Carting, a small, mob-free, Secaucus-based carting company in the Meadowlands, and tell him to sell his business to Jersey Carting, a mob-controlled rival private carting company. The request had come from Louis "Bobby" Manna, a Genovese underboss, who had been recorded giving the order to Zarra on one of our wires.

I drove to Piscaty Carting by myself and was shown into the boss's office. Charley Piscaty was a tough, old Polish businessman who had a reputation of not taking shit from anyone, including mobsters. He sat impassively behind his desk, a half-empty bottle of vodka and a filmy, topped-off glass by his elbow.

After introducing myself, I explained that Joe Zarra wanted him to sell his business to Jersey Carting. Piscaty promptly reached under his desk and emerged with a shotgun. A man of few words, Charley was.

"Whoa, Charley!" I said, raising my hands. "I'm just the messenger."

"Okay, shithead. Deliver this message: tell that fucking greaseball wop cocksucker Joe Zarra to go fuck himself. Now get the fuck out of here."

Which is exactly what I did.

I went back to the Cage and told Zarra what had transpired with Piscaty.

Zarra smirked. "How come no one got shot this time?"

"I left my black guy home."

"Very funny." Zarra shooed me away. "I'll take care of this."

The next day in the Cage, Sal Cetrulo told me to go back to Piscaty and lean on him.

"Sal," I said, "he's only got six trucks. All this bullshit for six lousy trucks?"

Cetrulo laughed. "That'll be six more than we have now, genius."

The greediness of wiseguys never ceased to amaze me. They'd steal air if they could cart it away.

I had no desire to get blown away by a shotgun, but I had to go back and see Piscaty again to maintain my cover.

I went back the next morning, this time entering the office with my hands raised chest high. Charley was behind his desk, as I supposed was his shotgun. "I come in peace, white man," I said with a smile. Didn't even elicit a giggle. Never trust a man with no sense of humor.

"What now, asshole?" He sounded drunk and it wasn't even close to noon.

I pointed to a wooden chair in front of his desk. "Can I sit down?" I opened up my jacket and did a pirouette. "I'm not armed."

"Sit, okay."

"Jersey Carting will make you a legitimate offer, Charley. Strictly legal." Which was true. Of course the offer would be a lowball price, but at least Piscaty wouldn't get the business stolen from him. "You don't like the offer, you can negotiate."

Piscaty looked at me through bleary eyes. "Okay, listen to me. This business: it's my life. My kids; I got three grown-up boys. They want nothing to do with this business. I leave here, what I'm gonna do? You seem like a decent guy, I'm sorry for yesterday. But I'm not gonna sell. Zarra wants trouble, he'll get it from me. You can tell him that. Now go." He reached for his drink. I was glad it wasn't the shotgun.

Back at the Cage, I gave Zarra Piscaty's message.

Zarra said, "Ah, balls," and dismissed me.

During the coming week, Piscaty's fate was discussed on the club's phones in Mafia code, which was really no code at all. Wise-guys think they're fooling someone when they call killing someone "taking him out to dinner" or referring to drugs as "shirts" or "suits." Helen Keller could figure out the gist of the coded conversation immediately.

The mob decided to lay off Piscaty for a few reasons. Zarra deemed it unfeasible to go to war over six trucks, and a war it would be. Piscaty's life was his business, and if it were up to him, he'd live in his office. He arrived there at dawn, drank all day, and drove home when he felt like it, if he went home at all. If anyone was going to take him out, the best possible scenario would be a full frontal assault on the office after business hours when he was alone and fucked-up on vodka.

"But this guy's a tough fucking Polack," Zarra said to Bobby Manna on the phone. "He's probably got a drink in one hand and that fucking shotgun in the other. There'd be too much heat, we went in like that. Fuck it; let's give him a pass."

Manna agreed.

Charley Piscaty got to keep his business.

Two days later at 1:00 p.m. I was standing on the sidewalk in front of my office when Cetrulo pulled up in his Caddy, parked it quickly, and haphazardly ran into the Cage. At the door he pointed at me and said, "Don't go nowhere, I'm gonna need you."

I didn't like the sound of this and went to my office. Billy was at his desk.

"Billy, looks like the shit's hitting the fan, call somebody." While I was there, I went to the bathroom. When I got out, Cetrulo was standing by Billy's desk.

"I thought I told you not to go anywhere."

"Hey, Sal, I didn't go to Michigan, I went to take a leak for crissakes." I sounded indignant but my self-preservation gene was kicking in. Why did I get the feeling all this urgency was directly related to me?

"Forget it." He threw the keys to his Caddy to me. "You're driving. Let's go."

The last time Cetrulo let me drive his precious Cadillac was . . . never. Now I was beginning to get worried. No better way to control someone in a car than to have him behind the wheel. The scene in the *Godfather* came to mind where Paulie, the don's driver, takes Clemenza and another wiseguy on a tour of the New York/New

Jersey area where they were supposed to be looking for safe houses due to an impending mob war. When they're passing the Meadowlands, Clemenza tells Paulie to pull over so he can take a leak. Within seconds Paulie is DOA, two bullets in his head. Clemenza infamously utters the line "Leave the gun, take the cannoli."

I was relieved to see Cetrulo wasn't carrying any pastries.

Cetrulo was in the Caddy before me, and I had a chance to glance at Billy, who mouthed the words "Sweeney is on the air." This meant Jim Sweeney was coordinating cover for me via radio and would be in constant touch with his men. Sweeney was a great street boss and I felt better already.

I got behind the wheel with Cetrulo in the passenger seat and started to pull out. "Where we going?"

Cetrulo grabbed my arm. "Wait for Joe."

Zarra waddled out of the club within seconds and heaved himself in the backseat.

"Now?" I asked.

"Yeah, now." Cetrulo gave me directions to travel on what seemed like every back street and alley in Newark. In the backseat Zarra grunted every time he turned around to look for a tail. My mirror told me there wasn't any. I began to get worried again.

That's when I heard the faint but reassuring whir of helicopter blades. I knew the chopper was part of my protection team, and I began to breathe a little easier.

As we began to leave Newark, Zarra tapped me on the shoulder. "Make a right on Summer Avenue and stop on the corner. We gotta make a pickup."

I did what I was told and waited in front of a dry-cleaning store, motor running. I still heard the helicopter above us. Our temporary stop would give Sweeney time to position cars on either side of us for a leapfrog surveillance. I was feeling better all the time.

Then the back door swung open and Andy Gerardo slid into the car. My stomach did flip-flops. He was dressed like a homeless person, unshaven and scowling. His attire was completely out of character, and then I thought, why get dressed up in your best stuff for a hit? Bloodstains don't come out easily.

"Hey, Mr. Gerardo," I said, trying to keep my voice from cracking. I was almost positive that I was gonna get another bullet in the head and this time I wouldn't survive.

Gerardo grunted.

No one greeted Gerardo, no one spoke at all. I sat there until Zarra began giving me directions.

"Take Route Twenty-one north, then east on Three towards New York, Mikey."

My throat was so dry I didn't dare verbalize an acknowledgment. I just mumbled. I was thinking to myself, The gang's all here. I wondered, Who gets to pull the trigger? What did I do? How did I fuck up to allow this to happen? I felt hope begin to fade until a yellow taxicab pulled up alongside us at a light. Sweeney and another cop were in the back passenger seat, and the driver I knew as a trooper from back in the day.

My emotions were all over the place. While the helicopter was comforting, it wouldn't help much if I was forced to suddenly pull off the road to take a bullet. Sweeney's being close by in the taxi was another story. Sweeney had the balls of an elephant, and I knew he would do anything humanly possible to save me.

I thought about the Newark riots, which occurred in 1967. A cop and a fireman had been killed in street gunfights, and the

Newark cops couldn't handle the level of violence and destruction that was being wrought upon an already devastated city. In came the State Police to the rescue.

I'll never forget seeing Jim Sweeney barreling down Springfield Avenue standing in an open-top military jeep grasping a mounted .50-caliber machine gun. We had been taking sniper fire from two housing project buildings for hours, and the Newark PD bosses couldn't make a decision as to how to deal with it. Apparently Sweeney knew, however.

Sweeney's jeep pulled in front of the projects and immediately began attracting fire. What happened next is still talked about and will be part of Big Jim Sweeney's legacy. He began strafing both buildings with machine-gun fire. A .50-caliber machine gun is a devastating weapon. Chunks of cement as big as shoe boxes were being blown away from the buildings' walls from the shattering firepower. The noise was so deafening, my teeth began to rattle.

After fifteen seconds of withering automatic fire, Sweeney ceased shooting. Not a sound came out of those buildings; not then, not the next day, not for the remainder of the riots, which ended the following week. During that week Sweeney patrolled in that jeep, draped over that machine gun as if he'd invented it. No more cops or fireman were killed, and civilian casualties were kept to a minimum.

This was the guy who was watching my back. I felt secure.

Zarra told me to switch directions, and we headed toward Hoboken through Jersey City, the Bell Huey helicopter with us all the way, but high enough to remain unseen.

We wound up at the abandoned railroad yard of the Erie Railroad. No one in the car said a word. I checked my mirrors for Sweeney's cab, but didn't see it, but I knew he was close by. Later he

would tell me he had deployed snipers to the rooftops of the abandoned buildings and green-lighted them to take out everyone in
the car who so much as raised a hand to me.

After fifteen minutes of total silence, a black Cadillac pulled in
behind us. Genovese underboss Louis "Bobby" Manna and big-time
hitter Richard "Bocci" DeSciscio got out. As soon as I saw them, I
knew I was safe. An underboss would never put himself at the scene
of a hit. I heard the helicopter peel off, but I assumed Sweeney still
had boots on the ground protecting me.

Apparently, Gerardo wanted a trusted guy to drive them. He
had selected me.

We got out of the car, and while the wiseguys exchanged cheek
kisses and hugs, I stayed back. I knew my place. Unless I was invited
to sit in, I'd have to be happy cooling my heels in the car.

The group started walking toward an abandoned building. I
stayed put. Andy Gerardo turned to me and said, "Come with us,
Mikey. Keep your eyes open for people that shouldn't be here."

As far as our case went, this was gold. I was going to be privy to
a meeting of top Genovese bosses. Christmas came early for the
State Police that year.

Manna ran the meeting like a five-star general. He didn't look
imposing; you look up the word *average* in the dictionary and you'd
find a picture of Manna. Rank in the Genovese family traditionally
stayed in New York. That New York had elevated a New Jersey wiseguy to the rank of underboss was enough for him to command
respect. Manna didn't have a volatile temper. He was the type of
boss who would deal with a problem by putting his arm around
you, telling you that everything would be okay. The next day you'd
be dead. Manna was a thinker.

Everyone stood around Manna while he ran down a list of problems. The meeting was all about garbage. The Genovese family ran the carting business in north Jersey and all of Manhattan. They also owned landfills and were making millions of dollars in this area alone. BFI, a huge publically owned carting company, was moving to New Jersey. They had vast amounts of money to invest and were looking to take business away from Genovese-backed companies by lowering prices to their customers.

"If we lose any of our accounts, I'm going to hold you personally responsible," Manna said, glancing at Gerardo. Manna was particularly concerned about the big accounts such as Home Depot and the Crazy Eddie electronic stores. "I want you to send your best guys to these places and explain our position. Lean on them if you have to. Explain how precious life is."

Gerardo chimed in, "I'll send my two best guys to talk to these mopes." He pointed to me and Cetrulo. Wonderful, I was going to intimidate a Home Depot executive.

Manna said, "Good, take Bocci with you." DeSciscio gave us a benign head nod. This guy had killed more people than Sergeant York.

Cetrulo told Bocci to meet us at the Cage in three days to begin our public relations push, Mafia style.

Manna threw around so many names, this was one of the few times I wished I'd worn a wire. The meeting lasted another twenty minutes, and by the time it ended we had enough basic information to add still more indictable counts to our ever-growing list.

Demus Covello called from Florida twenty minutes after we got back from the meeting with Manna.

"Mikey, I'm coming up tomorrow to talk to Sal. I'd like you at the meeting."

"Yeah, sure." I knew enough not to ask what the meeting was about. I'd find out soon enough.

The next afternoon Demus breezed into my office. It was a beautiful autumn day, sunny and mild. I was shuffling papers around my desk, and Billy was looking equally busy talking to no one on the phone. The first thing Demus did was bitch about the weather.

"Fucking freezing up here."

"And hello to you, too, asshole. It's fifty-five degrees. You gotta have water for blood."

"Mikey!" He smiled and extended his arms for the inevitable embrace and cheek kisses. He looked good. At about five feet nine inches, with an average build, he was tanned and dressed well. Today looked like Armani, but I'm Irish, what do I know? Demus's bow to vanity was a toupee that looked as if a squirrel had died on his head. All the money he had, I'd have figured him for a transplant or at least a rug that had a little more quality than an Earl Scheib paint job.

The sloppy guinea-greeting bullshit over, I introduced him to Billy.

Demus said to me, "Where can we talk?" He looked at Billy. "No offense."

Billy shrugged. "None taken."

"Sal's meeting us at the San Carlo on River Road. You hungry?" I said.

Demus replied with the standard Italian response: "I can eat."

Fifteen minutes later we were in the San Carlo, a decent Italian restaurant devoid of "friends of ours." Having a meeting like this in a crew hangout was like wearing sandwich boards with WE'RE UP TO NO FUCKING GOOD printed on them.

We ordered lunch and Demus got down to business. "Sal, I asked Mikey to join us today because he's an old friend and I'm more comfortable with him around. Is that okay?"

"Sure, Mikey's in solid with us. I like having him around, too."

Jesus, I was thinking, what bullshit.

"Okay," Demus said, "I'll get to the point. I want to make a move on Art Stock."

Art Stock was a former schoolteacher from Woodbridge, New Jersey, who had struck gold in the nightclub business after leaving teaching. Within ten years he owned seven prosperous clubs in south Jersey, all under the protection of the Genovese family. Stock had agreed to the offer the family had made him: pay us a percentage and we guarantee you a trouble-free business. Stock was probably paying the mob between $20,000 and $30,000 a month and doing so gladly. Any problems with cops, politicians, wiseguys from families, whatever, he went to the local Genovese crew. End of problem. A few years ago he had expanded to Florida and started two more clubs, one in Hallandale Beach, the other in Fort Lauderdale. They were doing well, and the Demus crew wanted to move on those clubs for a percentage of the profits. To do this he needed permission from Gerardo, who was still shaking down the original clubs and owned the Stock "franchise."

I kept my mouth shut. I couldn't be a party to extortion, and any contribution I made could be construed as entrapment. If the crew's lawyers could mount that defense, successful or not, it could hurt my credibility.

They batted around an approach for twenty minutes until they

decided that Demus could make the entrée and run the operation independently of Gerardo's crew, which would certainly get a
cash tribute.

"Tell him twenty large a month. He shouldn't go batshit over
that," Cetrulo said.

Cetrulo was right, Stock didn't bat an eye and was glad to have
the coverage—just in case. In addition to the political and law-
enforcement clout it would buy, the cocaine turf wars were bal-
looning an already-high South Florida homicide rate into the
stratosphere, and with gangs' looking to branch out into other illegal endeavors, having the country's most powerful Mafia family at
your back wasn't such a bad idea.

It had been a good week for truth, justice, and the American
way. Between the garbage thing and Stock, we State Police had our
best week yet. The Stock case would be another count in an already-
burgeoning list of crimes we could add to future indictments.

11

Fed Up

The wiretaps were supplying so much useful information that the regiment of detectives already assigned to the investigation was proving to be woefully inadequate. In two weeks, four new criminal cases were recorded, with one, a major drug-distribution and gambling ring, requiring immediate attention. We also learned that Gerardo's gambling operation alone was making $50 million a year. This case would be the first major investigation in New Jersey to use the federal Racketeer Influenced and Corrupt Organizations (RICO) Act to remove all financial assets garnered from criminality from the mobsters. My trip to Home Depot to straighten out the BFI garbage conundrum had to be put off for a few days. I had just gotten the phony cast removed from my arm, and I made some lame excuse about having to get a series of X-rays and bone-density tests over the next few days and not being available. Cetrulo swallowed the story. I was beginning to think I could tell him I killed JFK and he would've believed me.

The drug/gambling case was codenamed Operation Cheers, and the State Police moved to shut it down before it grew any larger or someone got killed. Initially the bosses debated if it would be a smarter move to let the ring flourish until the end of the undercover case against the Gerardo crew, lest we tip our hands that we had got the intel to shut them down through our covert wiretaps. But the greater good of getting drugs and dealers off the street outweighed the possibility that one of the targets would assume we were listening to their conversations.

The ring operated in Essex and Bergen Counties and was responsible for distributing fifteen kilos of cocaine a week, selling the stuff at bargain-basement rates because the purity was diluted by 80 percent. Coke was then popular, and if it was white and in powder form, people would shove it up their noses no matter what the quality. This grunt setup sold grams and eight balls in clubs, bars, and on street corners in the Meadowlands and Fort Lee areas. Quality lost out to quantity. The gambling operation was financed by the drug profits and raked in millions, too.

Arrested in the sweep were Tom Passante, age forty-eight; Larry Maturo, forty-six; and Joe Morra, twenty-six. This group fell under the control of Sal Cetrulo, who was not arrested or exposed in order to keep him a part of the undercover sting. A drug-conspiracy charge would be added to his list of crimes alleged when our investigation into the Gerardo crew was completed.

The second case gleaned from the wiretaps was a scam run by Sal Cetrulo and Joe Zarra. They had enlisted the aid of a larcenous dentist who was talked into a Medicaid fraud. The dentist's arrest was put off until the end of the Gerardo-crew investigation to avoid alerting the wiseguys to the presence of the electronic monitoring.

The next case, also a Cetrulo/Zarra brainchild, was the extortion of money from the Teaneck Pest Control Company. The owner was paying the wiseguys for being allowed to stay in business. We also waited until the end of our major case to expose what we knew about this one, as we did with the last case, a credit-card fraud run by Anthony DiVingo. In this case, credit-card receipts stolen by service help in restaurants were used to manufacture phony credit cards.

The five Home Depot superstores in north Jersey had their managerial offices on the second floor of the store locations. Cetrulo, Bocci, and I went to each store to impress upon the managers the benefits of not jumping ship to BFI. Bocci was with us as Manna's emissary to make sure the message was delivered to his liking. To that end, Bocci and I donned Jersey Carting uniforms to further look the part. Cetrulo wanted no part of the masquerade.

"Are you fucking kidding me?" he said when I asked him why he wouldn't wear a uniform. "I'm a made guy; I only wear good shit."

Spoken like a true connoisseur of fine garments.

Our plan was simple and began with the three of us bursting into the managers' offices unannounced. Sal did the talking while Bocci and I stood with our arms folded across our chests looking menacing. Bocci could've handled this part alone; he was six-five and had a face that could scare babies.

When we entered the first manager's office, Bocci tripped over a folding chair and almost landed on his ass. Pissed off at his clumsiness, he hurled the chair through the manager's hundred-gallon fish aquarium, spilling dozens of colorful tropical fish onto the floor. The fish flip-flopped all over the executive's polished wood floor while Cetrulo went through his sales pitch, most of which involved terms like *dirt nap, accidental death,* and *wood chipper.*

On the way out, Cetrulo gave the manager an innocent look. "You should clean this mess up, wet floors can be dangerous."

Other than the fish-tank fiasco, we went through the same act in the other stores, Cetrulo refining his pitch as he went along.

Two store managers quit immediately and went back to Omaha or wherever they had come from. All the Home Depot stores wound up staying with Jersey Carting. Cetrulo missed his calling, he was quite the salesman. We had the same results with Eddie Antar, owner of the Crazy Eddie electronic superstores.

We had a perfect sales record; we lost no accounts.

New York law enforcement was shining a light on the mob's involvement in the private-carting industry, but the New Jersey crews felt secure enough to try to hold on to accounts and secure new ones. The carting companies in New Jersey had one major advantage when it came to keeping contracts from the encroaching BFI: the New Jersey mob owned all the dumps in New Jersey and wouldn't allow BFI to dispose of their collected garbage there. BFI was forced to haul garbage to Pennsylvania and Connecticut. One such location was in Bozrah, Connecticut, which was a four-hour drive one way from the collection point.

* * *

Cetrulo began using me again as a driver to make the runs to New York with the shaving kit stuffed with tribute cash, only now the money was being delivered to Louis "Bobby" Manna instead of Fat Tony Salerno. Salerno, along with bosses Jerry Langella, Phil Rastelli, and Antonio "Ducks" Corallo had been indicted by the feds in the Commission Case. It was the government's way of putting away the high-ranking bosses of all five families under RICO. Corallo's Jaguar had been bugged while he was attending the Private Sanitation Industry Association Dinner and Dance on Long Island. The subsequent recordings helped get all the bosses convicted and sent away for a hundred years each, a veritable life sentence.

Bosses were running scared, but it didn't stop those who remained free from trying to make money and making sure what was due to them got delivered.

Our meetings shifted to the Lower East Side on Thursdays at 8:00 p.m., where we would initially meet Manna in an alley on Orchard Street and hand him the money-stuffed shaving kit. There would rarely be conversation; he'd materialize around a corner, take the money, and walk west toward Elizabeth Street. Every few weeks the meeting place changed, but it was always on the Lower East Side. Manna didn't want to meet in Jersey for fear he'd get pulled over in one of the tunnels on his way back to New York and have no place to stash the money.

One day we were instructed to meet Manna on Delancey Street. When he didn't show up after fifteen minutes, we became concerned. Manna was rarely late, especially when it came to picking up money. Cetrulo and I were leaning against an old Cadillac when the trunk popped open and out jumped Manna. I thought I was watching a David Copperfield special. I also thought Cetrulo was going to have a heart attack.

"What the fuck, Bobby!" Cetrulo said after he caught his breath.

"Just wanted to make sure you weren't followed." Manna held out his hand, and Cetrulo handed over the shaving kit. "Have a nice day," Manna said, and strolled away.

After every handoff Cetrulo and I went to Katz's Deli, which was in the neighborhood, for sandwiches. The conversation always drifted to Manna.

"He's a good guy to get on the right side of," Cetrulo said.

"And why's that?"

"He's the Chin's favorite guy, brought Bobby up to where he is today. You watch, he'll take over when Chin retires."

Vincent "the Chin" Gigante was the boss of the Genovese family, the largest of the five families. His claim to fame was that he was never convicted of a major crime. While all the other bosses were getting sent away under RICO, the Chin seemed immune. He had strict rules dealing with security. No one was to ever utter his name in conversation. To do so would result in an immediate death sentence for the violator. Instead of speaking his name you had to point to your chin. The Chin also pretended to be mentally ill and could be seen wandering around Greenwich Village, unshaven, in pajamas and a ratty robe and supported under each arm by his two sons. His lawyers argued that he wasn't competent to stand trial. The act worked for over twenty-five years, but the law finally caught up with him and he was convicted of numerous federal charges. He died in prison at age seventy-seven.

* * *

Due to our unprecedented workload, the New Jersey attorney general's office told us the hundred-member Organized Crime and Racketeering Task Force was coming on board to render assistance. I was apoplectic, as were Sweeney, Nick, Billy, and the rest of the handpicked cops assigned to the case. This was a blatant move to hijack our case and grab headlines after we had done all the work.

The Task Force was composed of do-nothing cops who had aligned themselves with politicians by campaigning and contributing money to their election coffers to help get or keep the politicos in public office. The cops were given appointments to the Task Force as payback. I called these guys empty suits because for the most part they weren't street cops and wouldn't know a wiseguy if one bit them on the ass. Some did twenty-five years on the job without making a single arrest. Too many agencies, too many politicians, and too many headline seekers were now involved in this case. Sweeney and I could see a train wreck in the making, and the first calamity occurred within days of Task Force involvement.

Sweeney called me in my office, said urgently, "Get to a phone," and hung up.

I did my usual tour of the neighborhood until I found a pay phone that worked.

"What?" I said, expecting bad news.

"Gerardo's gonna be locked up."

This was one of the few times in my life I was literally speechless.

"You there, Mike?"

"Yeah, yeah, I'm here. I hear you right? Gerardo's gonna get busted?

For what?" I expected something top level, like a homicide where he was caught with a smoking gun and covered with blood, the crime witnessed by a busload of nuns.

"Parole violation. Consorting with gangsters. Is this fucked-up or what?"

"Fucked-up? This is a fucking disaster. You can't swing a dead cat in Newark without hitting a freakin' gangster. Are they kidding? Don't these assholes know I'm meeting with him weekly? Gerardo's a wealth of intelligence. I'm in solid with this guy. You gotta stop this, Jimmy."

"Can't, Mike. I've been pleading with the boss for two days. He was told to do it. Came from somewhere, gotta be a political thing. I think the jerks in the Task Force want to show they're in control. Someone wants their name in the papers."

I felt numb, just like when I got shot in the head. Gerardo's arrest served no purpose except to hurt our investigation. When a boss gets arrested, day-to-day operations change dramatically. The crew might go to ground—clam up, shut down anything that might get them indicted, stop talking about pending scores for fear they were being recorded. I was envisioning my forward movement coming to a screeching halt.

Amateurs were now running our case.

Andy Gerardo was arrested the next day and proceeded to manipulate the system. Somehow he got himself placed in the Edna Mahan Correctional Facility for Women, in Clinton, New Jersey. He had his own private cabin in the rear of the property equipped with a pay phone and private bath. He had guards on his payroll that brought him food and booze from the outside and was allowed weekly visits from his wife.

Billy got himself a nice spot on the roof of the main facility and photographed Gerardo, Cetrulo, Zarra, and Peewee paying off correction officers.

I was on the wire in my office when Gerardo called the Cage complaining that the cops were taking pictures of him from the roof of the main prison building. Billy had been made, but through no fault of his own. Gerardo said he was tipped off by one of the correction officers.

Sweeney passed this information to correction officials, and Gerardo was transferred to Rahway State Penitentiary and placed with the general population for the remainder of his stay. The correction officers at the women's facility who helped Gerardo were indicted, convicted, and received long prison sentences.

The Task Force held weekly meetings at Division Headquarters in West Trenton, and my presence was requested. Sweeney politely told the Task Force honchos that I was a street cop and as such I worked the street.

"Mike isn't an office boy," he told them. After also defining the word *undercover,* he said, "We don't want anyone without a need to know who he is, or that we even have an undercover, in the loop."

I was never asked to attend another meeting.

With Andy Gerardo in the can, Ralph "Spuds" Vicaro took his place as acting boss. Vicaro was seventy-one years old and had been in the New Jersey wing of the Mafia all his adult life, holding the rank of captain for as long as anyone could remember. Sal Cetrulo once told me Vicaro's first crime was stealing wampum from the Indians.

"They built New Jersey around him," Cetrulo said on more than one occasion.

Vicaro was as nondescript as a mobster could possibly be. He was always in the Cage, but we had yet to get him on a wire because he rarely talked, and you couldn't pick him out of a lineup of two people if someone held a gun to your head. He was just a plain-looking, old man. Vicaro was good at hanging out and not much else, but I had to give him credit, when Gerardo went to prison, Vicaro stepped up and assumed command as ranking capo in the crew.

Vicaro lacked a major attribute that a boss must have: a commanding presence. He was insecure. From day one he latched onto me as if we were joined at the hip. I was required to be on the sidewalk in front of the Cage when he showed up every afternoon to make sure it was safe for him to leave his car. I also had to have lunch with him every day. I added to his insecurity when I reminded him of a quote from Al Capone, who once said, "You don't have to worry about the cops. It's always the guy underneath you that's gonna take you out."

My relationship with Vicaro was pissing off Cetrulo and Zarra because they were the made guys, and if anyone should have Vicaro's ear, it should have been them. But they couldn't go to Bobby Manna and complain because it was outside the chain of command. So they stewed while Vicaro relied on me for his security. Cetrulo and Zarra got the assignment of taking turns going to Rahway once a week on Tuesdays to visit Gerardo and exchange information.

* * *

Shortly after Gerardo's transfer to Rahway, the state attorney general issued a press release detailing how difficult it was for law enforcement to keep Gerardo from supervising his crew from behind bars. The AG further stated, "It is hard to bring such groups to their knees." In essence, the attorney general was saying that the mob is smart and efficient, and law enforcement agencies are a bunch of idiots; criminals are committing crimes while in custody and we're powerless to stop them. I don't know what the AG was thinking when he issued such a humiliating press release. It certainly wasn't going to get him any votes.

Less than a week later I was blindsided by the Great Finish Line Raid. The State Police, in conjunction with the Task Force, decided to raid the Finish Line restaurant on Roosevelt Avenue in north Newark without sharing their plans with me. The Finish Line was a bar/pizzeria hangout for the Genovese family. As a gambling and bookie location, it contained gambling records, cash, and guns. Every schoolkid in the neighborhood knew what went on in the Finish Line.

According to the attorney general, the purpose of the raid "was to stir up some action." My read on it was the only thing the raid would stir up was awareness that the family was under law enforcement scrutiny. It was a foolish idea and I made my feelings known to Sweeney.

"Mike, I agree," Sweeney said. "The Task Force assholes want some publicity. I tried to stop it. Couldn't budge them."

The raid turned out to be a fiasco. I was on the scene as a spectator, a short distance away in a van with blacked-out windows, and couldn't be seen. I videoed the entire raid, start to finish. The tape, along with other video I'd shot, was later included in an HBO special on the mob. I still watch the video of the raid to this day and am reminded of the old Three Stooges shorts. I also knew right from the beginning that the wiseguys had been tipped off they were going to be raided.

At 2:00 p.m., a small army of troopers and detectives descended on the Finish Line waving warrants and shouting, "Police, don't move!" to the seven wiseguys hanging out on the sidewalk in front of the restaurant. Three of the wiseguys shrugged and walked off. No one stopped them. One of the three, Mike DelGurcio, a known hit man, saw another crew member, James Calabrese, slowing his car to park and tipped him to the raid. Calabrese kept on driving. The four mobsters who remained could have wandered off in the ensuing confusion, but they were laughing so hard they decided to hang around for the rest of the show. One of the four, Tommy Sperduto, strolled up the block to a pay phone and made two calls. No one stopped him. A short while later, the four got bored, got in their cars, and drove away. And . . . no one stopped them.

Cops were running in and out of the restaurant, apparently not knowing what to do or where to look for the "gambling records" and other contraband. I saw a detective named Caramana search a car belonging to a wiseguy. When I saw how he was conducting the search, I swung the camera to him and recorded his movements for posterity.

Caramana had popped the unlocked trunk and went directly to the right side and rummaged around. The open trunk lid obscured what he was doing in the trunk. He abruptly closed the trunk and walked away. This is not how you search a car. Any rookie fresh out of the academy knows that the *entire* car gets searched; this means not only the trunk, but the interior, engine compartment, exterior, and undercarriage.

Something was beginning to smell rotten.

The cops never bothered to talk to the wiseguys; they were acting as if the wiseguys weren't there. The cops never covered the three exits, and instead of drawn guns they carried clipboards. It seemed as if the only reason the cops were there was to have pizza, and indeed I saw a few happily chomping into slices.

So let's tally the evidence collected. I didn't need a calculator for this . . . there wasn't any. The raid didn't produce one gambling record, not one incriminating piece of paper, or any guns, cash, or any other contraband. The mobsters had evidently been tipped off. The only upside to the "raid" was that none of the cops who participated knew of my existence or that an undercover operation was in place. I'm sure had they known, someone would've ratted me out to the crew for a nice payday.

About twenty minutes after the raid I got a call on a police radio from Assistant DA Harry Brett, who was on the scene of the raid. He told me everything had gone well.

"All we wanted to do was shake things up."

I let it alone. What I had seen had thrown me into a deep depression. This case was my life. I had devoted my existence to undercover work at nearly the cost of my life. I had a hole in my head to prove it. To see what I considered a bunch of corrupt cops going through the motions of a raid was making me physically ill. The case had been moving at warp speed and was unraveling just as fast. The Task Force, the AG's office, and even the Organized Crime Bureau were lost in a maze of bureaucracy, politics, and corruption.

On top of it all, the stupid, small-time, botched gambling raid would shortly come close to costing me my life.

A few days after the raid, three detectives who had participated were arrested and later convicted of stealing $70,000 in cash from the Finish Line. Detective Caramana, who had stolen a gold Rolex watch from the trunk of the car in which I had seen him rummaging around, was also arrested and later convicted. Someone told him about the watch and he went right for it, it being his sole reason for going into that trunk. The idiot was wearing the watch when he was collared. All four cops received stiff prison sentences.

I knew I had to get back to the Cage quickly after the raid. I was sure a few of the escapees from the Finish Line were already there recounting what went down. I wiped some petroleum grease on my face and hands—my cover for my whereabouts would be I was doing a furnace removal at the other end of town.

As soon as I walked into the Cage, Vicaro called me over to a corner.

"Mikey, you gotta strip down," he said. Sal Cetrulo and Joe Zarra stepped behind me.

I put on my innocent puss. "Huh, what's this about?"

Zarra said, "The Finish Line just got raided. C'mon, take it off."

I followed instructions and stood there in my underwear feeling like a jerk, all the time thanking my instincts for not wearing a wire when at this stage of the game it shouldn't have been dangerous to do so because I was one of the guys. While Sal searched my clothes, I decided to go on the offensive.

"You know, Sal, I was at the scene of a murder with you last month, and you think I tipped off the cops about a stinking raid? And at a bar I don't frequent? And did I say a fucking thing about who shot me? You guys should consider who I am before you do this shit."

Cetrulo just stared at me. While he might be a sociopath, he was far from stupid. These guys have survival instincts like gazelles on the Serengeti; eyes in the back of their heads, always suspicious, always questioning, always looking for the law enforcement lion that was going to pounce. I was good at what I did, and I knew I had to keep talking to put these guys at ease. Cetrulo was the type of guy who could pull out a gun and blow me away for the hell of it. He tossed my clothes to me and I began to get dressed.

"I don't see what you guys are so upset about," I said. "A couple of Newark cops want to score some money, so fucking what?"

Cetrulo started yelling. "They were fuckin' state cops!"

I laughed—try doing that when you're trying to save your life—and said, "That's an even bigger fucking joke. The guys with the funny stripped pants, giving out tickets on the Parkway? Somebody's missing the big picture here; you guys are dumber than the fucking cops." Then I turned it around. "You should be looking at Silvio DeVita, not me. The fucking guy's on lifetime parole. Maybe he took a bust and flipped."

They looked puzzled, but curious. At the start of my interrogation I had shifted my body so the crew would be talking to the wall microphone. I wanted their threats to be clear and understandable. Through the inquisition Vicaro looked embarrassed for me, and I knew I had him on my side, but he was the boss and he had to do what he had to do. Bottom line, I figured no one was going to whack me without his permission.

Everything began to calm down. Vicaro asked me if I could do more record checks. This request came out of nowhere, and I think he mentioned it to get everyone's mind off my grilling. Regardless, I answered it as if he were genuinely interested.

"Not possible. I'm not a cop anymore... I was fired. I don't want to be in police buildings."

Cetrulo and Zarra were looking to Vicaro to do something. Vicaro just shrugged.

I jumped in. "Let's go eat at Doc and Lou's. The special today is linguine with mussels and black olives with garlic."

Vicaro made a command decision. "Yeah, fuck it, let's go."

We all went to dinner in Cetrulo's Caddy.

I went from almost getting assassinated to having heartburn from too much garlic in the space of an hour. How can anyone not love police work?

The more I dwelled on the corruption I suspected in the Finish Line raid, and the meddling bureaucrats that were almost certain to ruin my investigation, the more I considered quitting; not just quitting the case, quitting the State Police. But I didn't have enough time in and didn't qualify for a pension. If I left, all I'd get is what the city and I had contributed to my pension account. With a wife and three kids I'd run through that quickly. But my level of frustration was such that I couldn't stomach seeing all my hard work go down the drain and being powerless to stop it.

"You're going to do what?" my wife, Angela, asked. The girls were in bed and we were working on a bottle of wine in the living room.

"Quit. I'm gonna quit."

"Police work is your life. And you're going to throw away a pension?"

"Yeah, honey, I am. Enough is enough. This patrol bullshit is going nowhere. Now's the time." Angela still had no idea I was working undercover.

"And what will you do when you get out?"

"I'll stay home and be with you every minute of the day," I said with a straight face.

"Great." She took a long hit on the wine.

Angela knew I was a hustler and would do well financially outside police work. Hell, I might even go into the oil-delivery business. I sure as hell knew enough about it by now. My wife and I were going through the motions of a marriage I didn't think would last much longer. My main concern was my girls, who were nine, eleven, and twelve at the time.

I had made my decision the night before. I couldn't take the incompetence of the bosses I was working for and the corruption I knew was pervasive, and it was eating me up inside. Plus, I was convinced it was only a matter of time before the jerks at the Task Force got me killed. If the Task Force bosses thought they could run this case, let them. I was going to Division Headquarters in Trenton and put in my papers, but not before I called Sweeney with my decision. He deserved at least a heads-up.

Oddly enough, Sweeney didn't try to talk me out of leaving. He shared my frustration and also feared for my safety.

"Fuck 'em, Mike," Sweeney said. "You're going out on top. There'd be no case if it wasn't for you. And you know what, buddy? I've got less than a year for my pension to kick in, and I'll be pulling the pin, too. Enough of this bullshit."

Well put, I thought.

I didn't inform anyone else I was quitting; I simply went to Trenton, handed in my gun and shield, and filled out a mountain of paperwork. No one at headquarters knew me; no one cared.

During the exit interview a captain asked me why I was quitting the job.

"Because I can't work for bosses who think it's more important to get headlines than it is to lock up the bad guys."

He knew better than to respond.

I left the headquarters building a civilian. Every cop thinks about how he'll feel when he leaves the job, no matter which department he splits from. I felt numb; not so much because I was walking away from a job that I loved, but because I knew the time I'd spent undercover would probably be for nothing. I was convinced the Gerardo-crew investigation would end up like the raid on the Finish Line, a travesty.

By the time I got home, panic had set in on all levels involved in the investigation. My wife had to unplug the phone, so voluminous were the calls.

I returned none of them, opting to take my girls to a movie instead. I'd worry about tomorrow when it happened. Somehow I knew I'd make out okay.

I'm a survivor.

12

Back with
a Vengeance

I was living in a surreal world. I had been involved in police work my entire adult life and knew nothing else. In what seemed the blink of an eye, I had thrust myself into the civilian world and I felt uncomfortable; I was a stranger in my own skin.

I was still operating in cop mode; it's something you can't turn off. I know former cops who, long after their retirement, still sit in restaurants with their backs to the wall, eyes on the door. They can tell by instinct who is carrying an illegally concealed gun, who has a carload of drugs, who just committed a crime, and—above all—who is lying. I was out of the job three days and my inner alarm was going off when I was in proximity to a bad guy, no matter how hard I tried to turn it off. This being Newark, that alarm was working overtime.

The majority of police officers planned meticulously for their retirement because many still had families to support when they left the job. Most got out when they were in their forties and first eligible for their pension—a veteran cop once told me that police work is no job for an adult. They wanted to transition smoothly into a new way to sustain their standard of living. Not only didn't I retire—I felt as if I'd escaped—I hadn't planned for the future. I had gone from the germ of an idea of quitting to actually doing it in less than a week.

Surprisingly, I didn't miss the job; I missed the cops I had worked with, particularly Jim Sweeney and the team of professionals, such as Nick, Billy, and Pat, who had supported me in my undercover assignment. I trusted these men with my life, and I'd be hard-pressed to think of any other line of work—other than the military in a time of war—where the bond among coworkers was as tight as what I shared with these men. To me, two things in the world have immense worth: children, if you're lucky enough to have them, and your partner, who will not only watch your back but take a bullet for you, too. I knew that no matter what I did from here on, no matter what kind of job, I'd never come close to that kind of camaraderie again.

I needed to invent a good excuse why I wasn't coming to the Cage, having rarely missed a day since the operation began. I told Sal Cetrulo that I had the flu and graphically described the symptoms.

"I'm all fucked-up, Sal," I told him when he called me. "Throwing up, diarrhea. Got the sweats. Feel fucking terrible." Cetrulo called me at home from time to time and in typical mobster fashion never shared anything with my wife as to who he was. Mob guys aren't much for small talk with wives or girlfriends; they're just one more person who'll rat you out. Women are not held in high esteem and are thought to be good for two things, and the other one is cooking. I passed him off to Angela as a cop I worked with.

"Well, you take care, Mikey," Cetrulo said. "The guys've been asking about you. See you when you feel better."

He'd be seeing someone, but it wouldn't be me. Sweeney told me the bosses were scrambling to salvage the investigation by brainstorming a way they could send in a replacement for me. Billy wasn't a candidate because he was supposed to be my helper in the oil business and as such allegedly wasn't privy to the inner workings of the crew. When the State Police bosses exhausted every possible scenario and deemed all of them implausible, I got a visit from the head honcho, Lieutenant Colonel Louis Toronto of the New Jersey State Police. The buck stopped with him, and he knew his reputation was at stake if the investigation went south. After four days of my being an official civilian, he showed up at my house alone.

We held our discussion in his department auto. Toronto was an imposing figure, in his fifties, over six feet tall, and built like the proverbial bull with a bad comb-over. We'd known each other for a long time. He was dressed in a black pin-striped suit and rep tie. I was in ripped jeans and a T-shirt, my uniform of the day. He diplomatically told his driver to get lost and got right to the point.

"Mike, we need you back, the case is going to shit."

Nice to feel wanted.

"With all due respect, Colonel, the case has been going to shit ever since the Task Force got involved." Whenever a cop is going to give a boss an opinion he might not like, it was mandatory to lead off with the catchphrase *with all due respect*. Sort of softens the blow. Same thing when talking to mob bosses; a boss is a boss.

He wasn't going to argue the point. He was a career cop, well respected and knowledgeable in the ways of politics as it pertained to police work. "I'm not here to discuss the Task Force. I want to know what it's going to take to get you back on the cops."

"A miracle sounds about right."

He stared at me. "Okay, you wanna be a wiseass? You have no choice, you're coming back. You just need to tell me what you want."

Of course I wanted to come back. I had a list of fantasy demands that, if met, would get me back. But they were just that, fantasies, both ridiculously demanding and far too expensive. I knew they would never get met. At least I didn't think they would. What the hell, I'd test the waters.

"I was working a sixty-hour week, Colonel, with no OT. I want the overtime . . . for starters."

He didn't bat an eye. "What else?"

"A raise, say twenty percent," I said with a straight face.

"Let me make sure I have this right; you want overtime *plus* a twenty percent raise?"

"Right."

"What, no car?"

Now he was busting my balls. You break mine, I'll break yours. "Yeah, a car, too. And throw in a no-show job for my wife, and relocation out of Newark for me and my family. The state would have to buy me a house; can't afford one on the shit salary I make." I was on a roll. You want me back? You're going to pay the price. I knew I'd never see any of it, but what the hell, it was cathartic.

"Any particular place you want to live?" Toronto asked.

When a cop graduates from the academy, he's given a form to fill out asking where he would like to work. It was called a Dream

Sheet because you never got what you asked for. Asking where I wanted to live brought back Dream Sheet memories.

I had once been to a seaside community in Connecticut and I fell in love with the town. Made perfect sense to me: be a Jersey state trooper, live in Connecticut, and commute to Newark every day. I was having fun with this.

"Funny you should ask. I'd like to live in Connecticut." I mentioned the name of the town. "I'm concerned about my family's safety when all this comes to an end." I knew the wiseguys would never find me in this dinky town.

"Is that all?" Toronto said.

I thought about it. "Yes, sir. That's about it."

Toronto extended his hand. We shook. "Okay, Mike, I'll get back to you."

I got out of the car and watched him drive away. What the hell just happened here? Was he seriously contemplating my demands? Could he be that desperate?

Two days later Lieutenant Colonel Toronto called me at the house. "You busy?"

"Very." I was watching a rerun of *Hawaii Five-0.* "What's up, boss?"

"I'd like to stop by and talk to you and your wife. She home?"

My wife? What did they want with Angela? Were the State Police contemplating what in essence amounted to a shakedown? Couldn't be. Virtually impossible. The overtime demand was doable, but I was a cop and couldn't demand a pay raise. Police pay is mandated by contractual agreement for every sworn officer. And buying me a house, in Connecticut no less, was so ridiculous I laughed out loud just thinking about it. The no-show job for Angela? The more I thought about it, the more it sounded like something Sal Cetrulo would demand of a shakedown victim.

"Yes, sir, she's home. Why do you need to know that?"

"You'll find out shortly. Half hour good?"

"Sure." I was going to tell him to bring the deed to my new house, but let it go. Even with a *with all due respect,* that wouldn't go over too well.

After I hung up, I called Angela into the living room. "We're having company."

"Who?"

I told her.

Up went the eyebrow. "*We're* not having company, *you're* having company."

"He wants to talk to you, too."

A confused look registered on her face. "What's he want with me?"

I shrugged. "Going to press me to come back to work, I'd guess. He tried a few days ago. Maybe he thinks he can enlist you into convincing me. He'll probably offer me unlimited overtime. Figures you'll go for that. It'll almost double my salary."

She was making herself a sandwich for lunch, but she stopped cold. "What did you tell him?"

I ran down my list of additional fantasy demands. "I made my requirements so ridiculous he'll have to turn me down."

"The department can't survive without you on patrol?" Angela's bullshit meter was on tilt.

There was no harm in telling her the truth now. My undercover days were over, and when Toronto made his pitch again, he would have to bring it up. I gave her the bare bones on what I'd been doing, leaving out selected parts, such as Lou Malavacca's eyeball floating in a shot-up bottle of vodka. When I was done, I prepared myself for the verbal abuse. Surprisingly, it never came.

"To tell you the truth, I'm relieved. I thought you had a girl-friend on the side. I knew you were lying to me, just didn't know why. I know you, Mike; you're an adrenaline junkie. You need the action, only I thought it involved a young bimbo. "

I let the remark pass. "Angela, I owe this guy the right to try to convince me to come back. He can authorize the overtime, but that's it. I'm going to politely turn him down, and that'll be the end of it."

She smiled. "What about the rest of it?"

I explained why any offer above the overtime pay was out of the question, indeed illegal.

"Sounds tempting," she said, "except for the moving to Connecticut part. I'd never move away from this area. To tell the truth, if I'm asked my opinion, they can stick their overtime."

This didn't surprise me. Money didn't interest Angela. With her it was all about family. As long as she was around the kids and her parents, and there was enough money to live on comfortably, she was fine. The only thing that could separate an Italian female from her parents was a crowbar.

I wanted to get away from the conversation, and the best way to do that with Angela was to mention food. She must've been a gangster in her former life. I gestured to her sandwich in progress. "Looks good, could you make me one of those, please?"

We ate in relative silence. As the years passed, it became increasingly obvious that we just didn't have that much to say to each other anymore. I respected her as a parent; I doubted there was a better mother on the planet. I know she respected me for being an honest cop and a good provider, but we both recognized that the fire had gone from our marriage a long time ago. The remaining embers had diminished to a faint glow, and they couldn't be reignited with a flamethrower. We were just going through the motions.

The doorbell rang and I was brought back from my reverie.

The three of us sat around the kitchen table. Lieutenant Colonel Toronto had brought with him a black leather attaché case. We had gone through the usual preamble with Toronto inquiring into the health of our kids, who were in school and would be home in about two hours. He complimented Angela on her looks and had nice things to say about the neatness of the apartment ("Tough when you have three kids running around"). Angela nodded politely and produced the requisite pot of coffee.

During a pause, Toronto pulled a manila folder from his case. "Angela, Mike told you about me trying to convince him to come back to work for us." This wasn't a question; he assumed I'd told her I'd been working undercover.

Angela nodded, but had no comment.

"We want him back in the fold because, quite frankly, with him out of the case we can't move forward. Not to get into issues, we find it . . . untenable to replace him." He opened the folder and spread out several official-looking documents.

I tried to read the papers upside down with little success. All I was able to make out was the official logo of the New Jersey State Police on every page.

Toronto turned to me. "Mike, your conditions for returning are . . . let's say, not within the department's power to grant. A few of them, such as the request that Angela here be put on the payroll is . . ." He groped for a word.

I helped. "Illegal?"

Toronto smiled. "Well, let's just say a . . . request like that has never been made."

I was confused and glanced at Angela. She seemed more baffled than me.

"With all due respect"—I couldn't escape that phrase—"why are you here then, sir? I'm not dropping any of my . . . requests." It sounded better than *demands*.

"We can give a lot more to a civilian than we can to a cop, Mike."

Now I was really confused. "But I am a cop . . . was a cop. What's this about?"

"It's about you being hired as an independent civilian contractor." He slid the paperwork in front of me. Angela leaned forward and we both started to read. I'd got as far as the word *agreement* when Toronto stopped me.

"Be easier if I explain what we're offering first. The legalese you can go over when I leave or show it to a lawyer, whatever. We're meeting all your requests except for the overtime. Contracted civilians don't get OT. You'll be getting a twenty percent pay boost plus a car. Don't expect a Ferrari, but it'll be paid for and it's yours to keep." He looked at Angela. "You'll be on salary for two years, at four hundred dollars a week. This is cash, by the way. Any objections so far?"

"Hell, no," I said, and looked to Angela, who just shook her head. She was amazed and speechless and I couldn't blame her.

Toronto said to me, "And we choose not to call this a no-show job. This is compensation to your wife for any inconvenience which this assignment might cause your family. Also—"

Angela cut him off. "What inconvenience? Mike'll be working the same case, right?"

"Yes," Toronto said, "that's true, but it'll ramp up from here on. Mike's getting in deeper and deeper, and I won't bullshit you, it can get dangerous. He's moving in circles with heavy hitters, and we want to make certain everyone is safe, including you and your kids. You know that move you wanted to make to Connecticut? We can do that; we *will* do that."

"Hey, I don't want to move to Connecticut," Angela said. "My parents are here; the kids' school, their friends." She looked at me, shooting me daggers. "You like Connecticut so fucking much, you move there."

Toronto was clearly uncomfortable. He cleared his throat. "Well, that's something you two will have to discuss. Think of the safety of your family, plus check out the area before you make any decisions." He mentioned the name of the town. "Great school district, low crime . . . let me rephrase that: no crime. The state will be buying you this house. It's a nice house, the kids'll love it." He looked around as if to imply. *It'll be a lot better than this closet you're living in now.*

"And me?" I interjected. "Helluva commute to Newark every day."

"We got you a garden apartment in Parsippany. You can go to your family on weekends or whenever else you can string a few days together."

Angela's left eyebrow shot up. I knew she was envisioning wild parties and an army of married cops using the place to bang their girlfriends. As if reading her mind, Toronto said, "The apartment will be monitored and the phones tapped . . . in case the targets call."

Before he left, Toronto answered a slew of questions. Yes, the house, as well as the car, would be ours to keep when the case was over; we would own them free and clear. Yes, Angela could visit her parents anytime she wished, but he would rather they not come to the new house until the investigation was over. It was expected to last another year, give or take.

"I need the contract signed by the day after tomorrow, Mike, if you're gonna come back. Up to you, but I know you'll do the right thing."

After Toronto left, Angela drew her line in the sand and refused to budge on the move to Connecticut; the rest she could live with. This was a sweetheart of a deal and she knew it, and after another hour of arguing, she agreed to take a ride with me to Connecticut the next day to at least check out the house and the town.

As I expected, she fell in love with the place. The house was a twenty-year-old, three-bedroom ranch on a quarter acre. What's not to love? We visited the local middle school and again she was impressed.

She agreed to the move. I called Toronto in Trenton the next afternoon.

"I'm in."

He let out a sigh I swear I could've heard without a phone. "Welcome back, Mike. You made the right decision."

That remained to be seen, but I was happy to be back. I was getting bored with being a civilian. Eight days out of the game was a bit too much. I was never meant to do anything other than what I loved.

* * *

Billy was sitting at my desk when I got back to the office the next morning. I'd driven to work in the new Olds Cutlass I'd been given by the State of New Jersey. I'd expected a Cadillac, in keeping with my mob persona, but I couldn't beat the price of the ride they gave me—free.

"Gee," he said with a grin, "you don't look sick."

"It's a friggin' miracle. Got up this morning, felt like a million bucks. What've you been doing?"

He sighed. "Besides playing with myself? Nothing. Can't do much by myself. I'd need one eye on the peephole, one eye on the door, and one eye on the wire. I'm good, but not that good. Bosses have been jumping through their own assholes trying to figure out what to do without you."

"Well, I'm back, only now as a civilian."

Billy's eyes went wide. "What the hell did they offer you, a blow job from Heather Locklear?"

I laughed. "Something almost as good." I made a zipping motion across my mouth. "Sworn to secrecy until this is over." Confidentiality was never mentioned, but I thought it best to keep the details of the deal to myself.

"Got it," Billy said. Cops can appreciate keeping one's mouth shut; more cops have gotten into hot water by talking too much than any other way. Billy knew that the less he knew, the better his chances of not getting caught up in some kind of interdepartmental bullshit rivalry, or worse, a criminal investigation into my actions.

I felt more secure working as a civilian than as a police officer. Law enforcement agencies are political and not above using leverage—usually the threat of a criminal indictment, or the termination of a police career—for real or imagined slights. I was immune to that type of harassment now. They could break my contract—something they couldn't afford to do—but that was about it. They needed me, I knew it, and I was going to run this case the way it should be run, by putting it back in the hands of the street cops who knew what they were doing.

I went next door to the Cage and was greeted warmly by the half dozen crew members who were doing what they do best: eating and gambling. Neither Cetrulo nor Zarra was present, but it was before noon and a bit too early for them make an appearance. I worked the room to pick up the latest gossip.

I learned that Andy Gerardo was having a rough time in Rahway State Penitentiary. Contrary to popular belief, prisons can't operate without the cooperation of the inmates. Prison officials look the other way at many infractions to keep the facility running smoothly. In return, the inmates promise not to murder the guards or riot, a promise that is kept most of the time. A fair trade-off for everyone involved. In Rahway, the Black Muslim cons ran the joint and couldn't have cared less about Gerardo's exalted Mafia rank. To them he was just another white asshole. Gerardo's cellblock was ruled with an iron fist by former middleweight boxing contender Rubin "Hurricane" Carter, who had been tried and convicted of a triple homicide in 1976—which was then overturned—and was then serving a life sentence. Carter reveled in giving Gerardo a hard time. Gerardo's mobster buddies and politically connected friends were hesitant to use their influence to help him for fear of public exposure. For the time being, Gerardo would have to tough it out on his own.

December 16, 1985, was a day that will live in Mafia infamy. On that day the Gambino crime-family boss, Paul "Big Paul" Castellano, was gunned down along with his bodyguard and heir apparent, Thomas Bilotti, in what was arguably the most publicized mob assassination in organized-crime history.

Not since the murder of boss Albert "Mad Hatter" Anastasia in 1957 had the head of a family been hit. What made the Castellano murder different from Anastasia's was that Castellano's assassination wasn't sanctioned. To kill a family boss, the Commission—the bosses of the four remaining families—had to give their okay.

The hit was allowed in Anastasia's case because his volatile, violent ways were bringing too much media and law-enforcement heat to the mob, which by definition is a secret organization and didn't appreciate the scrutiny. Anastasia's managerial style was to murder anyone who gave him a hard time, wiseguy or civilian. Castellano's killing, on the other hand, was engineered and carried out on the orders of Gambino captain John Gotti, who considered Big Paul a greedy boss, who eschewed contact with his Mafia underlings because he thought the rank and file were beneath him and took more than his share in tribute money. Gotti had asked for permission, was refused, and had Castellano killed anyway.

Castellano's murder sent shock waves throughout the five families. The streets of Newark resembled a ghost town for two days, and chatter on the crew phones was nonexistent. No one knew if Big

Paul's murder was the beginning of a power struggle and if other families would be dragged into it. Not until John Gotti spread the word that he was now the Gambino boss and no further violence would be sanctioned or condoned did things get back to normal, or what passed for normal in Gerardo's crew. Gotti's proclamation did not include taking credit for Big Paul's murder, which made the Jersey wiseguys even more unsettled because hardly anyone had heard of Gotti before Big Paul's killing. But the phone prattle resumed and we were back in business, the Cage crew adopting a wait-and-see attitude.

I overheard a phone conversation in which Bobby Manna instructed Sal Cetrulo to pay more attention to Port Newark and the Longshoremen's Union because he suspected John DiGilio of holding back money. Once this type of rumor got a foothold in the mob, the suspected thief started on the inevitable road to destruction, whether the rumors were true or not. In DiGilio's case, while his thievery was never proven, he would later be murdered in a traditional mob execution in 1988, shortly after he was indicted by the feds. The way the bosses figured, while DiGilio may have been totally straight, why take a chance? He had to go. The Gambinos, under the leadership of John Gotti, would take over Port Newark and the Longshoremen's Union after our undercover operation was over. Both had traditionally been Genovese turf.

Since Gotti's ascension to Gambino boss, I was seeing more and more new faces, a new breed of wiseguys who were smarter, more ruthless, bigger earners, and schooled in the ways of keeping more of the money they were supposed to turn over to the mob. Many

went into drug dealing, a sideline that was not permitted when Big
Paul was alive. He didn't object to dealing drugs on moral grounds,
he forbade it because drug convictions brought long prison sentences and prompted those ensnared to become informers for shorter
sentences. Under Big Paul's reign, dealing in drugs was an automatic
death sentence. Not so under John Gotti, who didn't care how his
family made money, just as long as they made it. Gotti was a degenerate gambler and constantly thirsted after more cash. In my opinion, Gotti's selfish leadership led to the weakening of the Mafia into
what it is today, an organization of turncoats. The mad rush for more
money and the violence that went with it was ushering in a new era
in the mob, with me a part of it. I knew that I was playing with the
big guys now, the heavy hitters, and I was concerned. I had to be
careful.

Sweeney set up a meeting for me with Ronald Goldstock, the director of the New York State Organized Crime Task Force. Goldstock
wanted to familiarize me with the new structure of the Gambino
family under Gotti, and how Gotti's tentacles were spreading across
the river to New Jersey.

Goldstock was a balding, fiftyish career crime fighter whose offices were near Penn Station in midtown Manhattan. After an initial cordial meeting, he turned me over to subordinates, who gave
me hours of current intel on the Gambinos and their likely move to
grab more power in Jersey. I was told that Bobby Manna would be
taking more of a leadership role in the family and to be wary of his
calm demeanor. Manna was small in stature, and I initially pegged
him as a status-quo guy who'd rather negotiate than fight. I was

wrong. He would turn out to be one of the most ruthless killers in both states. I was told of a Mafia hit a few years back when Manna and Salvatore "Sammy the Bull" Gravano ambushed their victim in broad daylight in midtown Manhattan and shot him to death. Manna did the shooting: two bullets to the head. No arrests were ever made. Manna was highly regarded, and the word on the street was if anything happened to Vincent "the Chin" Gigante, Manna would take his slot as head of the Genovese family.

The northern–New Jersey faction of the Genovese family was competitive and not to be trifled with. Men such as Tino Fiumara, Richard "Bocci" DeSciscio, and Louis Gatto were ready for anything that might come their way, and they had no fear of the Gambinos. During his reign, Fat Tony Salerno used violence only when he deemed it absolutely necessary because it was bad for business. With Fat Tony out of the picture due to his recent RICO conviction, there was no respected old-school boss to keep the peace. For the foreseeable future, disputes would be settled with guns rather than sit-downs.

Before I left, I was ushered back into Goldstock's office, where he shook my hand and said, "Watch your back, Mike. You're in deep and past the point of no return."

We were getting so much useful information from the wiretaps that the prosecutors figured we would have enough evidence of criminal wrongdoing by the end of the year to keep the court system busy for quite awhile. We still had awhile to go on the existing warrant, and we weren't slowing down. The evidence was great.

The attorney general's office was preparing the tapes for a special grand jury to hear evidence against eighty suspects.

I was told Billy's undercover narcotics expertise was required in another part of Jersey, and I was now basically on my own. While Billy held up his end of the investigation, he never had that much to do. I always felt I could handle the case by myself. I liked working alone and eased back into my original role as the lone undercover.

Over the next few weeks the wire was hot with talk of the Castellano hit. Bobby Manna was livid that John Gotti had taken it upon himself to take Big Paul out without being sanctioned by the Commission.

"That fucking Gotti," Manna said, "he's an imbecile and is bad for business for everybody."

We found out later that Vincent "The Chin" Gigante agreed and a plot was hatched to murder Gotti. Chin was notoriously paranoid about talking on the phone, so we had no idea that Gotti's days were supposed to be numbered.

A bomb was planted in Gotti's car while he and his underboss, Frank DeCicco, were in a social club in Dyker Heights, Brooklyn. When they were about to leave the club to get the car and meet their destiny, DeCicco decided to save Gotti the walk to the car by retrieving it himself and then coming back for Gotti. DeCicco was blown up and Gotti was spared. After that, cooler heads prevailed and no more attempts were made on Gotti's life, although he remained unpopular with everyone, including his own subordinates.

I began driving Sal Cetrulo to Manhattan social clubs to meet with Bobby Manna. We divided our time between the Dante Social

Club on MacDougal Street and the Panel Social Club on Thompson Street, both in Greenwich Village. Manna lived in Bricktown, New Jersey, but had rented an apartment in the Village to be close to another mob hangout, the Triangle Social Club, the Chin's base of operations. I would wait in the car during these meetings; what I wouldn't have given to be a fly on the wall or a "bug" in the bread-basket at those gatherings.

Cetrulo's meetings with Manna would get longer every week. He was trying hard to get close to Manna, aware that he was the Chin's right-hand man. This was the mob's version of ass-kissing.

After one such meeting at the Panel Social Club, Cetrulo emerged white as the proverbial ghost, and this is a guy who had a complexion the color of coffee. He was quiet on the way back, but I felt he was dying to share something, so I gave it a shot.

"What's wrong, Sal?" I asked as we entered the Holland Tunnel. Normally Cetrulo was ebullient after these meetings, his ego boosted by being in the presence of Mafia royalty.

"Bobby's got a source in Giuliani's office, some assistant prose-cutor. He's talking about whacking him." Cetrulo was shaking his head in disbelief.

I decided to play dumb. "Bobby wants to clip an assistant pros-ecutor?"

Cetrulo looked at me as if I had the IQ of a gnat. "No, jerkoff, he wants to whack Rudy Giuliani. Can you fucking believe it? You know what kinda heat that'll bring down? What it'll do for business? Whack the U.S. Attorney for the Southern District? Fucking insane."

At times like these I wished I were wearing a wire, but the unre-corded information was the second-best thing. I would pass what Cetrulo had told me to Sweeney before the night was over.

I didn't hear any more regarding the plot to kill Giuliani, but the particulars of the plan came out at the trial of mobster Phil Leonetti two years later. It never got past the talking stage, much to the relief of a lot of wiseguys.

The crew was on the move. According to Cetrulo, Nicky Scarfo of Philadelphia was getting tight with Bobby Manna, and Scarfo was moving into a power-broker position. Scarfo and Manna had agreed that Scarfo should begin collecting tribute money from the black gangs in south Philly that were selling drugs. When Scarfo began to push the gangs, the gangs started to push back. Initially, a lot of threats went back and forth, and after a year of trying to shake down the gangs, Scarfo backed off. No money was made and all that time was wasted. I found it amazing that the family was willing to risk war rather than continue doing business in areas they already controlled.

Apparently Bobby Manna thought the same thing, and the decision was made for the crew to expand its garbage-collection empire into Connecticut with Sal Cetrulo spearheading the move. Fortunately they wouldn't be operating anywhere near the sleepy town where my family was now living.

13

Gangsters "R" Us

The thing I've been asked most about regarding my life as an undercover is fear. How afraid was I to be involved with sociopathic gangsters, particularly after having survived an assassination attempt? Did my attitude change after I was shot? Did I fear for my family's safety?

I was more fearful before I started my stint with the wiseguys than I was when I was actually in deep with them. I had initially questioned my ability to pull off the charade and not make a stupid mistake that would cost me my life. Once I was in, I knew I could handle whatever was thrown at me. Confidence is a big part of successfully handling being an undercover cop.

Once entrenched, my comfort level increased every day. I also couldn't help but feel some empathy for the guys in the crew due to my constant interaction with them. This might be considered by some a version of the Stockholm syndrome. Certain mobster characteristics rub off, too. The role becomes real; you begin to talk, gesture, and think like your targets. I guess you can call it the guido syndrome.

The idea is not to empathize too much and go over to the other side, becoming a mobster. This is a constant worry for the handlers of undercovers, and it's happened in the past. It's known as *going native,* a term derived from similar circumstances during the Vietnam War when American POWs began to fight with the enemy against their own.

I was always focused, a few times fearful, but I felt in control at all times. While I may have come close to exposure after the Finish Line raid, I felt I had the situation under control. The ride with Gerardo, Zarra, Bocci, and Cetrulo in which Sweeney followed close by also caused some trepidation. I was fearful, but in control. The only upside to something like that is the adrenaline rush you get from fear of the unknown.

My concern for my family was born out of a fear of never seeing them again should I be killed. I accepted the dying part, it was part of the game, but whenever I thought about not seeing my daughters grow up, get married, and give me grandchildren, I'd get wistful. I didn't fear for their safety. Families are rarely touched by the Mafia in seeking revenge; it's against the rules. It pays to be cautious, however, because you never know when a young, hotshot, psychopathic associate might take out your family to make a name for himself. This lay-off-the-family decree doesn't necessarily apply to other ethnic organized-crime gangs who I might have been dealing with peripherally as an offshoot of my involvement with the Italians. The Mafia doesn't operate in a vacuum. They deal with any other organized-crime gangs who will make them money. The

Colombians, Albanians, Russians, Chinese, Vietnamese, and a few others will kill a family for revenge or to make a point.

"What I want you guys to do, is go to Connecticut and drum up as many garbage accounts as you can," Bobby Manna said to Sal Cetrulo and me as we sat sipping espressos in a diner in the SoHo section of Manhattan.

Manna had a plan to expand his garbage empire to Connecticut. He wanted the new accounts for Carmine Franco, who owned a mob-connected carting company in Bergen County, New Jersey. Franco had 120 garbage trucks, roll-offs, and street packers, a big operation. Franco was instructed to set up shop in the Stamford/ Greenwich area and wait for us to deliver new clients. Eventually, Manna wanted to expand throughout New England.

Another Mafia crew was in the area, under the control of William "Wild Guy" Grasso, fifty-six, but Manna didn't expect any problems when he made his move. Grasso had been unopposed in the area since the 1970s, but was considered weak and in loose control of his soldiers.

Manna referred to Grasso as "the Mild Guy," saying, "He's a pussy. I'll deal with him."

Cetrulo wound up dispatching professional—and legitimate— salesmen to the area to buy up small carting companies at fair prices for immediate takeover, while he and I visited their clients and introduced ourselves as their new garbage collectors. These people didn't care who picked up their garbage as long as it was picked up. Prices remained the same. Carmine Franco moved in right behind us and was in business in months.

Grasso never objected to the takeover, so Manna took it one step further and commandeered his entire gambling operation in nine weeks. Now it all belonged to Bobby Manna.

Carmine Franco would be indicted a few years later for overbilling Bergen County for trash collection. He served nine months in jail and was fined $11.2 million. A few months after the September 11 terrorist attacks, the *New York Daily News* reported that Franco was looting steel from the wreckage of the World Trade Center. These guys would steal anything.

William Grasso began to make some rumblings as he saw his empire collapsing, but made no overt moves to stop Manna. Members of Grasso's own crew, sensing weakness, made a power grab, and Grasso was found floating in the Connecticut River with a bullet in his head on June 18, 1989. The new regime stayed away from Manna, too.

We were now firmly entrenched in garbage—a good thing in Mafia circles—in two states.

Salvatore "Sammy the Bull" Gravano, Gambino family head John Gotti's underboss, began probing the north-Newark area for opportunities. Gotti's goal was to take over gambling operations, an area the Gambinos had sole control over until the mid-1970s, when law enforcement effectively shut them down. When the heat dissipated, New Jersey Gambino captain Joe Paterno rebuilt a decent-size gambling operation. Recent state crime-commission hearings, however, chased Paterno to Florida, where he reestablished himself as did my old friend Demus.

This left a power vacuum that Gotti took advantage of, and he sent Gravano to the Garden State to restore a gambling base. Gravano set up an operation that ran smoothly until he had to go back to New York and resume control of the construction industry. Before he departed, he put my old nemesis Bobby "Kabert" Bisaccia in charge, which turned out to be a tactical error of monumental proportions.

Kabert was a lazy slug, not too bright, and certainly not capable of sustaining a gambling operation of any size. He would drink sambuca and eat cannoli all day while the gambling action circled the drain. The Gambinos lost their business thanks to Kabert, while the rest of the operation's underlings—the smart ones—followed Demus and Paterno to Florida.

The Christmas season was rapidly approaching, always a good revenue-generating time for the mob. Consumers wanted to buy stuff and didn't care where it came from as long as they got a good price. The mob offered great prices on anything you might want, all of it stolen. Wiseguys had little overhead.

Cabbage Patch dolls were the craze that year, and legitimate retail stores were holding the little buggers for ransom, charging upwards of 100 percent over retail. Even at those prices, stores quickly depleted their inventories. Enter Gangsters "R" Us. If there's a fast buck to be made, the mob will become involved.

I was in my office when longtime made guy Vincent "Gimo" Calabrese called me.

"Hey, Mikey, I've got a truckload of those Garbage Patch dolls I want to unload. You want 'em?"

"You mean Cabbage Patch dolls?"

"Yeah, whatever. We boosted a truck in Port Newark. You want 'em?"

"Yeah, gimme three," I said, thinking of my daughters. One of the occasional benefits of being undercover: I get to commit a crime every now and then and get away with it.

"Three? What're you, jerking me off? You gotta take the whole load."

"And how many is that?"

"Seven hundred," Gimo said. "I figured I'd come to you because you have kids."

"I only have three kids, Gimo. What do you think I am, a fucking Mormon?"

"What about the crew? You can sell these things in a day. They can have 'em for twenty-five dollars apiece. Can you ask Zarra or one of the other guys?"

"Sure, I'll pass it along. Keep in touch," I said, about to hang up the phone.

"Hold up, Mikey, I've got another thing. I got a score lined up, a railroad car full of Mitsubishi big-screen TVs."

"Yeah, so?"

"Well, it's the Hudson County yards, the one between Hoboken and Jersey City. You know what I'm sayin'?"

Gimo knew I was a former cop and wanted me to act as a liaison between him and the Hoboken cops to smooth things over and let him steal the TVs without interference from them. The Cabbage Patch dolls were mentioned to sweeten my end. Of course I couldn't do it because I couldn't knowingly break the law, the three Cabbage Patch dolls I asked for notwithstanding. And I couldn't get involved even if I wanted to because Bobby Manna had many of the

Hoboken PD on his payroll, so Gimo would have to deal with him. I told him he had to reach out to Manna through the chain of command.

"Okay, Mikey, thanks," he said, and was gone.

I would add the Cabbage Patch doll caper and the plans for stealing the TVs to my daily report later that afternoon.

The next day when I arrived at the Cage, a box was waiting for me. Inside were three Cabbage Patch dolls. Santa had come this year for my girls in the form of Gimo Calabrese.

Manna, Chin, and Genovese capo Venero "Benny Eggs" Mangano switched meeting locations to Hoboken, where they felt more secure because Manna owned the police department there. The West Village in Manhattan, where the meetings were usually held because it was Chin's home base, was lousy with FBI agents and NYPD Organized Crime Control Bureau detectives. You couldn't drive down a street in the West Village without seeing at least two unmarked surveillance vehicles vying for parking spaces.

Benny Eggs and Chin would travel to New Jersey via the Hudson Tubes, the Port Authority Trans-Hudson (PATH)–operated subway that traveled under the Hudson River and connected lower Manhattan to Hoboken, and on to a private room at a Manna-controlled restaurant. They would make the trip during the day to confuse law enforcement, who knew that mob bosses traditionally traveled to high-level meetings by luxury automobile at night. Instead, Chin and Benny Eggs mingled on the train with whom they surmised to be citizens going to and from work. Once I got wind of the meetings, I tipped off Sweeney, and Chin and Mangano made the crossing with a trainload of New Jersey state troopers in civilian clothes. Oddly, the Port Authority Police, who were responsible for law enforcement on the PATH line, weren't made privy to the operation and weren't represented.

More cops on both sides of the river monitored movement. Corrupt Hoboken Police Department Lieutenant Frank Daniello provided security for the wiseguys. He was still a few years away from going to prison for life for an aborted hit on John Gotti.

Cetrulo and I met the mobsters on the Jersey side and were supposed to provide transportation to the meeting. One day I decided to chat up Daniello to see if I could pick up any useful information.

"Hi, Frank. How's it going? You got the street covered?" I said to him as both mob bosses exited the train station. I was referring to the obvious lack of security. No one was posted on the Jersey side to secure the area, not that much could happen with every homeless person, street sweeper, pushcart vendor, and baby-carriage pusher an undercover cop.

"Go fuck yourself, Russell," Daniello answered. "Go back to Newark where you belong."

Daniello was never a great fan of mine. I did notice, however, that for the next crossing he had two of his detectives waiting at the PATH exit.

Cetrulo wasn't permitted to sit in on the meetings because he wasn't a high-echelon boss. One time, however, he was invited in and was proud as a peacock when he emerged. All it took was a "What's up?" from me as we got into his car to have him blab about his role at the summit.

He pointed to his chin. "He wants me to keep my eye on Port Newark," Cetrulo said, sounding as if he were the secretary of state and was just asked by the president of the United States to whip up a Middle East peace treaty.

"No fucking way," I said, trying to inflate his ego by being impressed he would be entrusted with a mission of such magnitude.

"Lot of shit going on down there, Mikey. They need me to keep it operating."

What they had going on down there was extortion, murder, labor racketeering, gambling, hijacking, bid rigging, political corruption, and bribery.

Cetrulo had the backing of the bosses, but he knew he might need muscle to keep people, both civilians and wiseguys, in order.

"Can you handle some work for me if I need you?" Cetrulo asked me.

Work meant either murdering someone or busting him up so he couldn't walk. I looked at him and turned up the volume on the car radio, a gesture to show I was making sure no one could hear what we were saying if the car was bugged.

"What?" I said over the din.

"You're always thinking, Mikey. I like that. One of these days I'm gonna buy you and your family a house on Long Beach Island."

I just smiled.

I acted out every situation to maximum effect. I had to make my lies believable. On one of our trips back from a Hoboken meeting, Cetrulo said to me, "I know Zarra and Vicaro always ask you what goes on when we're together. I appreciate you never telling them anything. Really pisses them off." He laughed.

When I knew Cetrulo was watching me in the Cage, I wouldn't

respond to questions asked by anyone regarding what Cetrulo and I did on our road trips. I'd just smile respectfully and walk away.

Michael Perna, the Lucchese capo who ordered the hit on me, and a few of his soldiers began hanging around the Cage. Crews from different families often had mutual criminal interests, and to have them frequenting the same club wasn't unheard of.

One afternoon I was in my office doing nothing when Perna walked in, looked around, and said, "What the fuck kind of business is this?"

I played along. "Why would you want to know? What law enforcement agency flipped you?" I was calling Perna a rat and he didn't like it, but I was with another crew and couldn't be touched without permission of my crew boss. It took a lot more than a wise mouth to get clipped or a limb broken. He was doing a slow burn when Gerardo crew member John "Johnny Sausage" Barbato strolled in, went right to my desk, and removed a stack of cash without saying a word. Barbato left, nodding to Perna, who gave me a dirty look and followed Barbato out the door, but not before I hollered after him, "Any more questions, Detective?"

It had been Zarra's idea to keep the crew's operating money in my office in case the cops raided the Cage. To seize anything in my office, the police would need a separate search warrant.

Zarra heard about the incident, undoubtedly from Perna, and said, "Mikey, you should show the guy some respect; Perna's a captain."

I calmly answered back, "Respect is earned."

* * *

I decided to use the run-in with Perna to my advantage. I didn't want him or his crew anywhere near me. That'd be just one more way I could get exposed.

Later that day I wandered into the club and approached Vicaro. "How come Perna's hanging around the club asking questions? He also eyeballed Johnny taking cash out of my desk. You trust these Lucchese guys?" I could see Vicaro giving this some thought. I wouldn't let it go. "These Lucchese people are all rats. This could be the answer to who tipped off the cops about the Finish Line, maybe why Andy's still in the can. Let's not forget these are the mother-fuckers who tried to take me out."

Vicaro was nodding his head while I tore up the Luccheses. He summoned Zarra, who was watching TV. I took this as a signal to get lost and turned to leave: "I'm going down the street to get some eggs and Italian toast."

Vicaro grabbed my arm. "Hold up, I'm coming with you." He turned to Zarra. "Joe, I want all these Lucchese scumbags out of the club."

Zarra looked dumbfounded, but said, "Okay, Skip."

Problem solved.

After Vicaro bounced the Lucchese group from the Cage, they'd still come around occasionally, but only to hang out on the sidewalk and bullshit with Gerardo's crew.

I overheard a conversation that Ralph DeLuca and his two brothers, Randy and Rory—referred to on the street as the Three

Stooges—had with Vicaro. They had broken into a Department of Motor Vehicles office in Elizabeth and stolen blank state forms used in titling cars. Rory, if you recall, was one of the wiseguys that lured me into the alley and sucker punched me before Joey Ricardi shot me in the head. No hard feelings on my part, but I wouldn't mind seeing the asshole and his brothers locked up. The DMV forms would be gold to anyone trying to make a stolen car seem legitimate. While they were in the DMV office, they stole the IBM typewriter with the special font ball used to prepare the titles.

Meanwhile in the Meadowlands, an insider at the DeMassi Cadillac dealership would give them keys to cars on the lot, which they would steal, prepare titles for with the stolen forms, and sell on the street as legitimate for under-market value. The dealership was so big that a car's vanishing off the lot every now and then wouldn't be missed. The Stooges had a nice business going until I got involved.

Sweeney and I discussed an operational plan to put these guys out of business.

"I think you should buy a car," Sweeney said. "We'll use it as evidence and add Moe, Larry, and Curly to the list of indictments."

"Sounds like a plan," I said.

I contacted Ralph DeLuca the following day and asked him to meet me in my office. He showed up within an hour.

"How's your head?" he asked me, referring to the head shot that his brother was complicit in delivering.

"It ought to be examined for dealing with you."

DeLuca ignored the insult. "What do you need?"

"I'm in the market for a Cadillac."

DeLuca couldn't have been more helpful. "We just got in an Eldorado Biarritz. Brand-new, never driven."

"What color is it?"

DeLuca shrugged. "Who knows from color? It's a fucking Cadillac and the price is right. Does it make a difference what color?"

He had a point. "Not really, I guess. How much?"

He pretended to think about it. "For you . . . five large."

Five thousand dollars was a good price for a new Cadillac, but I didn't want to appear too eager. Wiseguys are notoriously cheap, and I didn't want to stray from the stereotype. DeLuca expected me to bargain him down.

"Too much, Ralph."

"Okay, okay, I don't want to lose the sale. What's it gonna take to put Mikey Ga-Ga in the driver's seat today?"

I cracked up, laughing so hard tears came to my eyes. DeLuca was laughing, too. He had been selling so many stolen cars he'd acquired the lingo of a legit car salesman.

"Fuck it, Mikey. Gimme three grand and the car is yours."

"Sold." DeLuca was being overly generous, and I thought he was paying penance for his brother's trying to take me out. I called Sweeney and got the buy money, which I handed over to DeLuca the next day.

I was the owner of a brand-new silver Eldorado Biarritz, which I'd gotten for the price of a used Ford. DeLuca gave me all the paperwork, which I examined closely.

"What's wrong?" DeLuca asked. "The paperwork's good."

"Just want to make sure you geniuses didn't spell *Cadillac* with a *K*."

"Yeah, very funny." He drove me to a warehouse in Elizabeth, where I was to take possession of my new car.

DeLuca handed me the keys. "Pleasure doing business with you."

It won't be so pleasurable when they slap cuffs on your ass, I thought as I drove away.

I was supposed to meet Sweeney at the State Police Barracks to turn over the car, but I decided to go home first to grab something to eat. My family had already relocated to Connecticut, and I was getting used to being a bachelor again, which required me to do all my own cooking. But I'd learned from the best, Angela, and I looked forward to my own meals.

I was ten minutes into leftover lasagna when the doorbell rang. Two uniformed cops glared at me when I opened the door.

"That your Cadillac out front?" one of them asked.

"Yeah, I just got it."

The cop whipped out handcuffs. "Well, you bought a stolen car. Assume the position."

I was cuffed, searched, and advised of my rights. I elected to keep my mouth shut and not identify myself as an undercover. New Jersey was riddled with corrupt cops, and I had no idea if these guys were straight. I'd go through the system like any other criminal.

Ten minutes later I was in Passaic County police headquarters being fingerprinted and booked. I was brought to an interrogation room and questioned by a detective who looked as if he had a hundred years with the cops.

"You used to be on the job?" he asked.

"Back in the day, yeah."

He smirked. "You've come a long way." He asked me where I got the car, but I remained silent, as was my right. As he was leaving, I had a question I had to ask.

"How'd the uniforms know the car was hot?"

"They didn't. They ran the plates when you were driving home.

They're transporter plates. Then they called DeMassi, and the manager said the car was on the lot. He found out different when he looked."

I was allowed a phone call, which I made to Sweeney.

"I'm in a Passaic County PD headquarters holding cell. Got locked up for GLA. Get me the fuck out of here." I waited four hours until Sweeney showed up with a bail bondsman, Hammering Hank Goldston, who would bail out anyone with a pulse.

Sweeney didn't identify himself, instead allowing Hammering Hank to prepare the necessary paperwork to spring me. But we did have time to talk.

"Once we walk out of here, it all goes away like it never happened," Sweeney said.

"Fucking humiliating. Every ten minutes a parade of cops comes by to gawk at the crooked ex-cop."

Sweeney chuckled. "You're not doing too good in civilian life, are you?"

I glared at him.

Sweeney dropped me off at my apartment and I got in my Olds and drove to the Cage. At least I could get some mileage out of my arrest, wear it as a badge of honor. Boy Scouts get merit badges, wiseguys compile arrests.

I cornered Cetrulo. "Got arrested in a stolen car. Posted bail."

He started laughing. "That bullet did really bad damage to your brain. What were you doing in a stolen car?"

I told him about DeLuca's stolen-car scam.

"Hey, they don't call those guys the Three Stooges for nothing. They'd fuck up a wet dream. Don't get involved with anything those assholes do."

"Yeah, right. Now you tell me."

"When's the return date?"

The court return date for me to answer the charges would never come. The entire case would get pulped, as if it never happened. I made up an arbitrary date two months in the future, knowing Cetrulo would forget about it by then.

Five more correction officers were arrested for helping Gerardo during his stay in prison. They were charged with accepting bribes and corruption. This wouldn't look good for Gerardo when it came time for him to be released on parole.

Cetrulo was lamenting Gerardo's problems when he asked me to take a ride with him. This generally meant he was going somewhere where he needed a show of force.

"Sure," I said. "Where we going?"

"Linden. Gotta scoop up Bocci on the way."

Now I knew it was a muscle job; you don't invite Bocci anywhere for his diplomatic skills. I didn't have time to call Sweeney, so I just jumped in Cetrulo's car and hoped I wouldn't be asked to kill anyone.

We picked up Bocci in a run-down bar by the river. He looked as if he had been out all night and smelled of booze and cigarettes. My deductive powers suggested that he might be in a foul mood. Bocci lumbered into the car and sprawled across the backseat.

"Hey, Bocci, nice day." I said. "How's it going?"

"Fuck you."

Now that the last of the merry men was present, Cetrulo told us we were going to evict a Bonanno captain who was poaching Genovese territory by setting up a sports-betting book and loan-sharking operation in the Port Newark/Elizabeth/Exxon-refinery area. He was using a local strip club as a cover, and the owner had dimed him to us.

"His name's Gabriel Infanti," Cetrulo said, "and he's a fucking scumbag like the rest of the fucking Bonannos."

The Bonanno family was the smallest of the five Mafia families and the least liked. They kept to themselves and didn't share or play well with the rest of the families. Any chance Gerardo's crew had to disrupt their lives, they seized it. This time they had a valid reason. If the Bonannos wanted to set up shop in Gerardo's area, they could've asked and something would've been worked out. I was hoping the impending confrontation wouldn't start a war, but I doubted it. The Bonannos were testing the Genovese resolve. This stuff goes on a lot among families, with the usurper usually blinking. This time was no exception.

We cornered Infanti in the strip club, which was gearing up for a late-afternoon opening. We could tell he wasn't expecting us. He was at the bar alone, unarmed, and apologetic.

"Sal, who knew this was your territory?" Infanti said. He was a big guy, around forty-five, well built, but no match for Bocci and me, and he knew it. "No disrespect intended."

"Well, your fucking ticket's just been punched. Time to fold the tent. Bye, Gabe," Cetrulo said.

Infanti grabbed his coat. "Hey, no problem, Sal. The next time you're in New York, give me a call."

"I'd sooner drink my own piss, Gabe. Have a nice day," Cetrulo said, and Infanti made for the door, never to be seen again on this side of the Hudson.

On the drive back, Cetrulo said, "That went well. Thanks for coming with me."

"Yeah, no problem," I said, happy I wasn't asked to break Infanti's legs.

"Like I had a fucking choice," Bocci said, and burped.

Cetrulo barged into my office the next afternoon. I'd just come off a wire, and he missed me with my eye to the peephole by seconds.

"Come with me, we have a problem." Cetrulo was normally pompous and cool; now he looked spooked.

"Okay, lemme make a call and—"

"No, *now*, Mikey. Joe's in the car. We gotta go to Paterson. C'mon, move." Cetrulo waited for me.

I wanted to call Sweeney with the code phrase for trouble, but couldn't. I shoveled paper into my desk and flew out the door. Zarra was in the front seat of Cetrulo's Caddy with his usual cigar jammed into his face, but he was rolling it around his mouth, unlit. He did that when he was upset. I got in the backseat, and Cetrulo left rubber leaving the curb. I kept my mouth shut until addressed.

Zarra did his best to turn around and talk to me. He looked like a landlocked whale. "We got a problem with Gatto, Mikey. He says we opened up a casino on his turf and he's pissed."

Zarra had had a run-in with Louis Gatto once before when Zarra had poached Gatto's territory by putting slot machines in Paterson, an area controlled by Gatto. I was the messenger back then when Bobby "Kabert" Bisaccia confronted me as I was making cash pickups from a candy store where we had some slot machines.

They had ironed out the problem back then, with Zarra blinking and removing the slots with a promise never to return. I wondered what the problem was now.

"So, we're cool, right?" I said. "There's no casino, right?"

Zarra hesitated. "Well, there is . . . sort of. Anyway, we have to clear out some equipment in a store I rented before Gatto busts in and destroys the joint, plus makes a liar out of me."

To my way of thinking, Zarra either had a casino in Gatto's area or he didn't. "Sort of" having a casino was like being slightly pregnant; either he had the casino or he didn't. Apparently he did and had once again tried to do an end run around Gatto, despite his promise not to poach Gatto's turf again. I would shortly find out that Zarra had a full-blown gambling mecca right in the heart of Paterson, including craps, slots, monte, and poker. I'm sure hookers weren't far behind.

"Joe, didn't we just go through this same shit with Infanti yesterday?" I asked. Infanti poached our territory, and Zarra was now doing the exact same thing to Gatto. As long as I had been involved with gangsters, I never totally understood them.

"Yeah, but the Bonannos are assholes," Zarra said.

Okay, I thought, that explains everything.

Twenty minutes later we pulled up to what appeared to be a deserted storefront in a run-down section of Paterson—and that was saying something because most of Paterson looked like a war zone.

Zarra fumbled with a set of keys while Cetrulo and I surveyed the area, looking for Gatto or any of his men. The streets were deserted. Never a cop around when you need one.

The store was musty and in disrepair, but gamblers aren't picky when it comes to décor. Two tables were set up for craps and monte, with one wall lined with slot machines, and a makeshift bar with shelves of booze in the far corner. Three poker tables were partially hidden behind a partition. A rotary-dial pay phone was on a wall adjacent to the bar.

"What do you want us to do, Joe?" I asked.

"Start breaking down the tables and put the booze in the trunk of Sal's car." Zarra looked at his watch. "I got a guy with a truck gonna be here in a half hour. He'll help us load this shit and get it outta here."

Cetrulo and I began breaking down the tables while Zarra gathered the liquor bottles by the front door.

We were there about ten minutes when the pay phone rang. I was closest to it, but deferred to Zarra, who was standing by the front door. "You expecting a call, Joe?"

He shrugged. "I don't even know the number to that phone. Answer it, okay?"

I grabbed the phone. "Yeah?"

A gruff voice said, "Who's this?"

"Mikey Ga-Ga. Who wants to know?"

"Louis Gatto. Put the asshole on the phone."

I held the phone out to Zarra. "It's for you."

Zarra looked peeved. "Who is it?"

"Gatto."

Zarra swallowed. "Take a message, Mikey." He double-timed back behind the bar and furiously began grabbing armloads of bottles.

Great, now I was the spokesperson for the crew. "He's unavailable, Mr. Gatto," I said pleasantly. "Can I take a message?"

"A message? Yeah, I got a fucking message. Look out the window, jerkoff."

I was standing next to a grimy, stained, curtain-covered window. I inched back the curtain and peaked out. All I saw was an empty, garbage-strewn lot. I got braver and drew back the curtain, glancing as far as I could see in either direction. Nothing.

"Okay, I did that. Nothing there. Now what?"

I heard Gatto exhale loudly. "The *front* window, asshole."

I let the phone dangle and walked to the front, past a silent Cetrulo. He didn't look so good. Zarra said, "What's going on, Mikey?"

I shook my head. "I dunno. He wants me to look out the front window."

I parted two slats on the filthy blinds covering the front window. I saw a black Lincoln with two gorillas leaning against it. One of them was Fat Tiny Manzo, easily the Mafia's biggest enforcer in Jersey. He had to weigh at least four hundred pounds. Fat Tiny and his buddy had their arms folded across their chests as if they were waiting for a bus. No Gatto. I looked to the left as far as I could and saw him standing in a phone booth near the corner. Then he stepped out of the booth and began walking toward the storefront. Zarra and Cetrulo joined me at the window. Something long, like a stick or a broom, was in Gatto's hand, but I couldn't make it out, because of the dirty window.

Behind me I heard Zarra, almost in a whisper, say, "Mother of God, he's got a fucking BAR."

BAR is an acronym for "Browning Automatic Rifle."

A machine gun.

Gatto was getting closer. He had a huge grin on his face.

"You're sure?" I said, realizing that my life might be over.

"Fucking right I'm sure, I carried one during the war." Zarra was backing away from the window. Cetrulo was now at the back window.

"Motherfucker," Cetrulo squeaked. "Three guys with guns back here."

I looked around for something I could use against a machine gun to defend myself. I spotted a table leg and grabbed it. If push came to shove, I might be able to beat myself to death before Gatto and his goons busted in and grabbed me.

I engaged two dead bolts on the front door, which was constructed of steel with steel jams, standard practice for illegal clubs. By the time cops breached the door during a raid, the help could destroy gambling records, which were usually written on highly combustible magician's flash paper.

"Either of you guys carrying?" I asked.

Zarra stood stock-still in the middle of the room, appearing to wait for the inevitable. He looked at peace with himself, while Cetrulo was running around the room like the losing rooster in a cockfight. "Motherfucker," he said to me. "You're the cop, where's your fucking gun?"

I shrugged. Even if I had a pistol, it would be woefully inadequate against a BAR.

I did, however, offer some advice. "Hit the fucking floor!"

I dove onto the grimy linoleum, trying to grind myself flat, followed by Cetrulo, who landed facedown with his hands over his head. Zarra still stood tall—as tall as he could get—in the middle of the room like a navy captain prepared to go down with his ship.

I jumped to my feet and tackled Zarra, knocking him to the floor as a fusillade of deafening machine-gun fire tore through the window and walls. The noise was so loud my eardrums felt blown out, and after ten seconds the sounds of gunfire became muffled. Then silence amid clouds of debris, broken bottles, demolished furniture, and wrecked slot machines.

I dared raise my head. "Everybody okay?" My voice sounded as if it were coming from a distance.

Cetrulo said something I couldn't make out, and Zarra wasn't moving. I low-crawled to where he was lying prone and shook him. "You okay?"

Zarra turned his head and looked at me. "He should've killed me."

I had no idea what he meant by that. I heard muffled voices from outside, then a barked command, and the entire world lit up once again. Apparently Gatto had to reload. After fifteen of the longest seconds of my life, firing ceased. After a few seconds the BAR fire resumed, only this time it wasn't directed at us. The rounds were striking metal, and I assumed Cetrulo's Caddy was going to rival Bonnie and Clyde's Roadster for most bullets fired into a criminal's car, but at least we weren't in it. After another reload, and another long burst into Cetrulo's Seville, I heard what sounded like a departing car.

Zarra and Cetrulo began to stir, but I told them to stay put. I envisioned an ambush if we left the storefront, but I had to assume after five minutes that Gatto and his crew had taken off. They wouldn't stay around if the cops were on their way.

I was first out the door, doing so cautiously. Cetrulo's car was blown to shit, what was left of the once-pristine Cadillac resting on its rims atop four shredded tires. The body was full of holes, and all the glass was blown out. Pieces of leather upholstery were strewn all over the street.

Cetrulo was behind me, screaming, "My fucking car! Those cocksuckers will pay for this!"

I stared at him, my hearing starting to return. "You're gonna go to war over a fucking car? We're the bad guys here."

Zarra shuffled out of the club looking old, filthy, and defeated. He'd heard what I'd said about us being in the wrong, which was his doing. I was totally disrespectful, but he made as if he didn't hear me. He knew he'd fucked up bad.

Cetrulo was ranting, "That motherfucker tried to kill us, Mikey. It's either him or us." A long stream of curses followed.

When he finished, I said, "Sal, if he wanted us dead, we'd be dead. The fucking guy had an automatic weapon for crissakes. He sent us a message."

"Yeah," Zarra agreed in a calm, relaxed tone, "a message. C'mon, let's get the fuck out of here."

Gatto had disabled the pay phone on the corner so we had to walk about a mile to find another one that worked. Cetrulo cursed and bitched every step of the way; Zarra just looked worn-out. Bocci eventually came and got us.

Three days later a sit-down was held in a club in the Bronx. Zarra and Gatto attended as did Bobby Manna, Fat Tiny Manzo, and a Gambino counterpart for Manna. It was agreed that Zarra would pay Gatto $30,000 for infringing on his turf and never set foot in Gatto territory again unless it was for non-family-related business. Zarra also agreed that he wouldn't take any retaliatory measures against Gatto or his crew. Zarra later told me privately that his venture in Paterson had cost him $70,000, including the loss of equipment.

During the sit-down Fat Tiny needled Zarra incessantly, but Zarra had to keep his mouth shut and take it because he was wrong for opening up the club without Gatto's permission. About six months later, Fat Tiny was found dead, stuffed into the trunk of his car. The summer heat had expanded the gases in Fat Tiny's body, making his already-huge body even bigger, and it took the medical examiner two days to extricate the corpse from the car.

No one knew for sure who had clipped Fat Tiny, but we all suspected Zarra, who in true Mafia tradition had waited for the heat to die down before he exacted his revenge for being disrespected at the sit-down. These old mobsters never forget a slight, but I was surprised Fat Tiny turned up dead so soon after the incident. I thought Zarra would have waited a few years, thereby distancing himself even further from being a suspect in the murder. But, then again, Zarra was getting old, and I guess he wanted to spill blood while he was still young enough to enjoy it.

The following week I got some bad news. The judge who had signed the wiretap warrant and extended it once refused to permit another extension.

"The judge says we have enough stuff on tape to get convictions," Sweeney told me.

Initially I was pissed, but I came to see the wisdom in the judge's decision. He was right; we had plenty of wiretap and video evidence, and to get more would seem like overkill, a possible reason for the crew's attorneys to say we were persecuting their clients and violating their right to privacy. Any more evidence we acquired would have to come from my personal interaction with the crew, something I'd been doing all along anyway.

We dismantled the equipment in the dead of night, just as we did when we had installed it. We had the mugging team in the alley in case some of the wiseguys stopped in for a late-night cocktail, but everything went smoothly. Pat, Sweeney, and I had the electronics out of my office and the club in under fifteen minutes. Patching the hole on the paneling took a bit longer. We left the camera brackets and telephone cables in place because they couldn't be seen.

I couldn't believe that I felt a bit sad to complete the first step in what would be the wind down of the operation. We still had a way to go, but I couldn't shake the bittersweet feeling.

I left the next morning for Connecticut for a weekend with my family and a jolt back to reality. It had been a rough week, but naturally I didn't share what had happened with Angela. The new house was my sanctuary, and I wasn't about to bring my work home with me.

14

Getting Bombed

The shooting at Zarra's casino never made the newspapers or any other local media. The police, who had no choice but to respond to the numerous calls about "shots fired" they had received, took their sweet time getting to the scene because they thought Louis Gatto ran the casino, since it was in his territory, and they were on his payroll. The cops wanted to give the shooters time to take off before they arrived. The investigation into what had happened never got off the ground, and the paperwork was probably buried alongside Jimmy Hoffa.

Violence within the Mafia is self-perpetuating; the more it occurs, the more violent the response. While Zarra was officially forbidden to retaliate against Gatto, someone had to pay for Zarra's humiliation, and that person was undoubtedly Fat Tiny Manzo (although that was never proven either by the police or by rival wiseguys). Eventually, all seemed to be forgotten, but with gangsters you never know.

Violence also becomes an easy way to handle a problem, and once used, it is applied exponentially more often, the rationale being "Hey, that shit worked. Let's do it again." It also becomes easier to kill someone after you've done it once, and it keeps getting easier as the bodies begin to pile up. This is one of the reasons serial killers become more prolific as time goes on.

Gerardo's crew was having problems with a small garbage-collection company in north Newark called Gazzo Brothers Carting. The Gazzos had stopped paying their monthly tribute to the crew and Vicaro was pissed, but as usual couldn't decide what to do about it. Enter Mario Mauriello, a made guy known for his violent solutions to most problems. Mauriello was in his forties, not too bright—which seemed to be a communal trait among low-level made guys—and he was told to teach the Gazzo brothers a lesson.

I attended a 2:00 a.m. meeting at Mauriello's house on Route 17 in Lyndhurst at which he, Zarra, and Cetrulo were supposed to brainstorm a solution to the problem. I was the driver and wasn't part of the think tank, although I took up a chair at their roundtable discussion. The meeting had to be the shortest in Mafia history. When everyone was seated, Mauriello said, "Let's blow up the cocksucker's trucks." Zarra and Cetrulo nodded in agreement, and the meeting was over. I didn't even have a chance to drink my espresso.

Normally, this wouldn't be a big deal. I'd report the plan to Sweeney and he'd make sure nothing happened to any of the company's four trucks. The problem was Mauriello wanted to do the deed *right then*.

"C'mon," he said, "I got gasoline in the garage." The plan was to make Molotov cocktails and toss them under the trucks to melt the hydraulic hoses that operated the lifting mechanisms of the vehicles. I needed to get to a phone and I needed to do it quickly; Sweeney had to get someone to the scene to prevent the conflagration. I tried every excuse to make a hasty exit, from a sick kid at home to chest pains. Nothing worked. They wanted me there to help make the bombs.

"Fuck chest pains," Cetrulo said. "You're healthy as a rich Jew in a steam bath. Probably some of that shit Irish food you eat."

I was trapped. Zarra handed me three empty soda bottles and I became the Mad Bomber. Molotov cocktails are crude firebombs, made by pouring gasoline into a bottle and inserting a rag for a fuse. The object is to set fire to the rag and toss the bottle at the intended target before the thing went off in your hand and you self-immolated.

Within a few minutes we had eight crude bombs, two per truck. The carting company was a few miles away, and unless I extricated myself from what was about to happen, I was about to commit numerous felonies, not to mention putting a company out of business.

We were on our way out the door when, to my utter shock, Zarra said, "Okay, Mikey, you can take off. We can handle it from here."

Even Cetrulo was surprised. "We don't need him, Joe?"

"Nah, he ain't feeling well, looks like shit, too. Go home, Mikey."

I thanked Zarra, wished them well, and walked as calmly as I could to my Olds. Once I was a safe distance from Mauriello's house, I floored the car and sped toward a deli on Route 17 that I knew had a pay phone. Within two minutes I was screeching to a halt in front of the phone and fumbling for change. I dropped a fistful of coins, salvaged a dime, dumped it, and waited for a dial tone.

The phone was dead.

Back in the car, sweating like the aforementioned Jew in a steam bath, I was back on Route 17 and barreling up the road at ninety miles an hour, skidding sideways into a gas station three miles away. The station had a phone that worked. I knew Zarra and company had to be at the carting-company site by this time. It would take a few minutes to make sure they were alone, survey for cops, stealthily approach the parked trucks, and let fly with the gasoline bombs.

Sweeney's phone rang six times before he picked up. He'd been asleep and sounded groggy.

"Jimmy, it's Mike. Wake up, we have a problem."

I envisioned Sweeney snapping to attention, head clear, ready for anything.

"Yeah, yeah, go," he said.

I told him what had transpired. "Time is of the essence, man, they gotta be there now. They're gonna put those guys out of business, plus maybe blow up a fireman or two when they respond." Molotov cocktails are notoriously unreliable, with delayed ignition, or often no ignition at all.

There was only silence from Sweeney's end. I thought we'd been cut off.

"Jimmy, you there?" I was becoming more panicky by the second.

A few more seconds of dead air. Finally he said, "Yeah, Mike, I'm here."

"Well, get someone up there!"

Another few seconds passed. "So what you're saying," Sweeney said calmly, "is you're the only other person who knows what's gonna happen, right?"

"Yeah, right." I was too wound up to see where he was going with this. Then it hit me. If the cops responded to the scene, the wiseguys would figure out I had dimed on them. Even if they weren't sure, I'd be in a bad spot. People have been killed for doing a lot less. On the other hand, we couldn't allow a crime to be committed.

"Okay," I said, "what do we do?" At times like this, I was glad I was only a lowly civilian and not a boss who was located where the buck stopped. "You're gonna make a call, right?"

"Of course I'll make the call," Sweeney said. "I'll consult my Rolodex and find an honest cop in Newark and tell him to get his ass over there. I'm gonna do that right now, drop what I'm doing."

Sweeney did his job and notified whomever he had to notify. Unfortunately, by the time responding police arrived on the scene, the four trucks were destroyed and the bad guys had made good their escape. There were no arrests.

Sometimes things don't work out for the good guys, but other times they do.

Things were quiet for the next few weeks. Gerardo was still in prison, and Vicaro liked routine as much as possible; heavy lifting wasn't his forte, and that was fine with me. I spent as much time as I could in the Cage without making it too obvious what I was there for. I got along with everyone, even visiting soldiers from other crews— except for Anthony DiVingo, a Genovese soldier who had always been suspicious of me. DiVingo would go so far as to leave a table if

I sat down in an empty chair. What probably saved me from his arousing the suspicions of some of the other wiseguys was that DiVingo wasn't popular, was combative, and would often get into screaming matches with other members of the crew both in and outside the Cage. DiVingo also resented reporting to Ralph Vicaro while Gerardo was in prison, but he was an old-time mafioso who went by the rules and grudgingly had a sit-down with Vicaro once a week.

DiVingo was a well-rounded career criminal in his late fifties whose rap sheet went back to the 1950s and involved gambling, loan-sharking, larceny, assault, possession of stolen property, burglary, and homicide. DiVingo was made by Gerardo in the mid-1970s after a friendship that began when they were kids in a tough Newark neighborhood known as the First Ward. The one homicide he was involved in—the murder of "Little Pussy" Russo—never resulted in a conviction because the evidence got "lost." I read it a different way. I thought he was given a pass by the feds as a reward for turning informer, and that my presence with the crew was stepping on his toes. He had no idea I was one of the good guys, but my law-enforcement background was spooking him and he'd rather not have me around, lest I discover an indiscretion involving cooperation with law enforcement going back a few years. I wanted him gone, too, but the guy was always around, particularly after Vicaro made him a member of Local #262 of the Retail/Wholesale Department Workers Union, the object being to remove union president Frank Smith from office and pave the way for a Genovese-family takeover.

DiVingo was also a leg breaker, used mostly to persuade low-level gamblers to make good on their debts. He ran weekly craps games from a club he owned on Bloomfield Avenue, but for the most part he was a fixture in the Cage. I always thought if I was ever going to get killed, DiVingo would have a hand in it. I had expressed this view on a few occasions to Sweeney, who nodded and told me not to worry about him.

"I'm not worried, it's just that the scumbag is a thorn in my side," I told Sweeney.

I don't know to this day if DiVingo got extraspecial attention from the State Police because of my concerns, but it sure looked like it. A warrant was sworn out for his arrest on a variety of mob-connected crimes, mostly from information emanating from my undercover work, but common knowledge enough for me not to get burned before the remainder of the crew went down. The plan was to collar him at Vesuvio's restaurant in north Newark, where he ate a few times a week. The small army of cops arrived in the middle of the lunch rush and announced to DiVingo that he was under arrest.

DiVingo, thinking he was dealing with corrupt cops on the Genovese pad, became highly agitated for having his lunch interrupted.

"You can't touch me!" he yelled. "Don't you know who I'm with?" Those turned out to be DiVingo's last words because he promptly grabbed his chest and went facedown into his bowl of linguine and white clam sauce. He was DOA on the spot. At least I didn't have him around to break my chops anymore, although some in the crew wondered why he was singled out for prosecution when there was more important game to go after.

* * *

A major food distribution company I'll call the Easy Eats had plans to build in a Bobby Manna–controlled area in north Jersey. The land on which it planned to build had been a major Genovese-family illegal dumping ground for toxic waste for years. The word came down from Manna through the chain of command—Manna to Vicaro to Cetrulo to me—that the land had to be cleared of the waste before ground was broken for the build. I got the job because I had no sense of smell, and the place reeked.

"And where am I supposed to put this crap?" I asked Cetrulo.

"Dump it at the bottom of Snake Hill. No one'll ever go up there."

"Wonderful." This was going to be backbreaking work, and I was the only person tasked to do it. Snake Hill was a granite mini-mountain in north Jersey that once had a working insane asylum at the top, long since shuttered. Snake Hill was a now barren eyesore that no one ventured near because it had no navigable access roads. The rumor for years was that Snake Hill was a mob burial ground, a rumor that was found to be true because in 2000 twenty-two bodies were unearthed there when an exit to the New Jersey Turnpike was constructed running near the hill's base.

For a solid week of twelve-hour days I excavated and dumped enough toxic waste to poison the population of Finland. I wore a surgical mask, took an immediate shower upon leaving the site, and hoped for the best. I was convinced that the Easy Eats were in bed with Manna and that's why he ordered the cleanup, otherwise why bother? I passed my thoughts along to Sweeney, who ran it up the line, but nothing ever came of it.

* * *

Around this time Cetrulo entrusted me with a major mission that indicated the ever-increasing trust the bosses had in me. The Genovese family had a New Jersey state legislator in their pocket, and Manna had sent the word down the chain of command that he wanted me to deliver the legislator's monthly payoff money. This legislator exerted influence over the weigh-in official where the Easy Eats was building. Genovese crews that had dumped toxic-waste material there were a part of an elaborate network of wiseguys, corporate investors, and numerous corrupt politicians planning to build substandard housing on contaminated land. Even though I'd cleaned out tons of toxic material, the soil remained tainted, and the Easy Eats buildings had numerous problems in ensuing years: sinkholes, river rats entering apartments through toilets, and a whole slew of other serious deficiencies due to the corruption in the building of the units.

"Who's the legislator?" I asked.

"It doesn't go further than this room," Cetrulo said as we sat huddled in a corner of the Cage. "Got it?"

I feigned being insulted. "Sal, what do I look like, a friggin' undercover cop?"

"I'm just sayin', it's gotta stay between us and those above us. Just so we got that straight."

"Yeah, no problem."

Cetrulo told me the name of the legislator.

I'd been doing this undercover stuff for a while, and standard, everyday police work for fifteen years, and not much shocked me, but my jaw dropped when I heard the legislator's name. I knew him *very* well and had no idea he was owned by the Genovese people. I'm not identifying him here because he's still active in New Jersey politics.

He shrugged. "Great, you'll have something to talk about." Cetrulo, in addition to being psychologically threadbare, was cynical to the point of thinking that everyone on the state payroll was corrupt, and that the legislator's conduct was business as usual.

I would deliver an envelope stuffed with cash to the weigh-in site, where I'd pass it off to a middleman, what we called a cutout. I never directly handed the cash to the legislator, but one time I waited until the cutout entered a trailer after I gave him the envelope, and while the door was open, I saw him pass the money to the legislator, who saw me and waved.

I've dealt with many corrupt people in Jersey—it was a fact of life during those years—but this guy's conduct upset me. Maybe it was because I'd bought the hype he was spewing. To this day I see the former legislator's smiling face in the newspapers or on TV quite often. He's a family-values type of guy and looks the part, taking available opportunities to parade his family in front of the cameras or talking up what a great place America is.

Since the 1960s, six state senators plus eight mayors from north Jersey have gone to prison. This legislator was one of the lucky ones who slipped through the cracks.

I was in my office gazing out the window when I saw Gambino underboss Salvatore "Sammy the Bull" Gravano and Bobby "Kabert" Bisaccia pull up in a black Jaguar. They entered the Cage for a pre-arranged meeting with Ralph Vicaro, who immediately sent Cetrulo into my office to get me to sit in on the meeting. Vicaro was still treating me like his personal bodyguard and confidant, which was fine by me because I was constantly picking up useful intel whenever Vicaro sent for me.

As I entered the Cage, Vicaro beckoned me over to where he and the two Gambinos were at a table in the corner. As I approached, Vicaro patted an empty chair next to him and said, "Sit here, Mikey."

I dragged a chair from another table and put it behind Kabert and Gravano. "I'll sit behind these two, if that's okay?" I said, immediately drawing Gravano's ire.

He turned to me and said, "I don't like anyone sitting behind me."

"Too bad, I like it back here."

Vicaro smiled. I was making a show of protecting him from the big, bad Gambinos.

Gravano eyed me up and down as if he were either measuring me for a coffin or considering asking me for a date—word on the street was he went both ways.

"You know," he said, "I box at Gleason's a few times a week."

I raised my eyebrows. "Excuse me while I catch my breath." I wasn't moving.

It looked as if Kabert didn't care if I rotated on the ceiling fan, and Gravano decided it wasn't worth it to get into a pissing contest with me. He was on our turf on business, decided to ignore my seeming lack of respect, and got right to it.

"Ralph," Gravano said to Vicaro, "we want to start taking back some of our old turf we lost in the seventies in this area. John asked me to come out and tell you what we're gonna do . . . you know, out of respect."

"John" was John Gotti, and after he murdered Big Paul Castellano, no one really wanted to disagree with him. He was the power to be reckoned with now and had a family with a lot of violent soldiers, some of whom were just getting out of prison after serving years for a variety of crimes. First out of the can were the Campisi clan; Anthony "NaNa," Peter "Petey Black," Carmine, Pipi, and another Peter "Petey White." These guys owned a chicken farm in Lakewood, New Jersey, which they used as a gangland burial ground. Piss them off and you sleep with the chickens, like sleeping with the fishes only you don't get to go for that final swim.

Gravano continued, "We're opening two bars with casinos on Bloomfield Avenue in the Branch Brook Park area. Our headquarters will be a social club on Sanford Avenue in East Orange." He paused for Vicaro to respond. When the old man stayed mute, Gravano went on, "Also two nightclubs in the Vailsburg section [Newark], four bars in West Orange, and two social clubs in Orange." He waited again for Vicaro to say something, and once again Vicaro didn't say anything.

Kabert said, "You got a problem with any of this stuff, Ralph?"

Vicaro shook his head but addressed Gravano. "No, no, Sammy, we don't have anything in that area. It's okay with us."

In reality, this was a high insult to Gerardo's crew. Gotti was effectively taking over a good portion of Gerardo's territory because he knew that with Gerardo in prison and with a weakling such as Vicaro in charge, the Gambinos could march in unopposed. The soldiers in the Gambino family were young and violent, while Gerardo's soldiers were mostly over fifty and soft. It was survival of the fittest, and Vicaro had to eat the humiliation. To go to war over Gotti's invasion would be suicide. Gotti wouldn't dream of making a move on Louis Gatto's crew, who were younger and a real force to be reckoned with as evidenced by their machine-gun reaction to Zarra's opening up a club in their area. The Cage crew, on the other hand, was easy pickings.

The remainder of the meeting was cordial with me keeping my mouth shut except when I was pouring espresso into it. Gravano told us that he'd just bought a horse farm in south Jersey and he liked the area.

After Gravano and Kabert left, Vicaro told me in private that he could do nothing to stop the Gambinos. He looked humiliated and broken.

"We're old men here, Mikey. Someday this'll change. You're our hope for the future." He shuffled off to the men's room after squeezing my arm.

In a few short years, Gotti would be in prison for life—because of Gravano's testimony. The Gerardo crew would retake north Jersey in a bloodless coup because it would be the Gambinos' turn to retreat due to their weakened position.

A few days later the crew got an ego boost of sorts. I was on the sidewalk in front of the Cage where a guy from the Philadelphia mob was showing off his new black BMW 745. Cetrulo came out of the Cage and tossed me the keys to his new Cadillac, the replacement for the Caddy shot full of holes by Gatto.

"C'mon, Mikey, we're going for a ride."

I drove him to Joey Harrison's, a club in Clifton, New Jersey, owned by wannabe wiseguy Joey Barcelona. Upon entering the empty club, we were directed to a back room where Bobby Manna and Nicky Scarfo of the Philadelphia faction of the Genovese crime family were seated at a table. I knew I had no place at the meeting so I veered left and made for the bar. Behind me I heard Scarfo's familiar bellow.

"Hey, you Irish prick, come in here!"

Scarfo had always liked me, probably because I laughed at his jokes. Truthfully, I'd never seen the murderous side of him I knew existed, and he'd always treated me well.

I entered the room, exchanged pleasantries, and sat down.

Manna, looking dapper in a suit worth more than the Olds Cutlass I'd gotten from the state, clapped me on the back. I wondered where this was going.

Manna said, "Mikey, you like Atlantic City?"

I shrugged. "What's not to like?" Atlantic City was what I considered the common man's Las Vegas: not as opulent, where gambling was legal, and the main demographic was East Coast residents who couldn't afford the trip West to gamble.

When the State of New Jersey gave the green light to legalize gambling, numerous politicians championed Atlantic City as free of organized-crime influence. Apparently Manna and Scarfo were going to change that.

In a joint operation, the Philly mob under Scarfo, and the Jersey mob under Manna, were going to move on the unions that controlled the maids and the bartenders, plus set up their own shadow gambling empire.

"Every bartender in every casino in AC will be ours," Manna said. "They'll be taking sports bets, promoting private poker games, and the rest of it." That meant loan-sharking.

Sports betting and poker were illegal in New Jersey. The poker games would be high stakes, held in hotel rooms by invitation only, and constantly moved with four games running at any time. The maids would watch for federal surveillance and would be on the lookout for high rollers they could alert us to so we could steer them to games; all this under the noses of the New Jersey State gaming commission.

"You and Sal," Scarfo said, "will make cash pickups and provide security for the poker games."

Involvement in Atlantic City would prove to be a huge money-maker for Gerardo's crew, who would get a piece of all the action. Manna was adamant that no other New Jersey crew be made aware of our participation in the operation. Keeping our mouths shut would be essential if we wanted to remain breathing. First chance I got, I called Sweeney about the Atlantic City takeover.

"Jesus, Mike, this is great stuff," Sweeney said, then he laughed. "This case would make a helluva movie, wouldn't it?"

I thought about that and dismissed it, but as time went on, the idea of a movie based on the investigation would reemerge in my head from time to time, although realistically I was aware that I was a cop, not Cecil B. DeMille.

15

No Second Takes

As we kept building a solid case against Gerardo's crew, interest in the investigation began to wane among the top brass. We had more than enough evidence to put a lot of wiseguys away for a long time, and after the judge who gave us three extensions on the wiretap warrants finally refused to allow another one, I knew the plug would soon be pulled on the investigation and the evidence presented to a grand jury. After testifying in court, I would be out of a job. I had no pension, no marketable skills, and would have to keep a low profile for the foreseeable future to keep myself and my family safe. For the time being I'd be kept busy because Sweeney wasn't about to go along with the cessation of the operation as long as I was producing, but there had to be a limit as to how much was too much.

Anthony "NaNa" Campisi, his son Peter "Petey Black" Campisi, and three other members of the Campisi clan had been inducted into the Gambino crime family one week after NaNa's release after ten years in prison. John Gotti knew a good thing when he saw it—the Campisis were ultraviolent—and he would use them as the spearhead for an all-out assault on gambling operations run by the Genovese family in north Jersey. They would run their budding criminal enterprise out of a Campisi-owned business, Peter Anthony's Coiffure, at 1883 Springfield Avenue in Maplewood, New Jersey. This legitimate hairdressing operation was a good front, but I couldn't imagine anyone who knew the history of the Campisi clan would allow any of those psychopaths near him or her with scissors.

NaNa had been a renegade, meaning he had no affiliation with any crime family after he was officially released from the Genovese family by capo Richie Boiardo in the 1970s for being too violent, which to my way of thinking was like being rejected from Weight Watchers for being too fat. But while violence is a good management tool, excessive violence attracts too much heat from the press and law enforcement. NaNa was given his walking papers rather than a bullet in the back of the head because no one wanted to try to take him out, such was his fierce reputation.

In the incident that sent him packing, one of NaNa's hitters, Irishman John Tully, shot and killed a coat-check girl at the Robert Treat Hotel in downtown Newark for giving him the wrong coat.

Within weeks of his release from prison NaNa and his family of misfits began taking over bars, sports-betting clubs, social clubs, and bookmaking operations, all previously under the supervision of paroled cop killer and Genovese-family soldier Silvio DeVita, whose job on paper was as a crane operator and member of the Operating Engineers Union. Somehow he had convinced his parole officer that he'd become an expert crane operator while serving thirty years in prison. He must've been good at it because within a short time he was "voted" in as a union rep. Another American success story.

While DeVita was a big guy, he was all mouth and no action. The Campisi's knew he had no stomach for violence and rolled right over him. The Genovese family was losing one business a week to the Campisi/Gambino consortium. DeVita immediately went into hiding and began missing his weekly tribute meetings with Vicaro at the Cage, but he had no money to give Vicaro anyway because NaNa had it all. This pissed Vicaro off, but he did nothing about it except bitch and moan.

As time went on, I thought Ralph Vicaro was going to have a stroke as the Campisi's systematically continued to take over every gambling operation the old man had. Vicaro was visibly shaken and thought it was just a matter of time before NaNa took him out. He became paranoid and took to arriving at the Cage with three bodyguards. Once inside, he would order everyone out onto the street to guard the front door should NaNa and his clan decide on a frontal assault on the Cage.

Vicaro summoned me into the club and ordered me to find Bocci: "I need him for security." Vicaro had enough soldiers now to guard a visiting head of state, and I didn't see how one more warm body would help. But it wasn't my place to have an opinion.

I found Bocci at the Veterans Club on Eighty-sixth Street in Bensonhurst, Brooklyn. He was lying low and would only venture outside to eat at Tommaso's, a restaurant next door. While Bocci was fearless, he wasn't stupid; he wanted to stay in Brooklyn until all the turmoil died down.

I was never able to figure out how Bocci managed to survive in the life. He had a heroin habit going back twenty-five years but was a functioning junkie, plus he was a bad drinker. He shot up twice a day, no more, no less. Addicts normally get mellow after a shot; not so with Bocci. He got wired and talkative. Being addicted to drugs is usually an automatic death sentence in the Mafia, junkies being notoriously unreliable and likely to flip when arrested. Hold out their heroin and they would turn anyone in for a fix. Bocci, however, was considered reliable and willing to do just about anything when ordered to do so, so he was given a pass.

While wiseguys had a thing for expensive, ostentatious cars, Bocci didn't. He didn't even drive. "I like public transportation," he told me on more than one occasion. "While all these assholes are stuck in traffic in their Caddys and Bimmers, I get to where I gotta go by subway in ten fucking minutes."

He had a point.

We got in my car for the drive back to Newark. It was Friday afternoon and I wanted to get back to the Cage and drop him off, then make an excuse to go to Connecticut and see my family. Bocci had other ideas.

"Mikey, take the Lincoln Tunnel and go to the Meadowlands. I got a tip on the double."

"Are you fucking kidding me? We'll have to fight traffic into Manhattan, then fight it again going out through the tunnel to Jersey, all because you want to play the horses?"

"I got a fucking tip, Mikey. Just do it, okay?"

We went back and forth for ten minutes, but I didn't see the upside to arguing with the guy. He was a made man and I had no choice but to do what he said. To the Meadowlands it was. It took three hours out of our way and he lost the races anyway. I think his horses are still running.

*   *   *

"So what do you think, is there gonna be a war?" Sweeney asked me at our weekly meeting. Every week we met in a different place, mostly parking lots and always far from Genovese territory.

I thought it was a toss-up whether the outgunned Genovese family would get tired of being humiliated by the Gambinos and start a shooting war regardless of the outcome, but they had no plans to do so. No one was "going to the mattresses"—hiding out in safe houses in preparation for a battle—and there was no talk in the Cage of fighting back.

But I had an alternative theory: "If it's gonna happen, it'll be because a hothead gets loaded one night and shoots up a Gambino club."

"And who do you think'll do that?" Sweeney asked.

I didn't hesitate. "Bocci. He's a lunatic junkie alcoholic with a vicious temper."

"I guess that might make him a likely candidate."

"You think?"

Sweeney decided to put Bocci under twenty-four-hour surveillance, which proved tougher than following the Invisible Man. Two surveillance teams were put on Bocci, but he was always being driven and was prone to switching cars, jumping out of a car and walking, doubling back the way he came, and walking up one-way streets the wrong way to shake any potential tails. When he wasn't doing that, Bocci was using public transportation, switching buses, trains, and cabs. The surveillance didn't work out.

Two weeks later someone—I had my money on Bobby Manna—sent a message to the Gambinos. Peter Campisi's body, shot numerous times, was found on Ninth Avenue and Forty-Second Street on the West Side of Manhattan. John Gotti, who would have retaliated under normal conditions, was beginning to have FBI problems and decided a gang war wasn't in his best interest. Things began to quiet down to the point where the Genovese crews got some of their turf back. It wasn't a total victory, but the Genovese family regained some self-respect.

I got a "forthwith" from Sweeney early one morning. In police parlance a forthwith means drop whatever you're doing and report in person. I had been on my way to the Cage but reversed direction and headed for the command-center trailer at the State Police Barracks to meet with Sweeney.

I arrived in record time; I was there but the trailer wasn't. Sweeney was leaning against his department auto in the parking lot where the trailer used to be. I was a little shocked; the trailer had been a part of the case since its inception. It was like home. I felt like a guy who leaves his house one morning to drive to work and finds an empty parking space. He knows the car's not there, but he stares at the parking space as if it'll materialize if he wishes hard enough. When that doesn't work, he looks up and down the street for the missing vehicle.

This is how I felt. I looked around for the missing trailer.

Sweeney just shook his head. "I know, where's David Copperfield when you need him?"

"What happened?"

"Everyone was pulled from the case. You're the only one left. The AG is presenting the case to the grand jury in a few weeks."

"What am I supposed to do if I need a backup?"

Sweeney shrugged. "Call 1-800-I'M FUCKED."

"Wonderful," I said, still trying to absorb the sense of abandonment. "I've still got you, right?"

"That you do . . . me and you against the world." I could tell he was pissed. I was that *and* disillusioned.

"How much longer do I stay under?"

Another shrug. "They didn't say. Keep gathering intel until you hear different, but this is the death knell."

I couldn't believe I felt such a sense of loss, such total emptiness. I'd lived and breathed the case for what seemed like an eternity, and it had become a part of me. I was having wiseguy withdrawal.

Sweeney handed me a business card for a party-favor/balloon store located on Route 46.

"What's this?"

"A bogus business you'll be meeting me at on a daily basis. You need to be closer to me now; I need to know what's going on at all times, where you are . . . all that. You're totally alone now, Mike. Be careful."

I returned to the office feeling like a man without a country, but still focused on getting the job done. What distraction I experienced came in the form of the fantasy movie about my life I was sure would put me and my family on easy street for life. I poked around a local library perusing books on freelance movie production, but that only got me more frustrated. I'm pretty pigheaded when I want to do something, and I thought this movie idea could become a reality if I could connect with the right people.

A few weeks later I was in my apartment watching the local TV news, concentrating more on my veal-and-pepper sandwich than I was on what was happening on the tube. Then something caught my attention.

John Roland, the veteran anchor of the ten o'clock news on Channel 5 in New York, was introducing a new reporter. "What better way to bring you a cop story than to have it reported by a NYPD police officer, now turned television reporter and new addition to our Channel 5 family, Frank Grimes."

All of a sudden I was paying attention. Grimes appeared to be in his early forties with a full head of blond hair. He was reporting on a vicious mugging on the Upper West Side and handled the story and interviews on the street very professionally.

Having good instincts—gut feelings—about something or someone is essential in the kind of work I do. An undercover has to be able to read people well or suffer the consequences. Within seconds of watching Grimes do this reporter thing on the street, I had a good feeling about him, that he'd talk to me if I called him and picked his brain about what it took to get a movie made, but there was only one way to find out.

The next morning I called some former and current cops I knew on the NYPD. I wanted the skinny on Grimes: Could he be trusted? What kind of a cop was he when he was on the job? There are cops, and there are cops, and I've seen the worst and the best. I wouldn't want to confide in some asshole that pushed paper for his entire career. Most of the cops I called either knew Grimes personally or knew his reputation. To a man, all said he was a "stand-up guy," police jargon—and wiseguy jargon, for that matter—for someone who could be trusted and was good at what he did. That was good enough for me.

I called the Channel 5 studio in New York, identified myself to a receptionist as a police officer, and asked to speak to Frank Grimes. I gave the name Mike Upton. While I wasn't a cop anymore, I knew identifying myself as one would open a door. Reporters love cops, especially reporters working the crime beat.

Grimes picked up on the first ring. "Frank Grimes speaking. Mike Upton?"

"That'll do for now."

I guess he was used to people giving phony names. "What department are you with?"

Ambient noise was making it difficult for me to hear Grimes. Behind him I heard multiple conversations, what sounded like a video loop, and a siren I assumed was coming from the street.

"Well, I'm not exactly on the job anymore—"

"Okay, hold on. No offense intended, but starting off even a causal conversation with a lie is telling me you might be some sort of nut. I'm a busy guy. Are you a nut, Mike Upton?"

"My wife thinks so." Grimes was an ex-cop all right; no bullshit, right to the point. I liked him already. "Listen, I'm former New Jersey State Police, Newark PD before that. I've got something you might be interested in."

"Okay, what've you got?"

"Don't want to get into it on the phone, but you'll like what I have to say."

"I'm not taking time out of my busy day to meet someone who may or may not have a story for me. I need a taste. What've you got?"

"Not on the phone. I've got to be adamant about that."

There were a few seconds of contemplative silence. If Grimes was anything but a former cop, he probably would've told me to go fuck myself and hung up. But good cops have a way of reading people that others don't. Grimes, from what I was led to believe, had been a good cop, and the instinct doesn't go away with retirement.

"Okay, I'll meet with you, but it's got to be today or tomorrow. I'll be out of town on a story for a few days after that."

"You tell me where and when and I'll be there."

He named a sports bar near the Channel 5 studio on First Avenue. "Tomorrow at two o'clock. We'll miss the lunch crowd."

"I'll be there." I hung up. I had no idea what I was getting myself into, but I felt good about Grimes. I was going to tell him an abridged version of my story and pick his brain. My goal was a movie, something that would give my family financial security after my undercover assignment ended. Whether this was viable, I'd find out when I spoke to Grimes.

With great trepidation I got into my Olds and made the trip to Manhattan the next day for my meeting with Grimes. I was in unchartered territory and questioned my movie idea all morning. I was a realist and had fleeting moments of doubt about the meeting. Was I way out of line here? Was I a dreamer or a pragmatist? Even if I got something off the ground, how would the New Jersey State Police handle it? There had to be rules about the media, but I had no idea what they were.

I parked in an underground garage on East Sixty-seventh Street and walked the two blocks to where I was supposed to meet Grimes.

The Upper East Side of Manhattan always mystified me. It was the middle of the afternoon on a sunny day, and the streets were packed with men and women in their thirties and forties wandering from high-end retail store to high-end retail store. Those who weren't shopping were entering and leaving restaurants, most dressed casually and seemingly carefree and happy, conversing with other like individuals. The neighborhood was the most expensive real estate in the world, and luxury apartment buildings abounded. Why the hell weren't these people working? How did they pay their exorbitant rents? I pondered these questions until I entered the bar where I was meeting Grimes.

While we may have missed the lunch crowd, the drinking crowd was still around. The place was packed with mostly male drinkers bellied up to the bar. I spotted Grimes at a table in the back. As I made my way through the throng, he made eye contact with me and nodded. Yep, he was a former cop all right; takes one to know one.

He was dressed in a dark suit and tie and stood up to greet me. "Mike Upton?"

"Yeah, well, we have to talk about that." We shook hands and sat down. "My name's Mike Russell. Sorry for the intrigue, but the phone is not my friend."

"They're part of my livelihood. Okay, tell me what you can do for me. I've got to be back at the office in an hour, so let's get to it." He raised a glass of flat beer and took a healthy hit.

"I'm working undercover with the Genovese mob in north Jersey, have been for a few years. I'm doing this as a civilian contract employee, but started while I was on the job with the New Jersey State Police. I'm thinking my experiences would make a great movie, and I know nothing about the business. I thought since you're in television and a former cop, maybe you could steer me in the right direction."

Grimes nodded and took another drink. I saw his eyes glazing over; he'd heard similar stories from cops before, both friends and strangers. I knew he was thinking to himself, why was my story any different from that of the myriad of undercover cops who had come before me?

"How old is this case you were working on?"

"What do you mean, how old?"

"You know, when did it end?"

"It didn't end, it's an ongoing case. I'm working it now."

Grimes's glass stopped halfway to his lips. He slowly lowered it back to the table. "You mean to tell me you're still under?"

I nodded. "Even as we speak."

A waitress came to the table and I ordered a beer. When she left, Grimes said, "Tell me more."

Grimes never made it back to his office that afternoon.

Grimes took notes as I went over the case and my experiences with the wiseguys. He agreed not to use any of what I told him unless I gave him my express approval. I told him about getting shot, how I shifted families after meeting Andy Gerardo, and a brief overview of the crew's heating-oil and other scams. I didn't mention anything about the wires we'd placed or the evidence we had gathered. He asked numerous questions about locations, mobster's names, north Jersey, lower Manhattan, and Fat Tony Salerno.

"You're looking for a movie out of this?" Grimes asked.

"I'm looking for a payday so I can take care of my family. I figure a movie is the best way."

Grimes shook his head. "The odds of getting a movie made are worse than for Fat Tony's becoming a priest."

"But the story . . ."

"Your story is great, but Hollywood is fickle. You could be shopping the idea around for years, get a lot of promises, and never get it done."

I was disappointed, but saw he was working an angle. "You have another suggestion?"

He smiled. "Funny you should ask."

Grimes's idea was to produce a documentary. He had a friend who had a connection at HBO, and he thought the cable giant would be interested in buying the finished product.

"I have no doubt we can sell it. We form a partnership: you, me, and a cameraman. We shoot it in real time as you're doing your thing. You think you can do that?"

I thought about it. "With just the three of us? Yeah, I think so, but we have to be careful. There're no second takes here; we gotta get it right the first time. The second take is a bullet in my head." And I already had one of those.

"You tell me what to do and I'll do it. I'm not looking to get you hurt here."

"What kind of money are we talking about?"

"No idea; could be a few hundred grand, could be more, could be less. We'd each throw in a few thousand to make the documentary."

This was a lot of information to absorb. I hardly knew Grimes, yet I trusted him from the outset, but I had to tell him the downside. "The brass would never go for it."

He sipped his beer, nodded. "Do they have to know? We'd make sure it airs after the case goes to court. It's better that way anyway. The viewers would want to know what became of the wiseguys."

I never expected that response, but he was right. I wasn't a sworn officer anymore. What could they do to me if they found out? As long as I didn't blow the operation and jeopardize the case, the first inkling they would have of the documentary was when they saw it on television, and that would be after the arrests were made and the case adjudicated.

I could see that Grimes was hot for the project; something like this had never before been done. To film an actual undercover operation as it occurred with real gangsters would be a first. I could see visions of Emmy and Peabody Awards dancing in Grimes's eyes. I liked the idea, too, but I couldn't jump on it. I needed to give it some thought. It was my ass on the line, not his.

"Give me some time to think on it."

"Sure," Grimes said. "How does tomorrow sound?"

He had a point. He was shooting the documentary in real time, and the operation could end any day. "I'll call you tomorrow afternoon, okay?"

Frank Grimes extended his hand. "Deal."

I was going to have a sleepless night.

I didn't give a damn about the hierarchy of the New Jersey State Police. I would do my job to the bitter end and do it well, and they could have no gripes about that. But law enforcement agencies are political and have the power to destroy careers. I didn't care about myself; I was a civilian and they couldn't terminate a career I no longer had. But I cared about Jim Sweeney and the repercussions the documentary might have on his livelihood. When the bosses found out I'd done an end run around them to make the documentary and I wasn't around to persecute, they'd go right for Jim Sweeney as the next-best target. He was my handler and would take the fall. Sweeney had told me a few months back that he was planning to retire, but I've known cops who've threatened to cut the cord for years and wound up having to be separated from police work kicking and screaming when they reached mandatory retirement age.

I called Sweeney and arranged to meet him in a diner in Passaic as soon as I left Grimes. He was in a booth waiting for me when I got there. I told him about my meeting with Grimes and his idea for a documentary.

"You think I should do it, Jimmy?"

"You going to tell the job if you decide to go with it?"

"No. They'd never allow it."

Sweeney rubbed his unshaved jawline. "So why ask me? Go with your gut. You trust this Grimes guy?"

"Yeah, Grimes is solid, I've checked. I'm asking you because once Trenton finds out, and they will find out unless no one there owns a TV, they'll hang you out to dry as my immediate supervisor, right? I can't jeopardize your career."

"Oh, yeah, they'll fuck with me any way they can, but what can they do to me? Force me to retire?" He laughed. "Be the best thing that ever happened to me. Maybe I need that push." He leaned across the table. "Listen, Mike, you've earned whatever kind of lemonade you can make out of this case. I say go for it. I'm bulletproof. My pension is vested and I need to go anyway. It's time. Just make sure you say good things about me when you mention my name."

I had Sweeney's blessing, but I still hadn't made up my mind. I'd spent almost half my life keeping my life a secret; such is the mindset of policing, particularly undercover policing. If the documentary ever got aired, the world would know who Mike Russell was, and I didn't know if I wanted that now, despite my movie fantasy.

I called Angela when I got back to my apartment and we discussed the documentary. She was insightful and probing, but best of all she gave me her perspective on the impact it would have on our family. She concluded as I thought she would.

"The money would be helpful, Mike, but the bottom line is, it's up to you."

The next morning I called Grimes with my decision. "Okay, Frank, let's do it."

"Great, Mike, you won't be sorry." He sounded relieved.

I sighed. "Okay, what do we do first?"

"I need to see the lay of the land: the Cage, your office, the restaurants, bars, like that."

"Okay, c'mon out here and—"

Grimes laughed. "I live in Manhattan, Mike. I don't own a car."

I told him I'd pick him up at noon. "You bringing anyone, a camera guy or someone like that?"

"Not yet, just want to look around."

I would give Grimes a tour of Wiseguyland over four days. I took him into the Cage after hours, showed him where the recording equipment had been placed, took him into my office, and explained how we'd planted the electronics. I made a rudimentary chain-of-command chart showing the hierarchy of the north-Jersey Genovese crime family from Bobby Manna on down, all their mug shots and locations of their hangouts. I gave him minimal information about the shootings, firebombings, shakedowns, and particulars of the heating-oil scams. This was going to be a real-life documentary, not a stroll down memory lane. The detailed indictments would speak for themselves when the arrests were made.

Grimes introduced me to the cameraman we'd be partnering with. I'll call him Bobby H. I told him that we had to be careful; no cowboy stuff or we could get seriously hurt or killed. Bobby was jazzed for the project, as was Grimes. I felt comfortable with him.

We agreed to contribute $1,500 apiece toward the venture, but understood more money might be needed. The money was mostly for equipment rental and videotape, these being the days before digital cameras.

"I doubt we'll need more money, but if we do, it'll be minimal," Grimes said.

We planned to begin shooting within a week. While Grimes and Bobby began scrounging up equipment, I got a lucky break. Sal Cetrulo was going to be in Montana for a few weeks hunting bear. Cetrulo was an avid big-game hunter and an expert shot with handguns and rifles, most of his expertise garnered from human targets I surmised. He entered many shooting competitions and was highly respected on the tournament circuit. Cetrulo went hunting out West several times a year. I was now freed up from having to be available to drive him, and I could devote most of my time to shooting the documentary.

We rented a van and began taping. First up was raw footage of the areas where the Genovese family lived and hung out. We checked for neighborhood lookouts and FBI surveillance and found none.

Grimes and I were in the front seats with Bobby shooting from the rear of the van. After a few hours, Grimes was like a police partner I'd been working with for years. He knew the enemy, and police work was still in his blood. Bobby was the consummate professional and did what he did best, shooting hour after hour of tape that would eventually be edited in a studio on Fourteenth Street and Union Square in New York.

"Can we go inside a place where these guys hang out, like a restaurant or a bar?" Grimes asked me.

I thought it was a good idea, but I had some conditions. "No cameras." The cameras back then weren't the compact devices they are today; they were shoulder-carried behemoths. We could have squeezed one into a barrel bag and brought it into a restaurant with us, but that was pushing our luck. "And it'll be only you and me," I said, and turned to Bobby. "No offense, but I'd rather only have to explain who one guy is; two would tax my mental capabilities." I smiled. I knew he wouldn't want to go with us anyway. I was giving him an out. He was a great cameraman but didn't have cop instincts should he need to think on his feet quickly.

"Hey, man, no problem," Bobby said to me. "I'll hold down the fort and shoot you going in and coming out. Walk a little spaced apart so I can edit Frank out later."

I decided to take Frank to the Casa Dante restaurant on Newark Avenue in Jersey City. It was a favorite among mob royalty because the food was great and the tables spaced far enough apart for private conversation.

"When do you want to go?" I asked Grimes.

He shrugged. "You hungry?"

"I can eat."

* * *

The restaurant was dimly lit and it took a few seconds for my eyes to adjust. The main dining room was half-full, but the adjoining, smaller room was sparsely occupied. I caught a glimpse of Bobby Manna at a table in the smaller room with what looked to be three other wiseguys. All were dressed in suits and ties and sat in huddled, subdued conversation.

Grimes and I were led to the smaller room and seated at a leather banquette. I made like I didn't see Manna, but I knew he saw me. Protocol dictated that if he wanted to talk, he'd make the first move.

We ordered drinks and Grimes made a show of looking at the menu. "Anyone here you know?" he asked in a hushed voice.

"Oh, yeah. Be cool." I concentrated on my menu.

"Hey, Irish," Manna said, just loud enough for me to hear.

I waved to Manna as if I'd just spotted him.

Manna beckoned me to his table with a wiggled finger.

"How're you doing, Mr. Manna?" I said when I got to his table. His three buddies were looking at me, but didn't say anything. I didn't recognize them. After a few seconds they went back to their food.

"Who's your buddy?" Manna asked, gesturing toward Grimes with a fork.

I knew if I ran into someone who knew me I'd be asked to identify Grimes, and I'd given the response a lot of thought before we got to the restaurant. I could bullshit and say he was my wife's cousin or some such nonsense or throw out an unexpected answer. I went with a response that no undercover in his right mind would say.

"That's Frank. He's a New York City cop."

The three wiseguys froze, waiting for Manna to either explode or order my execution before they ordered dessert.

Manna turned to stare at Grimes, who nodded at him.

"Huh," Manna grunted. "Well, Mikey, whatever score you guys are knocking down in the city, make sure I get my piece. You know the rules; just because Sal's away there's no freelancing."

"You know me, Mr. Manna."

"Yeah, I know you, Mikey. You're a stand-up guy. Go back to your pal, have a good meal."

When I got back to the table, it looked as if Grimes were going to jump out of his skin. I preempted any questions. "Save it for after they leave," I said, trying not to move my lips.

We left before Manna and company, and Grimes bombarded me with questions as soon as we cleared the restaurant's front door.

"Who was that guy? Who were the other guys? Are they bosses? You work with them?"

I answered his questions as we were pulling away in the van. Grimes was pumped; he was playing cop again and couldn't contain himself.

"You okay?" I couldn't pass up the opportunity to break his chops. "Your hard-on go away?"

"This is real big mob shit. Too cool for words."

It was cool, all right; I'd give him that.

We needed to shoot the inside of my office, and Bobby couldn't accomplish that without a lot of lighting equipment. We smuggled in about two hundred pounds of lights the night before the shoot, and I was beyond being a nervous wreck. My office was ablaze with lights that shone like a thousand suns—to me anyway. It was a miracle we didn't get caught. How would I explain away the lights and a camera as big as a guitar case?

By the end of the day we had some great footage of the hidden camera brackets, BX cables, connectors for the bugs, and phone lines hidden beneath the baseboard heaters.

We filmed for about two months, usually on the days Grimes was off from Channel 5, sometimes after he finished work. We caught the wiseguys riding around in their cars and running their criminal enterprises. We would change filming locations regularly and switch hours between day and evening.

I engaged Zarra, Cetrulo, and the rest of the crew in conversation while standing in front of the Cage, and Bobby would record it all with a long-distance microphone. Voices were clearly heard. At one point I decided to wire myself for sound and talked to everyone I could, but I stayed clear of talking business. To do that might arouse suspicion, and that would be the end of the documentary, although it would make great television to have an undercover cop whacked in real time.

Every day we filmed was a success; we had no down days when we couldn't find anything to do that would look interesting to future viewers. We were lucky.

We brought in C. Jeans, an Oxford graduate, to help edit the raw footage. Jeans had a friend at HBO who set up an appointment for us to pitch the project to their producers.

HBO was headquartered in a building on Avenue of the Americas and Forty-second Street. I met up with Grimes, Bobby, and Jeans outside the building and with great apprehension went to the meeting.

"Don't sweat it, Mike, they'll go for it," Grimes said.

Easy for him to say. I had a lot riding on the documentary; he had a full-time job with Channel 5, and I was going to be unemployed shortly.

We were led into a cavernous meeting room with a long, rectangular table. Four HBO executives were in attendance: three men in identical blue suits and a woman who looked as if she wanted to be elsewhere. They had already seen our finished product, and we would now tell them why they should buy it.

We had agreed before the meeting that C. Jeans was going to be the spokesperson because he was the professional editor, plus he had the hook at HBO.

Jeans began his presentation using his proper British verbiage and within minutes had the HBO execs looking at their watches. Listening to Jeans was like watching the yogurt in your refrigerator expire. He was one lackluster dude.

I decided to go proactive and took control of the presentation. Within minutes I had the HBO people enthralled and on the edge of their seats. I'm not full of myself enough to think I gave a powerful presentation; what I represented was a type of person the HBO producers never had contact with. I told the story from my point of view using street language and slipping in some nongratuitous vulgarity where appropriate.

One of the producers, a pencil-necked geek named Dalton, interrupted me while I was speaking.

"Mike, if we were to buy this documentary, would something in your past come to light later on that might embarrass HBO? Are there any skeletons in your closet?"

I responded quickly, "Look out the window. See the East River out there?"

Dalton didn't know if I'd just asked a rhetorical question or he was supposed to answer me.

I didn't given him the chance to contemplate a response, if any. "I'm an undercover cop, not a job where your hands stay clean, but I'll tell you this: Any secrets I might have are beneath the surface and will stay there."

Within thirty minutes we had a deal. HBO would lease the documentary for three years. They also wanted some footage of the arrests when they went down and, if we had access, interiors of the courtroom where the wiseguys would be brought for arraignment.

Shortly after the contract was signed, I got a call from Sweeney at my apartment. The indictments were going to be unsealed shortly, and the arrests would follow.

Now would come the fun part.

16

Takedown

I called Angela and told her that I wouldn't be coming to the house in Connecticut over the weekend, maybe not for a few weekends after that either.

"Any particular reason, or is this some of the usual mysterious cop shit?"

"Watch CNN, you'll see why."

"Be careful, Mike."

"I will. Kiss the girls for me."

Sweeney told me we'd be informed by Trenton when the arrests were going down, and we were expected to be notified any day now. For now I was to maintain my cover and do what I normally did with the crew, but I needn't gather any more evidence.

"Unless," Sweeney told me, "those assholes are planning something major, like a presidential assassination. Other than that, hang out and let me know who won't be in town anytime during the next few weeks."

I was wound tight, had trouble sleeping, and found myself jumping every time the phone rang. What wasn't affected was my appetite.

Since I had nothing better to do, I found myself going to lunch and dinner with the wiseguys almost every day. Zarra and Vicaro were more relaxed now that the Campisi threat had gone away. They joked around more, were convivial, and Zarra even reached into his pocket to pick up a restaurant check once. If Vicaro was in a good mood, the crew was in a good mood. I had more laughs with the wiseguys just before the arrests than I had had since we started the undercover operation. While I had no sympathy for them, I kept visualizing the expressions on their faces when they got busted and found out I was the law, and I felt pangs of . . . empathy? When that happened, I would think about my face being slammed into an alley wall in Newark, caused by a bullet parting my hair in the back of my head, and any empathetic feelings went away. While Gerardo's crew had nothing to do with that debacle, I could easily wind up on their hit list, too.

So I waited expectantly for the ax to fall.

I was being followed. For a few days several different vehicles had followed me wherever I went, from the time I left my apartment until I returned at night. The vehicles tailing me would constantly change, and for a while I thought I might be paranoid, but then I recognized a classic FBI leapfrog surveillance pattern. I confirmed my suspicions when I ran one of the license plates and it came back as nonexistent; it was definitely the FBI. I would even be followed to Atlantic City when I'd make my money pickups and do security for the poker games. The presence of many federal undercover cars was noticeable in AC.

The mob was aware of the increased federal presence in Atlantic City. Nicky Scarfo, who had AC locked up tight for the Genovese family, would provide a diversion for me while I made my rounds in the casinos by having hookers proposition the FBI agents, thereby giving me a chance to get lost while the agents fended off the women, who would grab their crotches and stick tongues in their ears.

Sal Cetrulo was back from his hunting trip to Montana, and I asked him about the FBI: "Any reason why the feds would be saturating AC?"

"I dunno, I'll check."

Rumors were floating about turncoats in Scarfo's crew, which might account for the FBI presence in AC, but why have a 24-7 tail on me?

Cetrulo got back to me, said there was nothing solid in the grapevine about federal investigations being conducted in Atlantic City.

"But watch your ass," Cetrulo said. "There're cops everywhere."

I met with Sweeney at his bogus party store and asked him about the surveillance the FBI had on me. "They're outside now. Why would the FBI be following me? I'm one of the good guys."

Sweeny looked out the window at the undercover vehicle, a Chevy Malibu. "They don't know that. Maybe one of the wiseguys flipped and named you as a real bad guy. But my best guess is there're rumors about an impending bust of massive proportions, and the feds figure it's got to do with your case. They're trying to see what we've got and steal some of the glory."

This made sense to me. There's nothing the FBI dislikes more than being shown up, and we were about to do just that. I thought this would be a great opportunity to have some fun, relieve a little of the tension and stress in my life.

"Great," I said. "I know exactly what to do."

"What?"

"Fuck with them."

Most FBI agents are from out of town. I don't care where you live; agents assigned to your city aren't from there. It's the way the FBI operates. When you get out of New Agents School, they ask you where you want to be assigned and then send you as far away from that location as possible.

I got a closer look at the agents who were following me by circling around behind their cars and passing them. To me they looked like farm boys from Middle America. I knew just how to make them wish they were back on the farm.

I took them on a tour of the black housing projects in the central and north wards in Newark. The projects consisted of eight to ten different locations of fifteen-story buildings and housed some of the poorest families in Jersey, with only one way in and out of the complexes. You could easily get trapped inside the developments if you weren't careful, and they were particularly hazardous if you wore a badge.

Crime in the projects was astronomical, and when the police responded there on a call for service or to make an arrest, they came in numbers and wore helmets. A common practice was to lure cops into the projects and hurl everything imaginable at them from the rooftops. Toilet bowls were a favorite projectile; get hit with one of those from a height of fifteen stories and your career was over, if not your life.

I was born and raised near the projects and still knew many residents there. While white people weren't too popular in that part of town, I was tolerated, even respected in some circles because I never abused my authority when I worked there as a uniform cop. I gave a lot of the inhabitants breaks when I caught them committing some minor crime, and now it was payback time.

I'd weave my Olds through the maze of streets that all looked the same, losing the feds in minutes. Sometimes the locals would do a quick roadblock for me and trap the agents in their cars. They tried calling for backup but were ignored by the local cops from the East Orange and Newark PDs per my request.

I was having a great time. After I lost them, I'd drive home and wait in front of my apartment in Parsippany until they arrived, them I'd exit my car, wave to them, and enter my building. We generally gave each other the finger as a parting gesture.

Interagency cooperation, you've got to love it.

The New Jersey attorney general notified Sweeney and me that the arrests were going to take place in ten days, on September 26, 1986. Two hundred state troopers were going to be used, a hundred in plainclothes and a hundred in uniform.

Frank Grimes and a Channel 5 camera crew were permitted to ride along in a command vehicle the night of the raids. I have no idea how Grimes set this up and didn't want to know. I know *I* didn't tell him when the raids were going down. No one in authority ever asked Grimes how he was privy to information about the case to begin with. Apparently our documentary and the HBO deal were more of a secret than the alleged top-secret New Jersey State Police investigation.

I told Grimes I'd call him with the location of the court where arraignments and bail hearings would be held as soon as I found out so he could cover them for our documentary. The location of the court was kept secret even from me until all the bad guys were rounded up. I wouldn't have been surprised if Grimes had wound up calling *me* with the location of the court.

Twelve hours before the arrests all the suspects were placed under continuous surveillance to make sure we didn't lose anybody. At the last minute Sal Cetrulo called me and said he was going hunting in Vermont for a week.

"You just got back from Utah, didn't you?" I asked.

"Montana."

"Whatever. Why go again?"

"Ah, things are slow, and deer-hunting season just opened up there. Why are you asking? You gonna miss me?"

"Oh, yeah, it's gonna be hell without you." I was considering inventing a scam I needed to work with him on in order to prevent him from leaving town. Cetrulo wouldn't care if the deer committed suicide in front of him; if a scam was going down, he'd make himself available. I decided against it, however, fearing if he got the least bit suspicious, it might screw up the raids. We could always have the Vermont cops lock him up if it came to that. What would probably happen is that Cetrulo would turn himself in. The mob knew getting arrested was part of the life they chose, and they rarely ran unless they were looking at a death sentence or the rest of their lives in prison. While the pending charges were pretty serious, and the penalty could be ten years, most mobsters were prepared to do that kind of time. There was a saying among the wiseguys: "I can do ___ years standing on my head." Pick a number.

We let Cetrulo go to Vermont to murder his deer, although we got a search warrant for his house to be executed during the sweep. Inside we'd find over $1 million in cash and $4 million in bearer bonds. Large amounts of cash were also seized at the homes of other wiseguys as well. Who said crime doesn't pay? Some troopers were later arrested and convicted for stealing some of Cetrulo's seized money. I was beginning to wonder if there was an honest cop left in the state.

I was told to stay away from the arrest operation and meet everyone in court later on. This was a military-style action and I had no place in it. I stayed in my apartment in Parsippany glued to a police radio, getting updates from commanders in the field.

Beginning at 4:00 a.m., a total of forty-one mobsters were locked up in a roundup that took nearly six hours. Most were home in their jammies when helmeted cops carrying automatic weapons came busting though their doors with battering rams. Some the targets arrested at the end had left their homes and were at other locations.

Ralph Vicaro, acting boss of Andy Gerardo's crew, was roused from sleep like most of the rest of his men.

Joe Zarra was collared in the Cage, a rare early-morning appearance for him. He was upset that the troopers had crashed through the front door, destroying it.

"Hey," he protested as he was being handcuffed, "you coulda fucking knocked! Look what you did to my fucking door!"

"You got a lot more problems than a busted door, asshole," one of the troopers told him.

Frank Grimes was on the street with his crew, camera lights blazing, recording it all. A crowd had also begun to gather as the word spread that the Cage had been hit by an army of cops wearing ski masks. The heckling began as the arresting officers led Zarra from the club. The cops ignored the chorus of boos and curses.

As Zarra was being stuffed into a radio car, he saw half a dozen troopers forcing their way into my office.

"You can't do that!" he protested. "You need a separate warrant for that place! It's a whole different business!"

"That location is a State Police undercover business. We don't need a warrant," a trooper sergeant said.

Zarra looked as if he'd been bitch-slapped with a tree limb. "No, no, you're wrong! That's Mikey's place! He's one of us!"

"I've got some bad news for you, Joe," the sergeant said. "Mikey's a cop, so's Billy and Pat. You've been stung, live with it."

Zarra still didn't get it. He insisted all the way to court that I worked for him and the troopers were lying to him. Not until he saw me in court did the truth hit him, and he got deathly quiet.

Andy Gerardo had been released from prison within the last month and placed in a halfway house for his "transition" back into society. Jim Sweeney arrested him at the halfway house. The only transition Gerardo would experience was being sent back to prison. Gerardo was stoic and kept his mouth shut.

"By the time you get out, Andy," Sweeney told him, "you'll be drooling and using a walker."

Gerardo just stared at him.

Sal Cetrulo heard about the arrests while in Vermont and, as expected, lawyered up, drove back to New Jersey, and turned himself in.

Elsewhere, everyone was rounded up without a problem, but one logistical snafu occurred in transporting all the wiseguys to court for arraignment. With over forty prisoners, they couldn't be arraigned separately if the sweep was ever going to end. The various arrest teams brought the prisoners to State Police division headquarters, loaded them onto a New Jersey State Corrections bus for the trip to the Essex County Courthouse, and arraigned them in groups.

Helicopters carrying top trooper brass, the attorney general, and politicians were now converging at division headquarters for the mandatory self-congratulatory news conference. I watched it all live on a local station from my apartment while reclining on a Barcalounger in my underwear sipping a beer. The brass were patting themselves on the back for a job well done when Frank Grimes began hitting them with hardball questions.

"Can you tell us something about Andy Gerardo and his role in the Genovese crime family?"

No answers, just a lot of stuttering and stammering from a sea of bosses. I was reminded of Jackie Gleason on the old *Honeymooners* TV show trying to explain to his wife why his latest get-rich-quick scheme didn't work. These guys knew nothing substantive about the operation; they were there for photo ops.

"Okay, then," Grimes said. "I understand this crime family was infiltrated by one lone undercover operative. Can you tell me how important a role he played in this case?"

After a lot of buck passing from boss to boss, but no definitive

answers, Grimes finally shut up. He'd made his point, or I should
say he made *my point:* police brass will do anything to grab the
limelight, but for the most part they have little idea about what it
takes to make a case, particularly one of this magnitude.

I arrived at the Essex County Courthouse on High Street in Newark a few minutes before the busload of wiseguys arrived. Normally, the crew would have been treated like royalty in Essex
County; most of the judges and prosecutors were used to dealing
with them and they would have been given minimal bail and sent
on their way. Today, however, a state judge was brought in to offici-
ate, and the prosecution was taken out of the hands of the locals
and given to the New Jersey State attorney's office.

The wiseguys' lawyers began arriving from their homes wearing
wrinkled suits, un-ironed shirts, and no ties. If it weren't for the
suits, you wouldn't have been able to tell them apart from their clients. I was sitting in the front row as the defendants were paraded in
front of the judge, cuffed and unshaven. I made sure I positioned
myself behind Zarra, Vicaro, and Gerardo. By this time all the wiseguys knew I was working undercover against them all along.

I leaned over the railing and said loud enough for all three to
hear me, "You know that as soon as you make bail, you guys are
dead, right? They're going to find your asses in long-term parking
at Newark Airport."

Any wiseguy who brings an undercover cop into a crime family
and vouches for that cop will almost certainly get whacked when arrests result. It's happened in the past numerous times, most notably
when FBI agent Joe Pistone, passing himself off as hoodlum Donnie

Brasco, brought down a New York Mafia crew in the 1970s after a nine-year undercover operation. Gangster heads rolled literally, and there was no reason to believe it wouldn't happen this time. Andy Gerardo was ultimately responsible as the boss, but his capos Ralph Vicaro and Sal Cetrulo, and soldier Joe Zarra, would also be held accountable because I had worked with them almost exclusively.

Vicaro looked as if he were going to faint, Zarra looked disgusted with himself, but Andy Gerardo stood stone-faced and erect. In true Mafia tradition he knew the buck stopped with him, and he appeared ready to accept the consequences.

I wasn't about to let up on them. "By the way, Manna, Gatto, and Sammy the Bull send their thanks for all the territory you're handing over."

Gerardo turned in my direction and glared at me.

Bail requests were made by the wiseguy's lawyers, each asking for ROR (Release on Own Recognizance) for each of their clients. The rationale was the same with all of them: Their defendants were all honest laborers with limited financial means and strong ties to the community. The judge actually laughed out loud at the requests, citing the millions of dollars seized during the sweep.

"Bail is set at one million dollars each," the judge declared, and banged his gavel amid groans and moans from the prisoners. The crew would spend a week in jail until their lawyers had bail reduced to $75,000 per man.

Frank Grimes was videotaping all of the proceedings. He was running around with his crew shoving a microphone under the nose of every wiseguy he could corner.

"What happened here, fellas?" Grimes asked a multitude of mobsters.

Thomas "Peewee" DePhillips pushed the microphone out of the way and said, "Fugeddabout it, get a real job."

Salvatore Napurano tried to dodge Grimes's cameraman with an eloquent "Did you get a picture of me fucking your mother last night?"

I introduced Grimes to Gerardo and Zarra as "Scoop" Grimes of Channel 5 news and a former New York City police officer. They couldn't get their coats over their heads fast enough.

The judge granted Grimes free rein and seemed to enjoy watching the wiseguys squirm. The prosecutor and the cops also watched Grimes do his act and were laughing at the wiseguys as they tried to avoid the reporter's aggressiveness.

Andy Gerardo's lawyer, Elmer H., was a friend of mine; I'd known him for at least twenty years. As his client was being led away, the attorney motioned me aside.

"How bad is this, Mike?" he asked.

"It's bad, Elmer. We've got them on video and audio simultaneously. There's no speculation about who's on the audio. They're fucked, all of them."

Elmer smiled and I started laughing. He said, "Well, thanks for the work, Mike."

I couldn't resist sticking around and gloating. I positioned myself by the door that led to the holding cells and waited for the crew to begin their processing and extended vacations, courtesy of Essex County. I knew I couldn't successfully needle Gerardo because he was taking everything on the chin and remaining stone-faced. I felt a little sorry for Vicaro; the old man had treated me well, and I'd given him enough shots for the night. Zarra, on the other hand, was fair game. I never felt an affinity for the greedy bastard. As he walked by me, I fell in lockstep with him as we were marching out of the courthouse.

"Hey, Joe, you know what I'm gonna do when I leave here?"

He tried to ignore me, but his curiosity got to him. "What?" he said, a weak snarl on his face.

"I'm going past your house and toss a Molotov cocktail right into your fucking living room," I said, just barely above a whisper. "You know, like you taught me to do with that poor schmuck sanitation guy's trucks. Remember that, asshole?"

"You wouldn't dare," he said out of the side of his mouth as he looked straight ahead. He tried to sound tough, but I heard the fear in his voice.

I got right in his face, stopping the line of wiseguys in their tracks. "Fuck you, Joe. Your house'll be a cinder in an hour. Have a good night." I turned my back on him and walked away.

As I strode down the grimy gray hall, Zarra began screaming, first at me, then alerting the corrections officers to what I was going to do. "He's gonna burn my house down! Stop him! He's a crazy cocksucker!"

The corrections people ignored him and urged the line of prisoners forward.

I smiled as I exited the building, breathing the cool night air and heading for my car. In twenty minutes I was at my apartment and on the phone with my family.

I had no intention of burning Zarra's house down, I just wanted to see the rat bastard squirm.

Epilogue

Andy Gerardo's crew had been decimated. Forty-five members and associates who had been arrested in the sweep were now free on bail, with the exception of Andy Gerardo, who was remanded. All were charged with felonies (see appendix, page 305) and were looking at some serious prison time.

I spent the next month with prosecutors going over evidence and preparing my testimony. It was assumed that most if not all of the defendants would request separate trials. Some requests might be granted, most would not. I was prepared to devote the foreseeable future to testifying at each trial. This would take time, perhaps years, but I was in no hurry.

While we had solid evidence against the defendants, it came as a bit of a shock to me when I got a call from Sweeney telling me the entire crew was going to plead guilty and would not be going to trial.

"You're shitting me," I said.

"I shit you not. They're all taking pleas; just got a call from the prosecutor's office. Seems the video, plus the simultaneous audio, convinced them it would be stupid to dispute the wiretaps. They'd rather not take their chances at trial."

Normally defendants caught on wiretaps dispute the contention that it's them on the recordings. The wiseguys couldn't do that in this case because we had video of them while they were being recorded on the audio equipment. A picture is truly worth a thousand words.

"What kind of time are they looking at?" I asked.

"Looks like it'll average five years they have to do. It'll save the state millions of dollars in trial costs."

I thought about that. The Cage crew was destroyed, and most of the wiseguys were past middle age; if they thought about going back into the life upon release, they'd have a hard time convincing the Genovese hierarchy that they still had the testicular fortitude to be effective. Allowing a cop to infiltrate their ranks also wouldn't speak well for their ability to be trusted or to make reliable decisions.

"I can live with that," I said.

"You did a great job, Mike. One lone Irishman took down an entire Mafia crew, and the evidence was so solid they're all pleading out. I'm proud of you, kid."

I was going to respond humbly, but thought better of it. To do so would be disingenuous. I did a great job, and if Sweeney's accolade was the only recognition I got, I should respond honestly. Jim Sweeney wasn't one to throw around compliments.

"I did, didn't I? Thanks, boss."

* * *

The undercover operation was the gift that kept on giving. Six months after the defendants in the Cage case took their pleas and began serving time, the collateral damage to the mob was proving fruitful.

Working undercover against Gerardo's crew, I had obtained enough information about criminal wrongdoing in other crews to have separate investigations initiated. In addition, some of the defendants in Gerardo's crew who faced more serious charges had flipped and were providing information against wiseguys in other crews for lighter sentences.

Capo Louis Gatto, responsible for the machine-gun assault on Joe Zarra's gambling operation, and an all-around thorn in the Gerardo crew's side, was sentenced to sixty-five years and died in prison. His son Louis Gatto Jr. died in prison in 2002. Another son, Joseph "the Eagle" Gatto, died a free man in 2010 after serving his time. Alan Greco, a mathematical wizard with a genius IQ and Gatto's top gambling man, was convicted, as was Robert Belli, also a top moneymaker for the group. Belli was also a suspect in numerous homicides.

Louis "Bobby" Manna and his crew didn't escape unscathed either. Manna and corrupt Hoboken police lieutenant Frank Daniello were sentenced to two consecutive life terms for an attempted hit on John Gotti. Two other Manna soldiers, James Napoli and Martin Cassella, got eight and twenty years respectively.

Richard "Bocci" DeSciscio, who initially escaped the mass arrests, was locked up a year later and convicted of numerous homicides, including the murder of soldier John DiGilio, and sentenced to multiple life terms. At trial it was learned that Vincent "the Chin" Gigante ordered the DiGilio hit and told Bocci not to shoot DiGilio in the face because his mother wanted an open coffin. Apparently DiGilio's mother knew about her son's impending demise. Having spent her entire life involved in the Mafia through friends and family, she knew she was powerless to stop her son's murder and had the one request that she see her son in death as she knew him in life. Gigante also ordered that a credit card be stuffed in the dead DiGilio's mouth as a message that he couldn't be trusted with money.

As of this writing Manna, Daniello, and Bocci are still in prison and are old men.

No one was hit as a result of my infiltrating Gerardo's crew. I can only surmise that given the age of the defendants and the likelihood of their mob careers' being over, and the desire of the Genovese family bosses to avoid more media scrutiny, Gerardo, Cetrulo, and Zarra were given a pass. Zarra would serve his time and die a free man. Cetrulo is still involved in the life and has been in and out of prison over the years, his perfect record of never having served time a distant memory. Andy Gerardo would live in semiretired obscurity in Florida until the natural death of mob boss Tino Fiumara brought him back into the life as Fiumara's replacement. Gerardo would run his newly acquired empire from his condo on the beach in Florida, returning to New Jersey occasionally for sit-downs, weddings, and funerals.

The documentary I made with Frank Grimes was broadcast approximately thirteen times a year between 1988 and 1991. The ratings were excellent even when going against *The Cosby Show*.

British Central Television (BCT) bought the documentary in 1989 to be used in a made-for-television movie. I went to England and commuted between Manchester and London once a week to work on the project. Ratings were off the charts for the finished product, and I became an instant celebrity, making the cover of the British version of *TV Guide*. I did a publicity tour around London and was interviewed many times on television and radio. I was often compared to Dirty Harry and Kojak. Brits love American gangster stories.

The interviews were often hilarious because half the time I couldn't understand the questions because of the hosts' British accents, and they couldn't understand me because of my New Jersey street jargon. We had a language barrier.

Back in the United States, I continued to work with HBO doing television promotional tours to pump up the documentary.

I enjoyed the hell out of these unique experiences, but I missed police work and being around cops. While I'm a realist and knew my cop days were undoubtedly behind me—a notion I would later discover to be untrue—I still wanted to be in the game.

In the midst of the media blitz for HBO, I was contacted by a cable-television station in Connecticut that wanted me to develop and moderate a talk show focusing on the exploits of police officers from various departments. I readily accepted and within three months was on the air weekly with *Behind the Badge,* a one-hour TV show. My cohost was Sergeant Johnny Ochakowsky, a hero cop who had been shot in the stomach with a .45-caliber pistol during a holdup, managed to kill the stickup man, and made a full recovery. A regular guest on the show was Pulitzer Prize–winning reporter Jack White from Channel 12 in Providence, Rhode Island, who was an expert on most things criminal.

To gather material for the show I rode on patrol with the local cops along with a cameraman, and we got involved in a lot of street crime, from robberies to drug deals, often having to get physical with the criminals. It made for great footage, and I loved mixing it up with bad guys again.

To keep in shape I began fighting in American kickboxing at a semipro level where I trained with Jerry Smith, a badass professional and the most dangerous man with his feet and fists I've ever encountered. We still train together to this day. Staying in shape has always been a serious part of my life and an essential element of surviving on the street. I'm in my seventh decade and still train religiously, concentrating on weights and cardio.

I never gave up the dream of having a full-length feature movie made of my experiences with the mob. To that end I continued to make appearances on local and national television shows, figuring I'd get noticed and create buzz. I made two tries at a book project, both of which never got off the ground. Famed NBC crime reporter and former assistant director of the FBI John Miller—the only American journalist to interview Osama bin Laden—connected me to yet another writer and two actors, Tony Lo Bianco and Alec Baldwin. Nothing came of it. I also met with Chuck Norris in Foxwoods Casino in Connecticut while he was promoting a kickboxing tournament. We discussed a possible movie project, but that, too, went nowhere. I was beginning to think it was tougher getting a movie done than it was to work undercover with gangsters.

While I wouldn't abandon my movie dream, it was time to take a breather. I decided to walk away from potential stardom for a while.

* * *

Angela and I divorced in 1998. It was inevitable. She relocated to where the American people were told Vice President Dick Cheney was throughout the September 11, 2001, terrorist attacks—an undisclosed location. We're better friends today than when we were married and are in touch often. My kids are married and have made me a grandfather several times over. Life was good and about to get better.

I met my present wife, Patti, an executive secretary for a law firm, in a gym in Connecticut, and we eventually married. Shortly thereafter, tired of the northern winters, we moved to Florida, where we remain today. I settled into a life of pleasant retirement, all the time yearning for the "good old days" of being a cop. As luck would have it, I fell back into police work by accident.

I opened a security firm—this is what retired cops do—that specialized in providing guards for high-rise residential buildings in the Hollywood, Florida, area. Part of my responsibilities was to supervise guards at these buildings. One day I got into an altercation with a young tough guy who thought he could make a name for himself by kicking my ass. I suffered bruised knuckles in the ensuing fight, brought about by crushing his larynx, breaking his sternum, knocking out several teeth, and fracturing an arm. Two Hollywood police officers responded and arrested the idiot, who would spend three weeks in the hospital.

Unbeknownst to me, the entire fight was witnessed by two Russian wiseguys who resided in the building. They later reached out to me and asked if I'd like to work for them as their personal security. I ran the offer by the local police department, who had the

Russians under surveillance for suspected high-level cocaine dealing, and the police promptly signed me on as a civilian undercover
operative. Déjà vu all over again.

I told both Russians that I was a former cop who got bounced
off the force for excessive violence, the exact same cover story I'd
used with Andy Gerardo. If it ain't broke, don't fix it.

I began my new assignment by "fixing" traffic tickets for the
Russians to gain their confidence. Within a short time I was involved
in huge cocaine buys, running guns, gambling, and prostitution.

I still ran my security business as my main cover. My contract
with the realty company that owned the buildings would allow me
to enter any apartment in the complexes they owned at any time to
uncover tenants who were involved in criminal activity. South
Florida at the time was the cocaine capital of the United States, and
I found numerous tenants involved in the drug trade. When I happened upon drugs or paraphernalia, I'd leave the apartment the
way I found it and contact my handler, who would get a search warrant and take the dealers down.

I was back in the game and loving it.

This time I told my wife up front, and she was fine with it as
long as I didn't launch another law enforcement career. I didn't.

These days I consult with various federal agencies and munici-
pal PDs. I'm asked to work when they need my expertise, but I often turn down assignments unless the particular case piques my
interest. It seems the older I get, the less I need the adrenaline rush
I required in my youth. I like to spend my days in the gym, nights
with my wife, and take my excitement in bits and pieces.

In 2011 I signed a book deal with St. Martin's Press. Shortly
thereafter, DreamWorks bought my life rights and green-lighted a

movie to star Jason Segel playing me. The movie will be called *Undercover Cop*, a title that about covers it all. Ironically, I'd stopped aggressively trying to get a book and movie deal; it seemed my story came to the attention of some important people in the movie business, Steven Spielberg and Steve Zaillian among them. I'm nothing if not lucky.

It had been years since I'd even thought about the Cage case, but it came back to haunt me in May of 2011.

I got some local newspaper and TV coverage surrounding my impending book and movie. Andy Gerardo, now eighty years old and living not too far from where I lived in Florida, apparently saw the stories about me and put out the word on the street that he wanted me hit because he was reliving the embarrassment I'd caused him whenever he saw my name in a newspaper.

I was informed by local law enforcement about Gerardo's desire to have me dead. The open contract was based on street talk only. Whoever killed me just had to approach Gerardo for a nice payday. South Florida has no shortage of guys who would murder you for a few hundred dollars. Gerardo would pay much more.

I was incensed; I couldn't believe the balls on that fucking Gerardo. I made one phone call, found out where he lived, and went to Aventura to confront him. Along the way I scooped up a Hollywood PD detective to act as witness in the event of a physical confrontation.

Gerardo resided in a twenty-story, luxury condominium. The building was secure with uniformed guards and a doorman. I was informed by the doorman that Gerardo wasn't home and wouldn't be home for a few weeks. The doorman was obviously on Gerardo's personal payroll and appeared to be an ex-con, the kind of muscle the mob uses as late notices for delinquent payment of loans. Don't ask me how I knew this, it was just instinct.

"Tell Gerardo that Mike Russell was here," I told the doorman. "You want me to write that down, jerkoff?"

I got a sneer for an answer.

"Then you can tell him if his threat against me isn't rescinded, I'm going to personally come back here and throw him off his fucking balcony." At this the detective who accompanied me pretended to be fascinated by a palm tree and made as if he weren't listening to anything I was saying. "You understand what I just said?"

The doorman nodded, his bravado dissipating. "Yeah, I got it."

"You can also tell that washed-up scumbag that if anyone close to me—my wife, my kids, my fucking cat—has an unexplained accident, I'm going to cut off his head and shove it up his ass." I was fuming. "Do you understand *that*?"

"Yeah, yeah, I got it." I could tell the doorman was scared shitless.

After we left and I bought the detective lunch, I contacted Jim Sweeney in New Jersey and told him what had transpired.

"I'll make sure the word gets out to the bosses up here, Mike. He's not authorized to whack a former cop, no fucking way," Sweeney said. "That said, he could go rogue and push the button on his own, but he'd get clipped for not asking permission. It might be all bullshit bravado, but be careful anyway."

I thanked Sweeney and hung up, but I wasn't finished just yet.

I composed a letter to Gerardo's condo board to apprise them of whom they had living in their building: a career criminal and a captain in the Mafia, currently active in organized crime. Luxury-condo boards in Florida are notorious for being selective as to who resides in their buildings; the more luxurious the property, the tougher it is to get in. I suspect someone on the condo board got greased to let Gerardo skate through the selection process. I signed my name to the letter and told the board it was okay if they told the tenant who wrote the letter. I also sent a copy to the local media. The notoriously private Andy Gerardo was about to be outed.

Pressure must have been applied to Gerardo because the word on the street was that the offer of money for my head had magically disappeared. I never heard from Gerardo or anyone else connected with the Genovese family. Gerardo died on January 29, 2012. The incident taught me a valuable lesson, however. I was taking for granted that because my undercover operation with the Cage crew was long behind me, I could relax and lead a normal existence. While I'm safe from most of the guys I put away, due to age, death, and incarceration, it only takes one Italian with a long memory—such as Andy Gerardo—to act on a decades-old vendetta at any time. A thought of revenge can fester for years before it's acted upon. With my name plastered all over the media I'm an easy target for someone who wants to settle an old grudge, or a young wise-guy associate who wants to get "straightened out" by killing a former cop who embarrassed the mob.

I take precautions. In addition, some names and locations have been changed in this book to protect those who are close to me. I've taken other steps, which I won't get into, that increase the odds I'll be around to live a long and uneventful existence.

Mine is not an ordinary life, but I wouldn't change my past and I welcome the future, whatever it will bring.

Appendix

Cage Crew
Ranks/Arrest Charges

Andrew M. Gerardo—capo—Conspiracy to commit racketeering, which encompasses labor racketeering, leader of organized crime, RICO statutes.

Ralph Vicaro—acting capo—Same charges as above.

Salvatore Cetrulo—capo—Same charges as above, in addition to criminal usury.

Joe Zarra—made—Same charges as Sal Cetrulo.

Thomas DePhillips—made—Conspiracy to commit racketeering, criminal usury, and conspiracy to promote gambling.

Thomas J. Sperduto—made—Conspiracy to commit racketeering, criminal usury, possession of an automatic firearm.

Salvatore Napurano—made—Conspiracy to commit racketeering and promote gambling.

Frank Bellazzi—made—Conspiracy to commit racketeering, and labor racketeering, extortion.

James V. Palmieri—high-level associate to Zarra—Conspiracy to commit racketeering and promote gambling, and criminal usury.

Philip R. DeNoia—made—Conspiracy to commit racketeering, leader of organized crime, conspiracy to promote gambling, criminal usury.

Mario Mauriello—associate—Conspiracy to promote gambling.

Nino G. Maccioli—associate—Conspiracy to promote gambling, criminal usury.

Michael DelGuercio—made—Leader of organized crime, conspiracy to commit racketeering and promote gambling, criminal usury, transportation of stolen vehicles.

Anthony Paul D'Acunto—aka Tony Orange—made—Conspiracy to commit racketeering.

Joseph Immerso—associate—Conspiracy to promote gambling, criminal usury.

John F. Ingauggiato—associate—Conspiracy to commit the business of criminal usury.

Joseph Cocuzza—associate—Conspiracy to promote gambling, criminal usury.

Joseph R. Carrino—aka Dukie—associate—Conspiracy to commit the business of criminal usury. *He was the only one who was acquitted; his brother was a Newark councilman.*

John Evangelista—associate—Conspiracy to promote gambling by running casino games and slot machines in storefronts, criminal usury, extortion.

Morris Boni—associate—Conspiracy to promote gambling. *This guy was a dipshit.*

Clement Valente—associate—Conspiracy to promote gambling.

Barry A. Zoppo—associate—Conspiracy to promote gambling. *This kid was a real fuckin' idiot.*

William Guido—made—Conspiracy to promote gambling (sports betting), criminal usury, and extortion. *Former professional baseball player.*

John B. Abidelli—associate—Conspiracy to promote gambling.

Don Dellemonache—made—Conspiracy to promote gambling, conspiracy to commit racketeering.

Joseph N. Patuto—made—Conspiracy to commit the business of criminal usury.

Anthony Naso—associate—Conspiracy to promote gambling, labor racketeering.

Frank P. Bucco Jr.—associate—Conspiracy to promote gambling, criminal usury.

Mario Cesario—made—Conspiracy to commit racketeering, promote gambling, criminal usury.

Frank A. Capasso—made—Hijacking, interstate transportation of stolen goods, labor racketeering, conspiracy to promote gambling.

Frank M. Coppola Jr.—associate—Truck hijacking, robbery, and conspiracy to commit racketeering.

Guillermo Rodriguez—associate—Conspiracy to promote gambling; *bookmaker to the Hispanic community.*

Leroy Milligan—associate—Conspiracy to promote gambling; *bookmaker to the Brothers.*

Peter A. Merola—made—Conspiracy to commit racketeering and leader of organized crime. *He was the owner of record of the Finish Line.*

Lawrence Caprio Jr.—associate—Conspiracy to promote gambling, criminal usury.

Dominick Damiano—associate—Conspiracy to promote gambling, interstate transportation of stolen goods. *He also was big into bringing cigarettes up from the Carolinas.*

Samuel DeNoia—associate (former made guy, semiretired)—Conspiracy to promote gambling.

Nicholas A. Rizzitello—associate—Conspiracy to promote gambling, criminal usury.

James Gammero—made—Conspiracy to commit racketeering, promote gambling, criminal usury.

Frank Esposito—associate—Conspiracy to promote gambling.

Salvatore Deleva—made—Conspiracy to commit racketeering, hijacking, AA&B (atrocious assault and battery), possession of numerous firearms by a convicted felon, possession of cocaine (four kilos), criminal usury.

Acknowledgments

I owe many thanks to the two Pats: Pat Picciarelli, my coauthor, and Patti, my wife and editor extraordinaire. Team Pat made the words flow, and an amazing story was expertly put to paper. Special appreciation to the late and great Sergeant Jim Sweeney, who appears in these pages. Jim had my back throughout my undercover years, and without his devotion to duty and my safety this book could not have been written.